Educating for
Creativity
&
Innovation

A Comprehensive Guide for Research-Based Practice

Educating for Creativity & Innovation

Donald J. Treffinger, Ph.D.,
Patricia F. Schoonover, Ph.D.,
& Edwin C. Selby, Ph.D.

Copublished With the

NATIONAL ASSOCIATION FOR
Gifted Children

PRUFROCK PRESS INC.
WACO, TEXAS

Library of Congress Cataloging-in-Publication Data

Treffinger, Donald J.
 Educating for creativity and innovation : a comprehensive guide for research-based practice
/ by Donald J. Treffinger, Patricia F. Schoonover & Edwin C. Selby.
    p. cm.
 "Copublished with the National Association for Gifted Children."
 Includes bibliographical references.
 ISBN 978-1-59363-952-5 (pbk.)
 1. Creative thinking--Study and teaching. 2. Creative teaching. 3. Creative ability in children.
4. Motivation in education. I. Schoonover, Patricia F., 1948- II. Selby, Edwin C., 1944- III.
National Association for Gifted Children (U.S.) IV. Title.
 LB1590.5.T72 2013
 370.15'7--dc23
                        2012027453

Edited by Jennifer Robins

Layout design by Raquel Trevino

ISBN-13: 978-1-59363-952-5

Printed in the United States of America.

At the time of this book's publication, all facts and figures cited are the most current available.
All telephone numbers, addresses, and website URLs are accurate and active. All publications,
organizations, websites, and other resources exist as described in the book, and all have been
verified. The authors and Prufrock Press Inc. make no warranty or guarantee concerning the
information and materials given out by organizations or content found at websites, and we are
not responsible for any changes that occur after this book's publication. If you find an error,
please contact Prufrock Press Inc.

Prufrock Press Inc.
P.O. Box 8813
Waco, TX 76714-8813
Phone: (800) 998-2208
Fax: (800) 240-0333
http://www.prufrock.com

Table of Contents

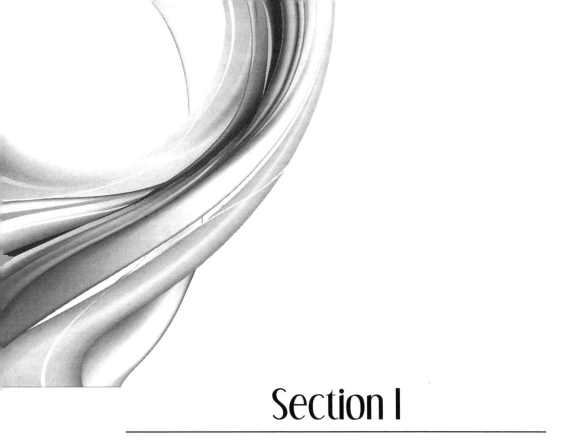

Section I

Understanding Creativity and Innovation

Chapter 1

Introduction

This book is for many different audiences. It's for you, for example, if you're an educational administrator, educational specialist (in any area), classroom teacher (present or future), or community leader who works with other people in any setting. The book primarily focuses on teachers and students, but it's really for any readers who want to extend their understanding of their personal creativity and to be able to nurture creativity in others. Even if you already consider yourself quite creative, this book will help you discover some useful tools and resources. On the other hand, even if you don't consider yourself very creative at all, you will discover that you can be creative in satisfying and rewarding ways!

For those of you who work with students—from the primary grades through adult learners—this book will help you find ways to incorporate creativity into your teaching, as you discover ways to recognize your students' creative characteristics and strengths, to nurture their creativity, and to evaluate their creative work. Let's meet three students. Think about ways they may be similar and different in their characteristics and needs and about how adults responded to them. From time to time throughout the chapters that follow, we will revisit these students and several others to explore their stories and to illustrate our understanding of creativity and creativity instruction in our schools.

Eric

Eric was a fifth-grade student in a small K–5 school in the Midwestern United States. He seemed to have trouble sitting still for long periods of time, and he could be very trying for the teacher. He seemed compelled to talk to other students even during quiet reading time, and he was prone to getting into mischief. If there was a commotion in class, Eric was often the center of it. When Eric's classroom teacher responded to a survey that inquired about the creative potential of the students in her class, she was not able to identify any interest on Eric's part that she could use to motivate him to be more productive in class. She had resigned herself to trying to get as much out of Eric as she could by placing him in productive cooperative learning groups and working with him to cut down on his talking and inconsistent work and behavior patterns. She shared this about Eric:

> His schoolwork is sporadic. At times he seems distracted, although when he does take part in class discussion, his answers are appropriate and show some thought. When assigned to a group, he will work with the others as long as they are working. He seems unwilling to take the lead in projects, but will carry out his assignment and do his share. Eric is popular with other boys and respectful toward adults. Even when he is being reprimanded, he is quick to acknowledge that he was in the wrong and will sincerely pledge to try to improve his behavior. On open-ended assignments, when he does hand them in, Eric's work shows evidence of originality and flexibility at times, but often lacks breadth or depth, and he will elaborate on his answers only after prompting by the teacher. In group assignments requiring creative thinking, he may offer some tentative ideas, but again will not take the lead. Although he will work with others to meet a challenge, he is not motivated to seek out challenges or ambiguous situations. His attempts at trying out new and original ideas are tentative at best, and he seeks teacher validation to make sure his efforts are "okay" or "right."

Eric's situation might have continued in much the same way throughout the year, except for the intervention of one of his friends and the willingness on the part of his teacher to broaden her view. The teacher announced her plan to begin a unit on the Civil War and was preparing to give the class an assignment when one of Eric's friends raised his hand and exclaimed, "Mrs. Lynch, if you want to know about the Civil War, you should ask Eric. He knows all about it!" Mrs. Lynch responded, "That's very interesting. Thank you, Jimmy. Eric do you know about the Civil War already?"

Eric responded that he did, and he proceeded to summarize the causes of the war as well as some of the battles and leading generals on both sides. Upon further questioning, Mrs. Lynch found that Eric's uncle was a Civil War reenactor and had involved Eric in his hobby for more than 2 years. Eric had a passion for all things Civil War and avidly read books about it that he borrowed from his uncle or the town library. He had recently been accepted as a drummer boy in his uncle's regiment. Mrs. Lynch was a bit stunned and mystified as a new view of Eric began to form. She had found a hook that she could use to more fully engage him in his schoolwork and channel his energy in positive ways. She also had found a tool to help him work toward expressing his creative potential.

Mrs. Lynch's first step was to invite Eric to put together a set of lessons about the Civil War and Civil War reenactors. She spoke to his parents and uncle to enlist their help. At Eric's request, his friend Jimmy also became involved. The project they planned involved research that would lead to a PowerPoint presentation accompanied by activities for their classmates to complete. The teacher taught the entire class to use some tools for thinking and problem solving. For instance, she asked the class to use the Brainstorming with Post-it® Notes tool to list the challenges that faced the nation in 1860. The students then created another list of challenges facing the United States today. The lists were compared to see if any of the issues of concern in 1860 were still of concern today. Students then worked in groups to choose one of those issues and develop possible solutions.

Eric and Jimmy began to generate ideas for their presentation. When they encountered some difficulty, Mrs. Lynch suggested they try to list the attributes of the Civil War that they wanted to emphasize, choose a workable set of goals for the lesson, and then develop a plan. She offered to check with them at each step in the process. The boys became engrossed in the project and worked on it during any free time that they could find at school, in the evenings, and on weekends. Their presentation was a great success. Both boys came in costume, one as a soldier for the North and the other as soldier for the South. Their PowerPoint presentation included slides from history books and old maps, as well as slides the boys created themselves.

Mrs. Lynch was so impressed that she told the other fifth-grade teachers about the presentation, and the boys went from class to class sharing their knowledge. When they had completed their rounds of the other classes, Mrs. Lynch took some time with the boys to review what they had done. They discussed how they had used the problem-solving process, which tools they had used, and what they might have done differently. She asked them to each write a short paper on the experience to place in their online portfolios.

Eric had become involved in class, taking a leading role in many classroom activities. Mrs. Lynch suggested that Eric try writing an article for the school paper, and he decided to write about Civil War reenactors. Mrs. Lynch told Eric that if he wrote a strong enough article, he could submit it to a local newspaper that ran a weekly history feature. With Mrs. Lynch's approval, Eric again enlisted Jimmy's help. The boys gathered all of the information about reenactors and decided to interview Eric's uncle and others in the regiment. When they were done, they had more information than they could handle. Mrs. Lynch suggested that they think about using some of the focusing tools to narrow their options, which they did. After several drafts and revisions, the full-length article was ready for the community paper and a shorter version was submitted to the school paper.

Throughout this experience, Eric's classwork and behavior became more positive and consistent. He began to volunteer answers and take the lead in cooperative groups. He also expanded his interest to other historical periods and maintained his interest in writing. In sixth grade, with the guidance of his social studies/language arts teacher, he created a similar presentation on ancient Greece, focusing on the Persian Wars. An article from that presentation was also published in the local paper.

William

William has studied piano privately for 6 years and the clarinet in school for 5 years. Now, as a high school freshman, he is excited about being selected for the concert ensemble. To improve his understanding of music, he has elected to take a music theory class. During his piano lessons, he has found learning about chord progressions and jazz improvisation a lot of fun, and he has tackled each assignment with a degree of confidence in his own ideas and ability, both in terms of his skills and attempts at originality.

His background has enabled him to approach assignments in his theory class from several directions. He is able to see patterns in different musical ideas and can pull from several genres. He has produced some interesting arrangements for small ensembles. These are usually played and then critiqued by William's classmates under the guidance of Mr. Trimble, the band director. Mr. Trimble has offered to work with William on an arrangement that might be played in the upcoming spring concert.

Mr. Trimble has also invited William to try out for the jazz ensemble. During lessons, William is not only developing his improvisational skills, but also gaining a wider understanding of the standard band literature.

William also does well in his other classes. A solid A/B student in most classes, he enjoys science and math most. In middle school, his science fair project won top honors. He is also thinking of trying out for the school musical. Watching the drama club's fall production, he remarked to his friend that he thought that he would enjoy being in a musical. The two boys agreed to try out together after the winter holidays.

Sue

Since she was in kindergarten, Sue has peppered people with questions. Today, as a high school junior in a northeastern suburban high school, she has become more and more enthusiastic after realizing that in science there are so many more questions than answers. Over the years, her parents have been supportive of her growing passion for science. While she was still in elementary school, her father built her a mini-research lab in the garage. In middle school, she consistently won science competitions, first locally and then on the regional and state levels. Today she corresponds regularly with other students around the world and with faculty members at several leading technical schools, exchanging ideas and receiving feedback on the progress of her experiments. One faculty member has become her online mentor.

Sue is an outstanding student in all of her classes and is captain of the school tennis team. Socially, she is accepted by her peers and respected for her achievements. She has a tight-knit group of like-minded friends but spends most of her out-of-school hours on her studies or exploring some new facet of science that she uncovered in her reading. She is very comfortable with adults and is able to hold her own in any conversation, especially on issues related to science and technology.

This year she is taking an Advanced Placement (AP) biology course. She has approached each assignment with passion and has been able to really motivate her two lab partners, Ida and Mary. Together they have become very interested in a particular disease from which Ida's grandmother passed away. During the course of the year, the three girls have developed a new process that may enable the early diagnosis of important indicators of the disease. After winning a state-level competition with the report on this process, they have now entered a national event. They have also published a paper on their process in a peer-reviewed journal, with Sue as first author.

Sue has been fortunate throughout her schooling. Her parents recognized her potential early on and encouraged her questions, actively supporting and nurturing her curiosity and her desire to explore both physical and biological science. Her school and teachers also recognized her abilities and placed her in accelerated classes whenever possible. Her AP teacher ensured that she and her classmates were well grounded in the problem-solving process and tools and supported opportunities for them to tackle open-ended challenges. Her fellow students usually supported Sue as the leader in taking on advanced projects. In her senior year, Sue will attend her high school classes in English, social studies, and Chinese and also enroll in college courses in math and science at a nearby university. Unfortunately, it is probable that this change in her schedule will make it necessary for her to give up her spot on the tennis team. She accepts this possibility, however, and is quick to explain that her first priority is her passion and enthusiasm for learning and creative inquiry in science.

Plan for the Book

In a nutshell, this book will be your resource guide for making creativity a viable aspect of your personal life and your professional efforts. The book includes 20 chapters, divided into five main sections.

Section I: Understanding Creativity and Innovation

The first section of the book, which consists of Chapters 1–4, sets the foundation for the book's approach to creativity and innovation in education. Our goal is to provide a common set of concepts, principles, and terminology that will guide you throughout the book. Chapter 2 describes and responds to several myths and misunderstandings that are widely held about creativity. Chapter 3 presents a number of definitions that have been used to explain creativity and innovation and synthesizes that body of work by offering working definitions that we will employ throughout the book. Chapter 4 explores several reasons for the importance of creativity and innovation and challenges you to consider their implications for education.

Section II: Foundations for Creativity and Innovation

The second section presents a systematic framework, using the acronym "COCO" for understanding the foundations of creativity in education. It includes Chapters 5–9. Chapter 5 presents an overview of the four essential factors in the framework, and each of the four subsequent chapters describes one of those factors in greater detail. Chapter 6 deals with personal creativity characteristics. Chapter 7 defines and explains the operations that are essential elements of creativity in action. Chapter 8 examines the context for creativity and innovation in educational settings, and Chapter 9 considers creative outcomes or products.

Section III: Identifying and Measuring Creativity

The third section includes three chapters that deal with practical questions and resources for creativity assessment and measurement. Questions on these topics are among the most common inquiries we receive and include:

- o Are there any creativity tests?
- o How do we know whether they have any value?
- o How can we document the effectiveness of our attempts to foster creativity or show that we are making a difference?
- o How do I determine how creative my students are?

Chapter 10 establishes a foundation to help you avoid common traps or trip wires in this area and understand how some basic educational measurement concepts apply to creativity. Chapter 11 describes basic principles and procedures to guide creativity assessment in instruction and to help you find, review, and use assessment resources appropriately. In Chapter 12, we describe a practical, contemporary approach for assessing creativity in ways that relate meaningfully to instruction.

Section IV: How Do We Develop Creativity?

This book builds on the basic commitment that the creativity of people—at all ages—can be enhanced through deliberate instruction or training. As a result, responding to the question of how to accomplish that represents a major commitment for us, and you may find that the seven chapters in this section (Chapters 13–19) are really at the very heart of the text. Chapter 13 guides you in establishing basic conditions for fostering creativity and innovation. Chapter 14 presents eight basic guidelines, organized into two complementary sets, that undergird all explicit efforts to promote creativity and innovation. Chapter 15 offers practical strategies for teaching the basic tools that are foundational to creative and critical thinking. In Chapter 16, we describe ways to build upon and extend knowledge of those tools into working with realistic problems, or structured practice tasks (e.g., case studies, simulations, practice problems). This chapter also includes an overview of several creativity and problem-solving models and their instructional implications. Chapter 17 describes a number of national and international educational programs that encourage and build creativity skills. In Chapter 18, we discuss real problems and challenges. Chapter 19 considers the rapidly evolving role of creativity and innovation in education today and highlights the role and impact of mentoring, working with at-risk students, technology, and the challenge of linking creativity and process tools with curriculum content standards.

Section V: Looking Ahead

The final section of the book consists of one chapter that we hope will stimulate you to look toward some exciting future directions and opportunities. In Chapter 20, we consider issues and future directions for research on creativity and innovation in education.

Chapter 2

Dispelling Common Myths

After reading this chapter, you will be able to recognize and set aside nine widely held myths and misunderstandings about creativity. You will also be able to clarify your own understanding of creativity and be a more critical consumer of educational materials and techniques that claim to foster creativity.

Common Myths and Misunderstandings

There are many misunderstandings surrounding the topic of creativity. These misunderstandings can hamper people's understanding and acceptance of creativity in general and their own creativity in particular. For example, recall Eric from Chapter 1. When Eric was in third grade, he seemed to have a knack for creating unique mechanical devices out of bits and pieces that he found around home and at the city's recycling center. The teacher called Eric's parents quite often because Eric also forgot important articles of clothing like his warm coat or hat and mittens in a snowstorm. Eric seemed to live in another world and was not always aware of what was happening in his environment. The teacher also found Eric very irritating because he often asked "impertinent" questions. The teacher wanted to move on to another topic, but Eric always seemed to have a question or an opinion that the teacher found obnoxious. It was easier for others to view Eric's unique behavior as troublesome than to consider that he might be showing signs of creativity, as they focused more on what Eric *wasn't* doing than on his imagination and inventiveness (two traits that Eric kept well to himself).

Misunderstandings can also influence people's attitudes, beliefs, and behaviors regarding efforts to recognize and nurture creativity in educational settings. Educational studies about creativity have consistently noted that some teachers tend to dislike personality traits they associate with creativity, which might be described as obnoxiousness, nonconformity, and questioning authority (Williams, 1968). They may ignore or overlook constructive personal creativity characteristics. Teachers may say that they recognize the importance of creativity and of providing a variety of methods and strategies to allow for creativity in the classroom, but there is debate as to whether teachers can actually recognize creative behaviors in order to enhance them (Aljughaiman & Mowrer-Reynolds, 2005). To help get started in a constructive direction, let's examine nine misunderstandings that are particularly important and seek ways to frame them more positively.

Viewing Creativity Only as a Rare Form of Genius

Marie Skłodowska-Curie

Many people think of creativity only in terms of the outstanding contributions of a Picasso, Rembrandt, Curie, Mozart, or Edison. Some may consider creativity as something that just happens—either you have it or you don't. Some of Sue's teachers in Chapter 1 may have viewed her as a "wonder child," not recognizing the support she had received from her parents and the effort she made on her own to prepare for her chosen career in science. Likewise, many of William's teachers might have been unaware that he had any special talent at all. Viewing creativity as a rare and special gift beyond the reach of most of their students keeps some educators from trying new approaches or recognizing the potential talents of the students sitting in front of them.

Educators who fall victim to this misunderstanding may say, "It's unlikely that I will ever have someone like that in my class, so I don't have to be concerned about creativity." Or, perhaps they avoid trying something new because they overlook or don't recognize the many ways we all use creativity in everyday life and work. We've all heard ourselves or others say, "I could never do that" or "I've never been good at art" (or music, theater, and so forth). But, consider what it is that you do very well. You probably do what you do very well because you enjoy it, have practiced it a lot, and feel satisfaction each time you do it. You may also have had a lot of support from others who recognized that this activity was important to you.

So, the constructive approach to this misunderstanding is to affirm the creative potential in every person. All of us can learn to use our imagination better, to manage successfully the change we encounter daily, to generate more and better ideas, and to solve problems more effectively. Rather than avoiding the topic of creativity, consider that you have some students who, with a little encouragement and support, could develop something very new and unique to them and—perhaps—to you, too!

Viewing Creativity as Madness, Mystical, and Mysterious

Mad Scientist

Next, some believe that a creative person may be slightly mad or neurotic. You can probably think of people throughout history (Van Gogh comes often to mind) who seemed to be mentally unstable but exceptionally creative.

Many people are creatively productive without being mentally unstable. Highly creative people who have mental illnesses tend to be more productive when their illness has been diagnosed and treated. It has also been noted (Bailey, 2003; Weisberg, 1986, 1994) that some mental illnesses, such as anxiety and depression, actually disrupt the cognitive and emotional processes necessary for creative thinking and production. However, Silvia and Kaufman (2010) suggested that very little consideration has been given to the person with mental illness or disorder who continues his or her creative pursuit, and how that takes great courage. We need to be careful about assumptions made about the mental or psychological health (or illness) of highly creative people. Very often the studies about the topic of highly creative people with mental illness focus on one highly creative person whose life and apparent mental illness is diagnosed by another person who then writes a book about it. Silvia and Kaufman also noted that most of the highly creative people posthumously diagnosed with a mental illness tend to be people in the arts. You will have a hard time finding literature about a wild and crazy mechanical engineer. Engineers, historians, mathematicians, and landscape architects (among others) seem to be excluded from this "mad genius" stereotype, yet there are many exciting innovators and creative producers within all of these fields. For example, George Ferris developed what was known as "the wheel" for the World's Fair of 1893. Although Ferris was admired, he was also considered crazy for even trying something like that. No one had ever attempted to design or build anything like it before. Just as with the Eiffel Tower, the "Ferris" wheel was first considered by many to be an eyesore; it was eventually moved to St. Louis, where it was also considered an eyesore and finally demolished. Although the public may not have appreciated the first Ferris wheel, it has been with us in many sizes ever since. For some time, London had the world's tallest Ferris wheel, the London Eye, which opened to the public in 2000. Now, however, the Singapore Flyer, constructed in Singapore's Marina Bay in 2005–2008, is 98 feet taller than the London Eye.

Attaching the concept of creativity to being crazy or mentally ill is like saying that elephants like peanuts and everything that likes peanuts is an elephant. It is far more likely that people who exercise their creativity are more mentally and psychologically healthy and stable than those who do not (Bailey, 2003). A person who others see as eccentric, strange, or mentally unstable may sometimes be called creative. But being eccentric or mentally unstable is not the same as being creative, nor is it a necessary condition for creative productivity. To attach a stereotype of a mad genius to anyone seen as creative is an exaggerated and overly general belief about one group of people (Sylvia & Kaufman, 2010). However, it does seem to persist for those who experience depression, anxiety, and social anxiety, as well as the bipolar family of disorders, the schizophrenia spectrum of disorders, and substance abuse (Silvia & Kaufman, 2010). So where does this belief come from? Some argue that mental illness causes creativity. In this sense, creative achievement comes from anguish and pain, which is the romantic stereotype of the mad genius. Some researchers have suggested that the idea that creativity causes mental illness should be given serious consideration. Perhaps it comes from the belief that anyone who would devote years to a solitary, low-paying domain, such as writing, composing, or creating artwork, may have a lifestyle with several risk factors for mental illness. On the other hand, high levels of creative accomplishment can put a person at risk for intense criticism and rejection. A third possibility, and probably the most likely one, is that creativity and mental illness merely happen to occur at the same time—but certainly not all the time. One study compared a group of people who had bipolar illness with another group of people who didn't and found there was no difference between the groups in terms of creative abilities. Another study found individuals with schizophrenia, manic depression, or psychotic depression were less creative than the control group. These stereotypes often persist into the classroom. Gowan, Khatena, and Torrance (1981) noted that the child often identified as creative is seen as different, odd, unique, strange, adventurous, and curious. The child may have a lot of curiosity, but others may see the child as a curiosity instead.

Some view the creative person as mystical, being unusually able to tap into his or her unconscious mind and express it in unusual ways—and often unable to control the appearance or disappearance of those powers. The Greeks believed that the gods or the muses breathed ideas into people who were considered creative. Even today you will hear some people talk about their muse and its elusiveness when they share what inspires them in their creative endeavor. Some people also believe that the mystical type of creativity will appear in words or products that suddenly emerge, whole and complete, arising out of nowhere. For example, some writers may talk about a character who just seemed to appear on the pages completely developed; songwriters describe rapidly writing a piece that just seemed to write itself. These reports often overlook the fact that their efforts have been incubating for a long time and emerge *finally*—not suddenly—building on a lengthy period of preparation and sustained effort.

A positive response to this misunderstanding is to affirm that sensitivity and openness to experience are important to creativity, but that creativity can also be the result of deliberate application of tools for thinking and sustained, focused, and demanded attention and effort. Creativity can be intentional, directed, fickle, elusive, and spontaneous.

Treating Creativity as Comic Relief From Real Work

Unfortunately, some educators think of creativity primarily as something to provide their students with some playful time away from the recall and recitation they consider the "real business" of school. This is illustrated in comments like, "Boys and girls, you've been working very hard this morning, and I'm sure your brains are really tired. Now we'll do some creative thinking." This kind of thinking fails to recognize that creativity is a part of effective inquiry and learning. In recent years, we have seen greater interest in authentic instruction, or in emphasizing the importance of what students are able to do with what they know, not just with how much they know. Constructively, then, creativity does build on memory and past experience, but goes beyond: It involves a forward-looking foundation for application, synthesis, and action. When students are empowered to think and work creatively on their own or in teams and groups, their confidence grows about themselves as learners and creative thinkers, and they engage in challenging tasks with energy and enthusiasm. Creativity makes work meaningful and energizing.

Restricting the Concept of Creativity to Arts and Crafts

A teacher once described a student in his class as "not really being creative," although the student did "nice work and was very neat." In explaining what he meant by creative, the teacher offered an example of a student who seemed artistically talented—and who was also the sloppiest, messiest person in the class. The teacher explained that, in his experience, most creative people were distracted folks who expressed their creativity through some artistic medium.

Creativity plays an important role in the arts, to be sure, but it is also vital in every discipline, including those that make up academic school curricula: writing, literature, mathematics, science, technology, the humanities, and the social and behavioral sciences. Although William, our musician in Chapter 1, fits well within this myth, Sue and Eric are obvious exceptions. People can (and do) express and apply their creativity in every domain of human endeavor, as they develop and test new theories, plan and conduct original inquiry, solve problems, create new products, communicate their ideas, and apply their efforts to improving the quality of life in countless ways.

Believing That Creativity Equals "No Boundaries"

Some parents and educators believe that creativity implies total, unrestrained freedom of expression and behavior without any boundaries, constraints, or discipline. This may still be reminiscent of the beatnik or hippie culture of previous generations. We saw a cartoon, for example, of a couple: a long-haired, bearded man and pigtailed woman, both in fringed vests, sandals, tie-dyed shirts, and frayed jeans, looking apprehensively at a small boy of age 6 or 7, wearing a suit, dress shirt, tie, and vest and carrying a briefcase. The adults were saying, "Where did we go wrong?" The counterculture of today may be exhibited with fully or partially shaved heads or bright pink hair, tattoos, body piercings, and pants seemingly on the verge of falling to the floor, but the suit and tie on the young boy would be just as disconcerting. Some people seem to be convinced that highly creative people need to escape from all boundaries. This can often arise from a misunderstanding about the kind or extent of freedom that people need in order to be creative. Boundaries and guidelines can help to focus and direct creative intent and energy, as well as to constrain or inhibit it (Sapp, 1997). Some people prefer to work with a very clear and detailed set of directions, giving them a way to channel their efforts and activities productively. By contrast, other people prefer to work with only a very skeletal outline of what might be expected or the pathway they will follow. Structure (provided for you or of your own creation) and the guidance of authority (close at hand or at arm's length) can be valuable for some people in certain circumstances, but they can be debilitating for others. Removing all structure and boundaries is certainly not essential for creativity for all people across all tasks and settings! Again, we are reminded of a cartoon in which a group of young children was pleading with an overly permissive teacher, "Do we have to do whatever we want to do again today?"

The constructive view is that creativity involves freedom of ideation and exploration, along with creating and maintaining environments in ways that respond appropriately to the person's need for structure, authority, and direction—not simply stripping all boundaries away or using structure rigidly to stifle curiosity and inquiry. The challenge is to construct and use structure and boundaries wisely, not just to strip them away entirely.

Employing "Dot-to-Dot" Creativity (Reducing Creativity to Exercises and Workbook Activities)

A few teachers who have learned only a little about creativity settle for simple, easily used classroom strategies and use them routinely or mechanically, without really challenging the students to put thought and effort into them. Some teachers have been heard to say they use these activities during the last few minutes of class before the bell rings. One teacher was happy to demonstrate her approach to creativity in her classroom by asking Jason to come to the front of the room and proceed with the day's creativity activity. Jason came to the front and said, "Pop, pop, pop." A girl said, "Bubbles!" Jason replied, "Wrong!" Then he repeated, "Pop, pop, pop." A boy called out, "Balloons!" "Wrong!" Jason said. Finally someone guessed "popcorn," and Jason said, "Correct." Then he went back to his seat. The teacher called another student, Daren, to come forward. Daren stood in front shuffling from one foot to another, trying to think of something to say, and finally said, "Pop, pop, pop!" A chorus of classmates called out, "Oh, we already know *that* one: It's popcorn!" Rather dejectedly, Daren noted they were right and returned to his seat. That was creativity time in the classroom. Superficial activities produce glib and meaningless responses and fail to capture the power of creative learning for students.

Today, there are many activities and exercises in books and on the Internet that are labeled as creative (or as 21st-century learning activities). *Caveat emptor!* These labels do not necessarily mean the activities are in any way creative or innovative or that they promote creative thinking, critical thinking, or deep learning and challenging inquiry. The buzzwords have caught the attention of the marketing gurus. Even if the exercises and activities might have potential for creative or critical thinking, relegating them to being used as isolated exercises or filler activities during a specific time of day or week is not productive. It may even promote the idea that creativity is something marginal, a frill that is detached from curriculum and instruction. The constructive approach is to investigate ways to incorporate and integrate creativity into the main ideas, themes, and challenges of the curriculum, blending content and process in a harmonious synthesis.

Looking Only at Creative Teaching and Not at Creative Learning

To many teachers, creativity is something different and seductive. The idea of *different* may also mean *unique* for many teachers as they define creativity (Smith & Smith, 2010). In our visits to schools, administrators sometimes say, "I really want to take you to see Ms. Soozy, who's my most creative teacher." This often leads to observing some unusual (and occasionally bizarre!) kinds of activity and much less frequently to classrooms with many visible indicators of students' creativity in action. At the elementary level, for example, it often leads into a classroom richly decorated with bright colors and busy bulletin boards made by the teacher. This is akin to the person who believes that a person can only be creative if he or she (or the classroom) looks creative. At the junior or senior high levels, the creative teacher is often the building's maverick or "eccentric in residence," and sometimes the most prominent feature of the classroom is incredible clutter (all kinds of things piled everywhere). Again, we may see some signs of the teacher's efforts to be creative, but very little indication of any creative effort or activity by the students.

Creative learning should be concerned with instruction that leads to student thinking. We do not consider it sufficient to talk about creative teaching unless it focuses on ways to stimulate creative learning. The constructive approach to this misunderstanding reminds educators that the focus of their efforts will best be devoted to recognizing, challenging, guiding, and supporting their students' creativity and innovation. Teachers' creative engagement and ideas can enable them to serve as role models and can be a source of creative opportunities for the students, not simply as a showcase for themselves. (It can also be remarkably exciting for educators to discover how rewarding teaching can be when students are passionately engaged in creative learning.)

Believing That Creativity Is Only "Thinking Out of the Box"

"Thinking out of the box" is a phrase is so ubiquitously associated with creativity that you may be surprised that we present it as a misunderstanding. In fact, it is one of the most overworked, overused phrases ever coined about creativity and is, at best, only partially accurate. It seems rooted in the fascination we have had for decades with the notion that creativity is entirely wild-and-crazy, no-holds-barred thinking or that brainstorming tells the whole story about creativity, innovation, or problem solving.

We'd love to put the phrase to rest. We can emphasize the importance of thinking that is "out of the box," thinking that is "better inside the box," and perhaps also thinking creatively "with shapes that aren't boxes at all." Some people do naturally prefer to look for different options that emphasize novelty above all else. But others who are equally creative, albeit in different ways, express and use their creativity by thinking better inside the box; by stretching, reshaping, or expanding the box; or by making the box quite a bit more effective than it was before. By the way—who says it has to be a box, anyway? Perhaps when people ask us to think outside the box they are already being limited; it is simply a perception and perhaps a very personal one depending on what a person's "box" might be. Either way, the box notion can be limiting, so we should be careful when we toss boxes about. The next time you are in a group and someone asks you to think outside that box, ask, "What box?" We need to learn to move past the slogans and buzz words and to respect the creative contributions of all people (Isaksen, Dorval, & Treffinger, 2011; Treffinger, Selby, & Isaksen, 2008).

Thinking in Terms of Left Brain, Right Brain, or Whole Brain

"My, you look so left brained!" This statement was directed at a woman wearing a suit and heels and carrying a briefcase. The very professionally attired woman was working on evaluations for a school district with another professor from a nearby university. The person making the statement knew the woman in the suit as an artist and was surprised to see her dressed up this way—but that's another part of the story ("Where did we go wrong?" from above). The idea that creativity is concentrated or located only in the right side of the brain is another misunderstanding, as well as an enormous simplification of the way the brain functions and the concept of being creative. Children learn with their whole brain. But we still hear people talk about someone being "so right brained" when they are describing someone as creative or artistic. On the other hand, we also hear people describe someone as "so left brained" when they are talking about someone who is very logical and sequential in her thinking. The risk of these statements is that they create caricatures of creativity (and people), and portray creativity as a fixed quality. Such descriptions of creativity also reflect personal style differences, not just assumptions about where in the brain certain processes occur. The reality is that we need both sides of the brain for everything (McGilchrist, 2010). Almost all brain functions are served by both hemispheres; however, each hemisphere deals with these functions in consistently different ways. McGilchrist (2010) stated that the right hemisphere "pays wide open attention to the world" while the left focuses on the details (p. 9W). As McGilchrist (2010) noted, "There is a reason we have two hemispheres: We need both views of the world" (p. 9W). The more constructive approach is to consider the possibility that everyone (including you) has the potential to be creative in some way—in their own unique way, using their whole brain, their abilities, and their personal style preferences. Your creativity, and that of your students, may not look like what you expect or what anyone else expects from you.

Our View

We believe there is creative potential in all of us. We each have a preferred and unique way to approach creative and innovative endeavors. With practice and consistent application, you can teach a deliberate process and the tools for thinking that will enrich any curricular area and certainly enrich the lives of your students. As noted before, we believe creativity can be intentional, sustained, and directed, not just unexplainable, fickle, elusive, and spontaneous. As you and your students apply creative thinking consistently, they will become not just better problem solvers, but also problem finders. Your students will have greater confidence in their own abilities as learners and problem solvers (and finders!). Your role as guide, facilitator, and role model will empower students to think and work creatively, whether alone or collaboratively in teams and groups. We know that you will discover and be energized by the passion students can have when they are engaged in creative learning.

Although creativity plays an important part in the arts, we believe it is vital in every discipline, especially those that make up the academic school curricula. As an educator, and even more so as a role model, you can find ways for your students to apply their creativity in every curricular area. We believe that it is important to understand how people respond to or need different levels of structure and that it is necessary to construct and use boundaries wisely. Likewise, we know it is important to understand that it's not whether you are inside or outside of a box—or whatever shape it may be—but that you (and your students) are actively engaged in using your whole brain, your abilities, and your own unique creative style.

Taking the Chapter Forward

o Now that you have read this chapter, begin to watch for some of the ways you see the term *creativity* and related words, such as *innovation*, being used in everyday life. Be alert for signs, stories, and advertisements that you see, as well as conversations you hear.

o Think about the following questions:

> Have you seen or heard some of the nine myths that you've read about in this chapter? How do those myths influence the messages we receive about creativity or their implications?

> Do you find some of the myths reflected in the beliefs or behaviors of some of your colleagues in the workplace?

> If you have your own classroom, think about your students. How might you identify those who are very creative? What might you do to affirm the unique abilities, styles, and characteristics of each person and use those to promote creative growth?

> How might creativity, quality, and rigor work in harmony?

Chapter 3

Defining Creativity and Innovation

A fter reading this chapter, you will be able to develop an inclusive personal definition of creativity and innovation. We hope that you will share our basic belief that all people can be creative and be able to explain the rationale for that belief. In addition, you will also be able to compare, contrast, and evaluate the various definitions of terms, including *creative, critical*, and *innovative*, that you may encounter in this text and elsewhere and discuss with others the importance of creativity and critical thinking, as well as the concepts of generating and focusing.

The Problem in Finding a Definition

Before we continue discussing creativity and innovation, we should spend some time figuring out what it is we are talking about. The dictionary on the computer on which this paragraph was written defines *innovation* as "the process of innovating." That doesn't help much, so looking at the word *innovate*, we find it means "to make changes in something established, especially by introducing new methods, ideas, or products" or to "introduce (something new, especially a product)." In *Creative Approaches to Problem Solving*, Isaksen et al. (2011) defined innovation as "the commercialization of new ideas" (p. 13). Innovation seems to be a subset—and possibly an outcome—of creative behavior, so we will focus our discussion on defining creativity, which is not an easy task! The *Funk and Wagnalls Standard Desk Dictionary* only defines the adjective "creative." The *Oxford English Dictionary* defines the noun as "creative power or facility; ability to create." The computer's dictionary defines it first as "the quality of being creative" (back to the adjective again) and second as "the ability to use the imagination to develop new and original ideas or things, especially in an artistic context."

Part of the problem may be the variety of ways the word is used in general conversation and in advertisements. For instance, an advertisement for the Division of Continuing Studies at a northeastern university tells us that "Creative Lifelong Learning Begins Here." There is no explanation as to what is meant by "Creative Lifelong Learning," but somehow we suspect that it is not using the same definition of the word creative as it is used to advertise a business such as Creative Edge Contracting. If you would like to see the extent of this confusion, just look under "creative" in the white pages (see sidebar).

For several years, we've asked teachers in creativity courses to gather responses from their students about what the word *creativity* means. By a wide margin, the most common responses from grades K–8 involved being artistic or musical (e.g., drawing, painting, writing a song). The word *imagination* was also

Entries Under "Creative" From the Authors' Local White Pages
(These are all real!)

Anything Creative
Creative Bedrooms
Creative Business Brokers
Creative Canvas
Creative Citrus Service
Creative Crystals
Creative Dental Resources
Creative Design Doors
Creative Edge Contracting
Creative Engineering & Manufacturing
Creative Fabricators
Creative Framing
Creative Group Travel
Creative Hairdressers
Creative Handyman Services
Creative Healing Center
Creative Home Improvements
Creative Host Services
Creative Image Studio
Creative Kidkare
Creative Kitchens & Baths
Creative Lending
Creative Loafing
Creative Mailbox Design
Creative Metal Works
Creative Packaging
Creative Painting
Creative Quality Time
Creative Realty
Creative & Response Research
Creative Sign & Graphics
Creative Style Nail Salon
Creative Technology
Creative Tile & Marble
Creative Touch Video
Creative Wetlands

used frequently. Other responses included being an inventor or inventing something, making or building things (in the words of one 5-year-old, "making stuff that nobody maked or helped you with"), doing projects that are different, having lots of ideas, and, of course, thinking out of the box.

After more than half a century of research, professionals haven't done much better in defining creativity in a clear and consistent manner; more than 100 definitions can be found in the research literature on creativity. Some researchers, including, for example, Marcia Delcourt (1993), believe that creativity involves the development of original products, while Eric Fromm (1959) proposed that creativity is an attitude that exists whether or not something is produced. Then there are those who have tackled the subject using entirely different terms. For instance, Edward de Bono (1970) wrote about "lateral thinking" rather than creativity. There are those who used the word *ingenuity* (e.g., Flanagan, 1963), while others focused on critical thinking, including the ability to correctly assess statements or situations (Ennis, 1987).

As a noun, creativity is the ability to produce high-quality, appropriate, and novel outcomes (e.g., Beghetto & Kaufman, 2007). To Fromm (1959), it is "the ability to see (or to be aware) and to respond" (p. 44). Creative ability has been linked to imagination, where one breaks away from the bounds of perception, using ideas and emotions in order to form new and unique structures (e.g., Khatena & Torrance, 1973). Going back to the computer dictionary, imagination has to do with forming "new ideas, images or concepts of external objects not present to the senses" and is "the ability of the mind to be creative or resourceful." Imagination and creativity are abilities that have been the subjects of study for many centuries, and innovation might be regarded as an outcome of both. Our modern quest to better understand creativity so that we could find ways to help people fulfill their innovative and creative potential is widely regarded as stemming from J. P. Guilford's 1950 presidential address to the American Psychological Association, in which he called for new and expanded research on creativity and its implications for theory, research, and practice.

Definitions Found in Current Research and Theory

After Guilford's call, several different groups of researchers began to study various aspects of creativity, which taken together contributed to our overall understanding of the construct. We might think of the study of creativity much like that of the water in a lake fed by many sources, such as rain, underground springs, and a variety of rivers and smaller streams (Treffinger, 1996). If you travel along any one of the streams around that lake, you might feel separated from all of the others and perhaps even from the lake itself. You might not even be aware that there are other streams or that a lake might be found nearby. Nonetheless, the water in your stream may play a significant role in forming the lake or influencing the quality of its water. Researchers investigating creativity are in a similar position. They might be operating within just one tributary of the larger construct, but they are nonetheless studying a significant part of what makes up the "lake" of creativity.

One major stream feeding the creativity lake is that of the "third force" psychologists who looked at creativity in terms of mental health, a way of living, and a major element in self-actualization. This stream feeds and comingles with the inquiries of those studying classical theories of personality (the individual characteristics and styles of highly creative individuals) who seek to understand how individuals are creative in their own unique ways. Another stream running from the third force waters is the study of social and interpersonal factors, looking at how context might either facilitate or inhibit creativity. Traveling around the lake would also bring us to other feeders. The cognitive-rational approach includes scholars who investigate creative thinking, problem solving, metacognition, and remote associations, as well as visual perception, divergent thinking, and preferences for asymmetry or complexity. Finally, there are investigations into the nonrational conceptions of creativity: consciousness, mind expansion, imagery, meditation, spirituality, and brain function.

We must study these streams individually if we are to understand what the lake is made of, but if you dip a cup in the middle of the lake, the water will have mixed to the point that you can no longer separate the water of one stream from another. As a result, we end up with many definitions developed by researchers who have followed different streams of inquiry. Because of the complexity of the concept, finding one universally accepted definition of creativity is a daunting task. We'll try it anyway.

Many lists of informal and formal definitions of creativity have been compiled over the years (e.g., Aleinikov, Kackmeister, & Koening, 2000; Treffinger, 1996, 2011; Treffinger, Young, Selby, & Shepardson, 2002). Although some writers look at creativity as an ability, others look at it in terms of either products that result from creative behavior or the creative process that leads to those products. Prentky (1980) described characteristics of a creative product and then immediately included elements of process in his description. He suggested that creative products reflect originality, the synthesis and reformulation of existing ideas or experiences, spontaneity, incubation leading to revelatory insight, the influence of social context, the presence of worth or redeeming features, and sustained change.

Those who look at products often use the term *innovation* rather than creativity, with innovation referring to the commercialization of new or novel ideas—in other words, viewing innovation as a practical application of creativity (e.g., Isaksen et al., 2011). In this view, there can be creativity without innovation if creative potential is not fulfilled or if nothing results from a creative effort. Innovation requires some outcome or product resulting from creative thinking. Hennessey and Amabile (1987) suggested that to be creative a product must be novel and appropriate, resulting in a useful or valuable response to an open-ended problem. In a similar vein, Wallace and Gruber (1989) declared that works that are original, purposeful, and harmonious or compatible with human needs and values can be described as creative.

Earlier, Amabile (1983) described creativity as the point of interaction among three components: domain-relevant skills, including domain knowledge, technical skills, and domain-related talent; creativity-relevant skills, including working styles, thinking styles, and other personality traits; and task motivation or intrinsic motivation, growing from a deep interest or need an individual experiences at a point in time. Her definition seems to approach creativity in conjunction with an individual's personal characteristics. As early as 1961, Rhodes tried to address this difficulty, writing: "Creativity cannot be explained alone in terms of . . . any other single component, no matter how vital that component may be" (p. 306). He proposed four factors to help us better understand the concept. These four factors are often referred to as the "four Ps": *person* (personality characteristics or traits of creative people); *process* (elements of motivation, perception, learning, thinking, and communicating); *product* (ideas translated into tangible forms); and *press* (the relationship between human beings and their environment). Although many studies of creativity tend to emphasize one of these elements or treat them as if each existed separately and in isolation, it is important to keep in mind that they are always in dynamic interaction and that creative behavior results from the integration or synthesis of the four factors (Keller-Mathers & Murdock, 1999).

Treffinger (1988, 1991) described four similar factors in a slightly different way. He considered the *characteristics* that a person brings to a problem-solving or change management situation; the *operations* he or she is able to perform; the *context* in which the problem, challenge, or question is situated; and the *outcomes* that result (COCO). We will discuss these four factors in detail in Chapter 5.

Vernon (1989) returned to the consideration of ability but went a step further. To him, creativity is the "capacity to produce new or original ideas, insights, restructurings, inventions, or artistic objects, which are accepted by experts as being of scientific, aesthetic, social, or technological value" (Vernon, 1989, p. 94). This idea that identifying an individual as creative depends on some outside acceptance of that person's productive output as creative or innovative is found in various writings on the subject. For instance, Gardner (1993a) defined the creative individual as "a person who regularly solves problems, fashions products, or defines new questions in a domain in a way that is initially considered novel but that ultimately becomes accepted in a particular cultural setting" (p. 35). Sternberg (2006) seemed to agree that creative ideas are often seen as novel at first, but later become generally accepted. His "investment" theory of creativity suggests that, when it comes to new ideas, creative individuals are willing and able to "buy low and sell high." According to this theory, creativity is the result of six interrelated resources: intellectual abilities, knowledge, styles of thinking, personality, motivation, and the environment. Each of us has differing levels of these resources based on, among other factors, intelligence, knowledge, thinking styles, personality, and motivation.

Rogers (1959) emphasized three major inner conditions of the creative person: an openness to experience that prohibits rigidity, the ability to use one's personal standards to evaluate situations, and the ability to accept the unstable and to experiment with many possibilities. Rogers believed that individual creativity is usually a sign of psychological health, and similarly, Maslow (1976) viewed creativity as a path to self-actualization or fulfillment. Maslow held that creative people are able to overcome their fears and free themselves from social pressures as they attain personal integration or wholeness. He described creative, self-actualizing people as bold, courageous, autonomous, spontaneous, and confident. Creativity in his view is as much concerned with people and the way they deal with their daily lives as it is with impressive products.

Mednick (1962) proposed that creativity involves a process in which the individual associates ideas that are already in the person's mind in unusual but original ways to form new ideas. The creative person needs to dig deeply into the associative structure of the mind, probing beyond obvious connections, to find the novel or remote associations between ideas. From these associations original solutions are formed. Torrance (1974, 1987) also looked at creativity as

> a process of becoming sensitive to problems, deficiencies, gaps in knowledge, missing elements, disharmonies, and so on; identifying the difficulty; searching for solutions, making guesses, or formulating hypotheses about the deficiencies; testing and retesting these hypotheses and possibly modifying and retesting them; and finally communicating the results. (p. 8)

In the past, the creative process often was looked at as a natural gift available only to the geniuses among us. It usually followed a general pattern of inspiration enriched by a period of incubation leading to execution. Alex Osborn, in his 1953 work *Applied Imagination*, proposed that this process could be expanded, taught, and used deliberately in solving problems and meeting challenges. He initially identified three procedures: fact-finding, idea-finding, and solution-finding. He suggested that no matter what sequence they are taken in, each step "calls for deliberate effort and creative imagination" (Osborn, 1953, p. 86). Over the years, these steps have been reexamined and the process restructured. Several process models have evolved from Osborn's work (e.g., Basadur, 1994; Isaksen et al., 2011). Most process models include a discussion of two main types of activities and thinking, referred to as divergent and convergent (following Guilford's approach), creative and critical (drawing more on Torrance's approach and work in the 1970s), or generating and focusing (seen in more contemporary approaches).

Treffinger, Isaksen, and Dorval (2006) and Isaksen et al. (2011) pointed out that successful creative problem solving and decision making require a harmony or balance between creative and critical thinking. Creative thinking involves "encountering gaps, paradoxes, opportunities, challenges, or concerns, and then searching for meaningful new connections by *generating* many possibilities, varied possibilities (from different viewpoints or perspectives), unusual or original possibilities, and details to expand or enrich possibilities" whereas critical thinking involves "examining possibilities carefully, fairly, and constructively, and then *focusing* thoughts and actions by organizing and analyzing possibilities, refining and developing promising possibilities, ranking or prioritizing options, and choosing or deciding on certain options" (Isaksen et al., 2011, pp. 36–37).

"Big C" and Ordinary Creativity

Today many scholars view creativity in a much broader and more inclusive way than the early emphasis on "rare genius." In a more nuanced approach, however, some writers today (e.g., Gardner, 1993b; Simonton, 2010) distinguish between two types of creativity, commonly referred to as "Big C" and "little c" creativity, and others (e.g., Kaufman & Beghetto, 2009) distinguished among as many as four levels of "C" (big, pro, little, and mini). Early understandings of creativity were based on research involving those who are outstanding in their field, individuals whose works contributed to a major change in one or more areas of human endeavor—the type of creativity often referred to as Big C creativity. There are those who consider this level of innovation or creativity as the only approach worthy of study. As mentioned above, their definitions of creativity require that some larger audience recognize an individual's creative products as having value (Goleman, Kaufman, & Ray, 1992). For some, this approach is taken in order to better understand how others can reach their own potential (e.g., Dacey, 1989). By describing the characteristics of highly creatively productive individuals or discussing how they may have become who they are and what they are like, readers can better understand how to enhance their own creativity or help others to realize their creative potential. The downside of this is that many people come to believe that unless they can create that type of change, they are not creative and that there is nothing that they can do about it.

It is for this reason that others in the field view the human capacity to be creative more broadly. Maslow (1958) wrote:

> a fair proportion of my subjects . . . were *not* productive in the ordinary sense, nor did they have great talent or genius, nor were they poets, composers, inventors, artists or creative intellectuals . . . a first-rate soup is more creative than a second-rate painting, and that, generally, cooking or parenthood or making a home could be creative while poetry need not be. (p. 53)

Maslow was talking about what we might call little (or perhaps even mini) creativity, everyday creativity (e.g., Richards, 2007, 2010), or ordinary creativity (Ripple, 1989).

According to this perspective, creativity is not confined to a special few. One need not be a mad genius to be creatively productive, nor is it some magical gift from the gods. It is a complex form of human behavior and, as such, most individuals (about 68%) have an average level of creative potential. Most healthy people, including children, have the capacity to function creatively (Runco, 2003b). Psychologist Richard Ripple (1989) called this ordinary creativity: "Ordinary creativity involved in solving everyday real-life problems of less than heroic proportions helps us get through the day better and/or more effectively" (p. 190). Richards (2010) defined everyday creativity in relation to "human originality at work and leisure across the diverse activities of everyday life" and viewed it as "central to human survival and . . . found in everyone" (p. 190).

Although very few individuals may have very little potential for creative ability, others have the potential to change entire domains or even the course of history. However, the majority of human creative and innovative activity takes place more in the middle ground. It is of the more mundane, ordinary, every day little c sort that is nonetheless valuable. Much of human progress is the result, not of major paradigm shifts, but of small, almost unnoticeable, incremental improvements on existing practices, products, and human understanding. Most creators of these incremental improvements have gone completely unnoticed by history, but the cumulative results of their contributions are part of the bedrock of human civilization. We might view the creative productivity of the three students described in Chapter 1 as being little c. Of course, we cannot know the extent of their potential—only that each of them does exhibit potential.

Our View of the Matter

We think that this complex concept of creativity can and should be clearly defined. First, we work on the basic belief that creativity is a natural survival trait, much like running. We are not all Olympians, but the vast majority of people are able to run to some degree and, with proper training, practice, and self-understanding, could become better runners. Not all of us have the creative potential of Martha Graham or Albert Einstein; however, with the proper training, practice, and self-understanding, we can move closer to fulfilling our creative potential and to becoming more effective creative thinkers, problem solvers, and innovators. The belief that the skills and behaviors associated with creativity and creative problem solving can and should be taught has been supported by years of research and field application carried out by hundreds of practitioners, trainers, and teachers all over the world in every domain of human endeavor with people of all ages.

So, we end pretty much where this chapter began. Creativity is the ability to produce novel and appropriate outcomes to problems, challenges, or opportunities. Innovation is the successful change or product that results from creative effort brought to application and use. Creative ability manifests itself at different levels for different individuals. For many, the ability is emerging. They are aware that from time to time they are able to solve personal or work-related challenges with unique, appropriate, and innovative solutions. Some of us are at a point where we are expressing our creativity. Such individuals are able to apply their creativity in personal ways. A few have creative abilities that excel. These individuals are secure in their ability. Their products are recognized by those who are knowledgeable in their domain, and often more widely, as highly innovative.

A creative or innovative product is a novel and appropriate outcome for a problem, challenge, or opportunity. The creative process is the path that is followed in applying ability to reach a creative outcome. This applies to both Big C and little c, as well as any and all "Cs" in the middle. The ability to create novel and appropriate outcomes is innate. We can use it or ignore it. We can work to develop it to the fullness of our individual potential or let it go to waste. The fact that some people never use their creative ability—or that some have developed their level of ability far beyond the norm—is not an indication that the rest of us lack creative potential.

Taking the Chapter Forward

○ Now that you've seen a number of definitions, ask your students and some of your professional colleagues how they would define creativity and innovation or what it means to be creative. Perhaps you might ask them to list products or inventions they consider creative or innovative.

○ What is your own definition of creativity? How would you define innovation? Think about the connections between the words creative, critical, imagination, and innovation. How are they the same, and how are they different? When you are engaging in conversation, ask people whose opinion you respect to define these terms, especially the word creativity. Compare and contrast their definitions with your own and with the discussion in this chapter.

○ Ask at least four people you don't know in occupations different from yours how they would define creativity and innovation. Share your definition of creativity with others, and note their reaction. As you do, we hope that you will become confident in you own definition and that confidence will inform your thinking as you continue in this text and work with others to help them realize their own creative potential.

Chapter 4

The Importance of Creativity and Innovation in Education

After reading this chapter, you will be able to describe the overall importance of creativity, especially in educational settings; discuss creative problem solving and innovation as 21st-century skills; understand the relationship between creativity instruction and talent development and the importance of an educational commitment to bringing out the best in every person; discuss change and the role of creativity and innovation in managing change; and build and present a case for schools to make a commitment to working on and applying creativity and creativity instruction (for adults and for students).

21st-Century Skills

If you haven't yet heard someone mention "21st-century skills," you have either been living on a desert island or you just haven't been paying attention! On the other hand, the same might be said if you haven't also heard about high-stakes testing, standards, or No Child Left Behind.

Although the focus in education seems to have been riveted on accountability as supported by test scores, the goals associated with 21st-century skills emphasize the long-term development of a dynamic and productive population of thinkers and problem solvers who are comfortable with many kinds of technology. These appear to stand in sharp contrast to many current policies and priorities in the educational system. Short-term, test-driven goals seem more likely to result in more graduates with the ability to compete successfully on game shows such as "Who Wants to Be a Millionaire" rather than young adults with the confidence, competence, and commitment to be creative in tackling the long-range challenges facing the nation and the world. If you put this apparent conflict into historic context, you may discover some interesting and maybe even deeply disturbing patterns.

Consider, for example, several reports published and widely circulated over the past three decades. You have undoubtedly heard of the basics of education like reading, writing, and arithmetic. What else might "the basics" mean?

Begin with this quotation from a report entitled *Educating Americans for the 21st Century* by the National Science Board Commission on Precollege Education in Mathematics, Science, and Technology:

> We must return to basics, but the "basics" of the 21st century are not only reading, writing and arithmetic. They include communication and higher problem solving skills, and scientific and technology literacy—the thinking tools that allow us to understand the technological world around us. (p. v)

The striking feature of this quote is that it was published more than a quarter-century ago, in 1983! Another set of "basics of tomorrow" from the same decade included "evaluation and analysis skills, critical thinking, problem-solving strategies, organization and reference skills, synthesis, application, creativity, decision-making from incomplete information, and communication skills" (Gisi & Forbes, 1982, p. 6).

A decade later, the call persisted. In the early 1990s, a study for the United States Department of Labor focused on skills that business leaders identified as essential for applicants to be employable ("workplace basics"; Carnevale, Gainer, & Meltzer, 1990). That list included knowing how to learn; competence in reading, writing, and computation; listening and oral communication; creative thinking and problem solving; personal management (involving self-esteem, goal-setting, motivation, and career development); group effectiveness and interpersonal skills, negotiation, and teamwork; and organizational effectiveness and leadership.

The widely publicized SCANS (Secretary's Commission on Achieving Necessary Skills) report of the 1990s (United States Department of Labor, 1991) echoed the same ideas. The report proposed that business leaders would like their employees to possess the following skills:

- ○ creative thinking (generating new ideas);
- ○ decision making (specifying goals and constraints, generating alternatives, considering risks, evaluating them and choosing the best alternative);
- ○ problem solving (recognizing problems and devising and implementing plans of action), seeing things in the mind's eye (organizing and processing symbols, pictures, graphs, and the like);
- ○ knowing how to learn (using efficient learning techniques to acquire and apply new knowledge and skills); and
- ○ reasoning (discovering a rule or principle and applying it to solving a problem).

Nearly two decades later, calls continue for schools to become better able to meet the challenges of preparing students to deal with creativity, innovation, and change. The Partnership for 21st Century Skills (2009), a consortium of government, business, and community leaders, highlighted the need for instruction in survival skills in a new and growing global community; these skills include: creativity and innovation (thinking creatively, working creatively with others, implementing innovations); critical thinking and problem solving (reasoning effectively, using systems thinking, making judgments and decisions, solving problems); and communication and collaboration (communicating clearly, collaborating with others).

Looking at this history, and considering the lack of real progress compared with our expectations in 1982, we are compelled to ask, "Is it tomorrow yet?" In truth, the "new basics" have actually been around for a long, long time. There is nothing really new about the new basics, although their importance is consistently reaffirmed. We might ask, "When do the new basics become old basics?"

We fear that if our current test-score-driven practices reflect our true values and priorities, "tomorrow" may never arrive. Creativity, innovation, critical thinking, and problem-solving skills will not be genuinely recognized and nurtured as being basic to a complete education. Time and again we hear from schools and districts around the country: "We know the importance of the higher level thinking skills, especially creativity and problem solving, but we don't have the resources to fund that type of instruction. We are totally focused on improving or maintaining our test scores." They often express their fear that instruction in the skills of creativity, innovation, and change management will take away from time spent on test preparation, resulting in lower scores and possibly lower funding.

We have to ask what would have happened to our three students in Chapter 1 if their teachers did not recognize that they needed opportunities and instruction that went way beyond test preparation in order to nurture their passions and potentials. What if Eric's teacher, fearful of a poor evaluation, ignored the comments from Eric's friends and instead had the class pull out their books and start reading in order to meet the required time for reading across the curriculum? It is likely that Eric would have continued to be a bored student and a thorn in her side. What if William's school district did away with its music program so the resources could be redirected to preparing students for the graduation examination? Would his talent for composition and improvisation go unexplored? Sue's interest and success in science was supported throughout her schooling. She was able to demonstrate her knowledge and ability through productivity. Are there standardized tests capable of measuring the full extent of her knowledge? Luckily, her school and teachers understood that her time was better used in expanding her skills. In too many school, students like these have had their passion drained from them while being "drilled and filled" with standardized answers to standardized questions with the apparent goal of standardizing each individual student.

Nonetheless, we are optimists. It doesn't have to be this way! Although much work awaits us if we hope to ensure that creativity and problem-solving skills are being taught, nurtured, and applied effectively, it can be done. The knowledge, tools, and resources exist to address those goals successfully. The skills, processes, tools, and techniques of creative problem solving can be taught (Treffinger et al., 2006). In all schools, such instruction can indeed support our efforts to have students meet the standards while at the same time improving their higher level skills. (At the Center for Creative Learning website, http://www.creativelearning.com, you can find more than 80 specific activities, for example, that illustrate ways to integrate content standards with tools for creative and critical thinking.)

We are long overdue for the basics of the future to become the basics of today. The 21st century is no longer some far-off time in the distant future; it is now. This is the time that skills needed for 21st-century thinking, learning, and productivity take their place throughout education. In this chapter, let us look closely at several reasons that make this challenge vital to the future of education (and perhaps to global peace and survival).

Reasons for the Importance of Creativity in Education

Based on your past experiences and readings, we hope you already believe that creativity and innovation are important and that you have some good ideas about why that's the case. In this chapter, we present five reasons why creativity and innovation are important in teaching and learning in any educational setting. These may help you to understand why they are important, reinforcing your own initial ideas and helping you to explain them to others, or add some new perspectives that you might not have considered previously. They may not be the only reasons, but they certainly can provide a useful beginning on which to build.

Creativity and innovation help us to deal effectively with the rapid pace; constant, accelerating change; and unpredictability of modern life. As today's students enter their adult lives, they will need the intellectual and personal resources provided by creativity in order to cope successfully with opportunities, challenges, and concerns that no one has ever faced before and that neither they nor we can even anticipate at the present time. Change is a common experience for everyone, and it continues to occur at an ever-increasing rate. School-age children today take for granted many innovations that were unknown—perhaps even unheard of as anything other than fantasy or science fiction—when their parents were their age. Giving students the skills and tools of creativity helps them to be more effective in dealing with change and prepares them to be participants in the fast-paced world of change in which they will continue to live (and work) in the future. For better or for worse, then, change is a reality. The change we know today will not suddenly come to a halt or end at any time in the foreseeable future. We must be prepared to continue to accept that it's part of almost every aspect of our life. But, that doesn't mean we have to be passive, helpless creatures, tossed about in every direction by change. Creativity gives us the skills and tools we need to respond effectively to the changes around us, to make them work on our behalf, and even to enable us to be active participants in creating change to improve the quality of life itself. Creativity is important, not just because of novelty (although that may often be an element of its worth to us), but also because of the effectiveness or usefulness—the value—that can accompany its results. Creativity enables us to harness the novelty of change and shape or direct it in constructive, valuable ways. Creativity challenges us to build learners who are thinkers, innovators, and problem solvers who are masters of change from an early age.

Change also reminds us that increasingly, not only do we lack all of the answers, but that we are not even certain about what the questions will be. Once upon a time it might have been possible for us to say to students, "If you will just learn and remember the wisdom we share with you, you will have all of the ideas and information you will need to enable you to be successful in life." Perhaps, as the phrase "once upon a time" suggests, that has always been a fairy tale—never quite true, really. One conclusion is very clear, however: It is no longer true in today's world. Change teaches us that creativity is important because it will provide the skills and tools people need to frame new questions and then construct new answers for challenges we do not now envision.

Creativity and innovation help students to deal effectively, independently, and resourcefully with many complex opportunities and challenges. In a world of rapid change, we often find ourselves in situations that we have never encountered before, and we cannot simply draw on memorized facts and strategies to deal with them successfully. As William Easum (1995) wrote, "Nothing in our past prepared us for the present. . . . Simply learning to do old chores faster or to be able to adapt old forms to more complex situations no longer produces the desired results" (p. 21).

Teaching that enables students to think creatively and critically and to be effective problem solvers increases the range of situations, goals, and challenges with which people can deal successfully. It helps individuals become effective, autonomous, and competent with many different people and situations. Creative learning provides specific tools and strategies that students can use on their own whenever they encounter situations or challenges requiring them to generate or analyze new ideas. The popular term for describing this today is *empowering* people—helping them to recognize and apply the ability to think and act constructively on their own.

We live in an increasingly global society and economy, with more accessible technology and instant, exploding information at our fingertips. But our educational curriculum has not kept pace, and the ambitious goals and expectations put forth nearly two decades ago have not been attained (Wagner, 2007).

So, the new old (or is it the old new?) basics are still with us and much more necessary than ever before. We need curricula and instructional approaches that engage students in finding, working with, and producing information creatively and sorting it critically. In addition, we also recognize that the concept of career is changing, as new kinds of employment opportunities, career pathways, and disciplines are emerging continuously.

It is true that content is important. In order for our students to be able to contribute as citizens in the future, in any discipline or field, they need to know history, the sciences, literature, math, and economics. We cannot neglect the arts and languages "in a world that cries out for far more humane connections with others" (Hersh, 2009, p. 52). Emphasizing content reveals only part of the picture. Eventually our students will be launched into the big, wide world, and they will need important skills to help them continue their learning, solve problems, and make important judgments about the meaning and accuracy of what they read and hear. Students need learning that stimulates the imagination, teaches them *how* to construct meaning, and enables them to put information to work in innovative and coherent ways. Effectiveness in establishing creative education will require commitment from parents, teachers, and administrators. This education must involve our students actively, too, giving them ownership of content and helping them to discover and pursue energetically their strengths, talents, and sustained interests. In short, we need to engage students in a curriculum that promotes the processes of creativity, innovation, purposeful reflection, and effective decision-making, and that engages both mind and spirit—the passion for learning—that leads to success.

With the appropriate tools for thinking and a deliberate creative problem-solving process, we can actually begin to move education forward into the present century. Using tools for thinking, students can learn new complex ideas and concepts and present ideas with rigor and creativity. Feedback and evaluation by peers and teachers can be affirmative, constructive, and meaningful and emphasize both innovative and disciplined ideas.

Creative learning can have a very powerful, positive impact on students' preparation for future careers. There is clear support from the business world for the importance of creativity and innovation, both within today's workforce and in relation to its priority for education. Susan R. Meisinger, former president and CEO of the Society for Human Resource Management, described, for example, the need for "a talented workforce with communication and critical thinking skills for organizations" for future success (eSchool News Staff, 2006, para. 6). Bob Watt, a Boeing executive, asserted that "creativity and imagination are both job requirements at the Boeing Co. We make our living imagining things that never before existed. Creativity is at the heart of what Boeing does" (Associated Press, 2007, para. 11–12).

We need a concerted effort among the total "village" (educational practitioners, researchers, and concerned parents and community members) if our educational system is to move beyond the rhetoric and meet the challenge of providing all students the opportunity to learn the basic skills of the 21st century. Throughout the world, business and corporate leaders have realized in growing numbers that the success, and most likely even the survival, of their companies depends in many important ways on the creative resources and productivity of their people. These leaders have learned to value and nurture creativity at all levels: in individuals, teams, and work groups, as well as in the larger structures of their organizations.

A recent nationwide poll of voters revealed that 99% of survey respondents agreed that addressing a wide range of 21st-century skills in our schools—including critical thinking and problem-solving skills, computer and technology skills, and communication and self-direction skills—should be an important priority (Partnership for 21st Century Skills, 2007). As corporations continue to compete in an ever more complex and changing global marketplace, they, too, recognize the need for education for creativity, problem solving, and innovation; our economy urgently requires creative workers and innovative leaders (Eger, 2004). A survey (eSchool News Staff, 2006) polled more than 400 employers on the readiness of new workers in areas such as teamwork and critical thinking. Nearly three fourths of the respondents rated recently hired high school graduates as deficient in critical thinking and judged creativity and innovation as among the top five applied skills projected to increase in importance for future graduates. Business leaders agree they need employees who have a higher level of skill than typical employees currently demonstrate, including the ability to communicate, reason, problem solve, make decisions, function within a team format, and become a leader (Adams, 2005; Coy, 2000). Creative and critical thinking are included within all of these skills.

Creative learning offers rich and varied opportunities for personal growth, expression, and talent development. When people in a group talk about the best, most significant learning experiences they have ever had, it is common for them to describe their encounters with creative learning. When people discover and use their creativity, they find that they feel healthier, happier, and more productive in a variety of ways. They discover their passions as learners, and they accept the challenge of discovering and developing their own best selves. In short, creativity and innovation are important in education because they help us (as well as parents and students themselves) to recognize, develop, and apply our personal talents and gifts.

Traditional approaches to gifted education have focused on identifying, labeling, and separating a single, homogenous group (typically students who score high on standardized tests of ability or achievement). Then, identified students participate in a common gifted program that may focus on creative enrichment, alternative and rigorous content, or advanced content topics. We believe that a more compelling opportunity and challenge is to recognize the many (nearly infinite) ways in which students can grow and attain significant productivity through deliberate efforts to find and nurture a variety of strengths, talents, and interests in creative ways. We believe that the exciting, but plausible, challenge of programming for talent development is to bring out the best in every learner (Treffinger, Young, Nassab, Selby, & Wittig, 2008; Treffinger, Young, Nassab, & Wittig, 2004). Creativity can be very important in discovering, developing, and expressing varied talents among many students who, on the basis of traditional procedures alone, might receive little or no consideration for gifted programs.

Creative learning is not always easy, but it does lead to great satisfaction and reward. Creative learning is both demanding and fulfilling. The word *fun* often comes up in discussions of creativity. Unfortunately, as you read in Chapter 2, that often feeds some myths and misunderstandings—that creativity is frivolous and that it lacks substance and meaning. We avoid describing creativity as fun because this may cause the very real importance of creativity to be underemphasized or overlooked. Our long-time colleague, Dr. Sidney J. Parnes, often said, "Creativity can often *be* fun, but it's not *for* fun." Informally, his point is well taken, but rather than fun, the language we prefer observes that creativity contributes to meaning, integrity, and personal satisfaction, both in one's personal life and one's career.

After a period of extended work on a creative project or in a problem-solving group, it is always very common for people to report, "I'm exhausted. I would never have believed thinking could be such hard work—but it was worth it!" They experience this paradox: They're "drained" from the amount of focus and effort they invested in their work, but at the same time, they're energized and excited by the results of that work, and they're eager to carry out their action plans or put their new ideas to work. There is often a strong experience of joyfulness and excitement in the discovery of a new idea or product, the solution of a complex problem, or the sharing of an original creative expression. Creative involvement in a task is often characterized by an intense, sustained sense of focus, engagement, and persistent pursuit that athletes describe as being in the zone and some psychologists characterize as flow. We believe, then, that both adults and students in the educational setting can thrive and grow as a result of opportunities for creativity and innovation.

Taking the Chapter Forward

- Think about the role that creativity and innovation play in your life. How often are you called on to address some open-ended challenge? What difference does it make when change just happens in your life, as compared to those times when you were able to manage that change? How have innovations improved your life? Has innovation made your life simpler and better in some ways or more complicated and challenging in others?

- Review with your students the impact that creative young people can have on the world. Ask your students to research and report on the creative contributions of a person of their choice that were made before that person was 25 years old.

- Look closely at the myths in Chapter 2, the definitions in Chapter 3, and the reasons for the importance of creativity in this chapter. Take stock of your own current beliefs and practices. Share your beliefs with others and note their reactions. Are you able to argue convincingly for deliberate provision for creativity and innovation in education?

Section II

Foundations for Creativity and Innovation

Chapter 5

Four Essential Factors: COCO

After reading this chapter, you will be able to refine your description of creativity as a concept. You will be able to identify and define four essential factors that contribute to creativity, discuss the ways in which these factors similarly affect students and adults, and describe ways in which these factors are experienced differently by students and adults in their efforts to be creatively productive.

An Overview of Four Essential Factors

You have by now become more aware of the complexity of creativity, especially in the many ways this concept is defined by each of us and how differently creativity can be expressed. It is our own complexity and individuality that can account for the enormous variability of the ideas we generate and the solutions to challenges we might develop. As shown in Figure 1, creativity is a function of the *characteristics* of people and the

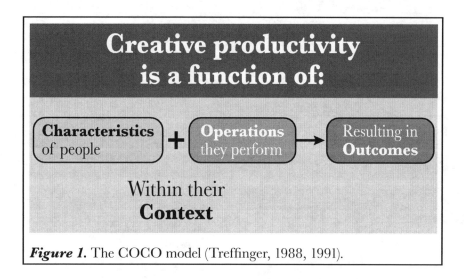

Figure 1. The COCO model (Treffinger, 1988, 1991).

operations they perform, resulting in *outcomes* all within a unique *context*. We call this the COCO model.

It has long been recognized that creativity is not just one kind of person or a certain kind of process, environment, or even a product, from the presentation of the four Ps of creativity (person, product, process, and press) by Rhodes (1961) that we discussed in Chapter 3, to more recent global discussions, such as that of Law (2007). Law summarized her view of creativity as follows: "creativity is understood as a multi-dimensional model such as process vs. product, individual vs. social, and domain-specific vs. domain independent" (p. 368). We concur about the multidimensional nature, although we don't see the issue as being one element versus another. We see a complex, continuing interplay between and among all of the factors. This interplay is made more complex due to the human element. Because we are all unique, people will see a challenge, problem, situation, or opportunity in very different ways. Now apply this idea to your classroom. Each student has his or her own characteristics and context. Some of these characteristics and contexts will be beneficial for learning and others will be barriers. Add another layer to this by adding your own characteristics and context!

Characteristics

The first C in the COCO model stands for characteristics. Creativity is influenced by the personal traits, characteristics, preferences, skills, abilities, and interests that each of us bring to any task or situation. These include:

o   creative thinking skills and abilities,
o   personality traits or attributes (or personal characteristics),
o   learning and problem-solving style preferences,
o   knowledge and competence within a particular domain, and
o   curiosity and sustained interests.

For many years, theorists and researchers believed that creativity was primarily, or even exclusively, determined by internal traits or characteristics, and that high (or "true") creativity was found only in a few rare "geniuses" who were endowed or gifted with the essential characteristics. An all-or-nothing mindset prevailed in many views. More recently, however, many theorists and researchers have viewed creative characteristics differently, emphasizing that all people demonstrate a variety of creative characteristics and preferences, varying in degree and expression in relation to tasks and situations. We approach creativity as a set of characteristics that we can use to differentiate learning, training, or instruction effectively for individuals and groups, and that helps people learn to recognize and nurture creativity in personally effective ways. There is no prescriptive list or a one-size-fits-all set of characteristics.

Every observant teacher knows students who are creative, but they tend to differ in many other ways. Some are quiet and reflective. Others are outgoing and, like Eric, our Civil War expert, love interaction—sometimes (if not positively directed) to the distraction of others. Some, like William, express their creativity spontaneously in writing, art, theater, music, or a combination of those. Students like Sue apply their imagination carefully in science and the exploration of ideas. They may even give up other interests to pursue their passion. Because of the infinite ways creativity can be expressed, we prefer to work toward understanding the complex contributions of personality, interests, and style to the huge variety of creativity effort. We'll examine characteristics in greater detail in Chapter 6.

Operations

The first O in the COCO model stands for operations. By operations, we mean the specific methods, tools, and strategies that people learn and use, working individually or in a group, to think, work, or perform creatively. These include:

○ tools for generating options,

○ tools for focusing options,

○ structured approaches for defining and solving problems, and

○ metacognitive (or executive) strategies.

Effective problem solvers also know and use a number of general inquiry strategies (e.g., research methods and tools within a discipline or domain), expression and productivity skills (e.g., time management, scheduling, presentation skills), and specific methods and strategies that are based in the content of a discipline or domain.

Sometimes students surprise us with their insights, as seen by one of this book's authors who had an interesting experience in a fourth-grade classroom. The students were working on a sample problem to practice process. It was a problem about a prince who had been changed into a frog by a witch's spell and had to live at the lily pond until a beautiful princess came to kiss him. Alas, no princesses had visited the pond in years. The students played the role of the frog prince, stating the problem as, "In what ways might I get some princesses to come to the lily pond?" The students were not able to come up with many ideas. The teacher looked puzzled—she knew what to do when ideas came quickly, but not what to do when they didn't. Our fearless author came to her aid, asking the students, "How many of you have ever had a garage sale?" Almost all said yes. "Did lots of people come?" "Oh, yes, all day. It was great." "How great would it have been if no one came?" "Oh, that would be terrible!" "Well, what did you do to ensure that lots of people came?" Many ideas flowed quickly. Although the visiting author was now ready to turn back to the problem, one student, Kathy, began to wave her hand frantically and said, "Oh! Oh! Maybe some of the things we do to get people to come to the garage sale, the frog prince could do to get princesses to come to the lily pond!" Excitement prevailed as they prepared to go back to work, but Kathy wasn't finished. "Wait!" she protested. "That was great. You just showed us that when we are working on a problem and get stuck, we can take another problem that's like it, but easier. We can get ideas for the easy problem and then use them on the harder problem." Could any of us have explained it any better?

In this book, we will look more closely at the operations factor in Chapter 7, and in subsequent chapters, we will provide much more extensive information and resources about a variety of process tools, strategies, and resources.

Context

The second C in the COCO model stands for context. Context includes the personal or internal situation that people make for themselves when thinking about or dealing with creativity and the external or social situation and environment in which everyone's behavior takes place on a day-to-day basis. Context factors may encourage and support creativity, or they may discourage and stifle it.

The internal, personal dimension of context include:

○ habit-bound thinking,
○ personal blocks and barriers,
○ motivation or "investments," and
○ attitudes, dispositions, and confidence.

The external, social dimensions of context include:

○ organizational blocks and barriers,
○ organizational culture and climate,
○ group and collaborative skills,
○ leadership dynamics, and
○ teamwork.

No matter the age, each of us brings our own context to every situation. Elements of our context may enhance or inhibit creativity and innovation. In the classroom, some teachers work very specifically on creating an environment that provides challenge, excitement, and opportunities, time, and resources for students to engage in learning creatively. Other classrooms may be less supportive. Personal factors also influence context. Some researchers have discussed the fourth-grade slump that occurs when students no longer want to stand out and do want to know the "correct" answer. Students may also come to school carrying support and encouragement for creativity from home—or may bring less positive "baggage" from home or personal relationships that may be inhibiting. Meet Tyrone and Francine, two students with very different contexts, to gain insight into contrasting examples.

Tyrone was a student enrolled in a gifted program in an inner-city school. He lived with his grandmother, who received support for raising him and his four siblings. He never spoke about what had happened to his parents. The small apartment was crowded with children. As the oldest, he had many responsibilities. There was little to enrich his environment beyond a television and no academic stimulation at all. Still, his eighth-grade teachers saw something and recommended him for the gifted program.

He had to walk to school. To get there safely each day, he would walk about a mile out of his way to avoid trouble. If he took the short route, he would be pushed around, bullied, or even mugged. Often this detour would make him late for school.

As a freshman, Tyrone was street wise, but academically naive. He was easily distracted and was unable to study away from the school setting. He was easily antagonized, took offense, and, at first, found group work difficult. At the same time, he lacked independence. Tyrone needed approval before trying anything new. He would take no risks and lacked self-confidence. That freshman year was spent catching up with his peers, both socially and academically. With the concerted help of his teachers, he did catch up academically, but still lagged socially until almost the end of his senior year. Through hard work, he was able to win several scholarships and admission to MIT where he studied computer science.

Francine lived in the same city, but in a one-family home. She was an only child and was also being raised by her grandmother. Her parents, both college graduates, died together in a car accident. Francine had her own room, and the home was filled with books and classical music. She came to the gifted high school program one year early at age 13. She would either take the bus to school or was driven by her grandmother.

In school, Francine was popular and self-confident. She sang in the choir and played viola in the string ensemble. Francine was a natural leader and participated in every school project, adding ideas and helping to work out details. Throughout her 4-year high school career, although the youngest in a class of capable students, she remained in the top five.

In addition to her music, Francine loved to write. She organized the gifted program's first newsletter and became its editor. She also entered works in several literary competitions and twice won first prize. Whatever she tried, her grandmother supported her. Francine's grandmother attended each performance and school activity and also served on the school's parent advisory committee. She was very proud when Francine was accepted to college to study medicine.

We'll examine several important aspects of the context for creativity and innovation in greater detail in Chapter 8.

Outcomes

Outcomes, the second O in the COCO model, reminds us that creativity is often in the eye of the beholder. The results that we obtain may often be used to assess or evaluate the creativity of our work. It is tempting to say, "My process was really creative, even if the results weren't so great." Sometimes, especially as a learning experience, an emphasis on process may override our examination of product, and it can be important and valuable to consider process in its own right as a dimension of creativity. It is also true, however, that anytime a teacher, coach, or supervisor says, "I really hope you will do something creative with this task or assignment," there will also be some expectations about the results or outcome.

These should be appropriate to the age and experience of the group, of course. (A community volunteer who served as a judge at an elementary school once reacted negatively to a kindergarten student's invention idea that other judges thought was great. He explained, "That idea isn't so original; I was just recently reading a very similar idea in a mechanical engineering journal." Apparently he didn't realize that not many primary students read engineering journals!) We should also consider the lessons we might learn from theory and research on criteria for creativity or innovation and the assessment of creative products. We'll examine outcomes in greater detail in Chapter 9.

Even though the next four chapters of this book discuss each of theses factors separately, please keep in mind that we do this only for organizational convenience. In real-world creativity and innovation, all four factors are continually in interaction; they are always elements of a dynamic system.

Taking the Chapter Forward

- How do the four COCO factors impact your life and your own efforts to think creatively, innovate, solve problems, and manage change? Think about times when you have been most creatively productive. Make a list of attributes that encouraged (or inhibited) your creativity. How did these attributes work together to either block or assist you in reaching a productive conclusion?

- Have your students define these factors, and discuss their relationship to one another. Ask them to think about their own situations and identify how each of the four factors came into play. Have the students make their own list of attributes that contribute to their creativity, and describe ways that each factor is experienced differently by students and by adults when making an effort to be creatively productive.

- What is the impact of creative complexity in the organizations to which you belong? In what ways might this knowledge improve your creative effectiveness as a member of those organizations? Engage your colleagues in discussion about the four factors. What are the different ways each factor impacts different individuals?

Chapter 6

Personal Characteristics

A fter reading this chapter, you will be able to describe our contemporary understanding of the personal characteristics associated with creativity and innovation, define each of the four main categories, and give examples of characteristics in each category. You will also be able to compare and contrast the concepts of level and style of creativity in relation to their implications for educational practice. You will be able to discuss styles of creativity and problem solving, define three main dimensions of problem-solving style, and explain the two styles in each dimension.

Three Additional Students

In this chapter, you'll meet three new students—Lucy, Michael, and Cheryl—who were part of a 12-member playwriting group working on an original script. You will follow them throughout this chapter to see how personal creativity characteristics are expressed in a variety of ways.

Each student in the group was selected for his or her writing skills and demonstrated interest in theater. Although all of the members showed creative potential, each approached the combined challenges of writing an original script and working in a group differently. Their responses to one assignment stand out as an example of these differences. The group had been working for several weeks, first generating hundreds of ideas for a story, and then focusing, regrouping, refocusing, and finally reaching consensus on a story idea. They were assigned to take a week to develop their ideas for a completed story outline, describe who the main characters might be, and write a brief description of their main characters.

At the next meeting, group members took turns reading their plot outlines and character descriptions. Cheryl's work was neat, well thought out, and orderly. She had written a complete outline. Although her characters fit logically into the outline, they did not stand out and seemed drawn largely from current movies and television shows.

When it came to be Lucy's turn, she pulled out a large bundle of typewritten pages and announced proudly that she had spent the week writing a completed script. She summarized her plot and character ideas and noted that there was no need to do any more work. The rest of the group was taken aback by this announcement, and the students were concerned that Lucy's script would be adopted without consideration of any of their input. Lucy noted that their input wasn't really needed since the script was done, and it made no sense to continue working and wasting time. Lucy was usually very vocal about her ideas, and this situation was no exception. Trying to hold off a possible conflict, the teacher pointed out that not all of the group members had been heard yet and that it was not appropriate to make any decision until everyone had been heard. Reluctantly, Lucy agreed, and others went on to report.

When it came time for Michael to share his thoughts, he pulled from his jeans a crumpled piece of paper with notes scrawled all over it. He proceeded to outline a completely new story, with entirely different characters from what had been agreed upon at the previous session. The group exploded all at once, with Lucy leading the charge. How could he even think of changing the story after so much work had gone into what had already been decided? Michael replied, "Easy: This is a better idea. People will really like it."

After the teacher had again gained control of the meeting, discussion continued, with the group breaking into camps around Lucy and Michael. Cheryl quietly followed this back and forth for some time, and then pointed out that Michael had some good ideas that could be worked into the story that they had decided on. She also suggested that using the structure of Lucy's script would save a lot of work and help focus their ideas, while bringing all of best ideas that had been presented together to make a stronger story. She noted ideas from several members of the group that she thought would fit together. After some discussion, the group adopted Cheryl's plan, and while not entirely happy, both Lucy and Michael were brought on board and work on the first draft got under way.

Each of these three students was able to make positive contributions to the overall effort of the group. All three were beginning to explore their abilities as writers and as potential problem solvers. Each had demonstrated skill in writing to at least one nominating teacher and had demonstrated real interest and commitment to the school's theater program. Yet, they were all very different in their approach to the assignment and in the ways they interacted. Each student brought very different personal characteristics to the creative efforts of the group.

Level and Style: Contemporary Perspectives

How creative do you think you are? Think about a vertical line numbered from 9 (*creative genius*) to 0 (*absolutely no creativity at all*), as depicted in Figure 2. Where would you place yourself on the line to represent your level of creativity?

When we ask this question to groups, we will have someone answer 9 from time to time—at least until we share the examples. We're confident that there are no zeros in our audience because they are listening and raising their hands, two behaviors not available to rocks. Most people in our workshops answer in the middle of the scale (or even slightly below the middle—being modest, we suppose).

This question has to do with *level* of creativity, that is, giving it a rating, from high to low. In terms of level, all 12 members of the playwriting group had demonstrated above-average writing or acting skills. During the time of the project, they were beginning to realize their creative potential. As you understand by now, we believe that all healthy individuals

9	Pablo Picasso, Louisa May Alcott, Marie Curie, Thomas Edison, Albert Einstein, Wolfgang Amadeus Mozart
8	
7	
6	
5	
4	
3	
2	
1	
0	A rock

Figure 2. Creativity number line.

have the potential to be creatively productive. For some, that potential has yet to be explored. For others, it has been realized quite extensively. As with running, some people have the potential to win many races, perhaps nearly every one they enter, while others are happy just to finish. The writing group students were just beginning, but with each challenge they gained competence and also confidence in each other.

The sources of these differences in level are as varied and complex as the concept of creativity itself. Early thinking viewed creativity as a gift from the gods. These concepts formed the basis of some of the mythology discussed in Chapter 2. Generally, the belief was that you either have it or you don't. In the Victorian era, a darker view evolved in Western culture. Sigmund Freud (1908/1959) wrote, for example, of the creative impulse as the product of the unconscious mind struggling to resolve or sublimate conflicts between fantasy and reality; the basic characteristic of the creative individual was inner turmoil.

Several theorists who followed looked more positively on the creative impulse (Selby, Shaw, & Houtz, 2005). Looking at creativity as natural and positive allowed for closer study of those positive traits that define the creative person. Carl Rogers (1954) described the creative person as being open and self-confident, displaying the courage of his or her own convictions. Creatively productive individuals may be set apart from others by the level of their motivation, vigor, intensity, dedication, and commitment

(Abra, 1997; Amabile, 1989; Renzulli, 1977b; Torrance, 1987, 1995). Both Lucy and Michael had the type of self-confidence described by Rogers, but without mediation, their clashing views could have brought the work to an end.

A great deal of energy was spent searching for those characteristics that highlighted high creative potential, asking the simple question, "How creative are you?" If we could identify those with a high level of creativity, we could give them appropriate instruction and resources. The problem with this is that many of the descriptions were contradictory. Or, worse, the same individual might exhibit opposite traits at different times (Selby et al., 2005). Some researchers and theorists began to wonder if we were asking the wrong question.

If we agree that all healthy individuals have creative potential, at different levels, influenced by differing characteristics, then asking "How creative are you?" provides only limited understanding. Perhaps we could learn more and better use our resources if we asked "How are you creative?" When we ask this question, we begin to act, apply instruction and resources, and conduct research based on our basic assumption that all individuals are potentially creative. Our search for creative characteristics goes beyond sorting, ranking, or separating individuals based on their (presumed) level of creativity. This alternative approach enables us to consider ways in which individuals express and use their creativity in unique and varied ways. It leads us to consider *style* of creativity and manifestations of personal preference that promote, or prohibit, creative productivity. Building on a growing body of research literature on learning and thinking styles, beginning in the mid-1970s, research on creativity and problem-solving styles has opened new pathways for research and practice and contributed to our understanding of the personal characteristics associated with creativity and innovation.

Categorizing Characteristics

For more than a hundred years, people have been studying highly creative individuals and making lists of their personality characteristics. Numerous lists, checklists, and rating scales have been used, encompassing literally hundreds of characteristics. Davis (2005) surveyed and catalogued more than 200 characteristics often reported as indicative of creativity and summarized them in 16 different categories. These excluded seven categories of negative traits. His 16 categories are: Aware of Creativeness; Original; Independent; Risk Taking; High Energy; Curious; Sense of Humor; Capacity for Fantasy; Attracted to Complexity, Ambiguity; Artistic; Open-Minded; Thorough; Needs Alone Time; Perceptive; Emotional; and Ethical.

Treffinger et al. (2002) reviewed similar lists of traits in three major areas: cognitive characteristics, personality traits, and biographical events. They found that

> often the specific characteristics do not fit neatly into just one of the three areas. Characteristics vary within and among people and across disciplines. No one person possesses all the characteristics nor does anyone display them all the time. . . . Many of these characteristics can be taught and nurtured. As a result it is difficult to predict which students may become creatively productive adults. (Treffinger et al., 2002, p. 7)

Considering how these characteristics might help us to identify creative potential and inform classroom practice, Treffinger et al. (2002) regrouped the extensive list of more than 300 characteristics from the literature into four categories, depicted in Figure 3. They concluded that creativity and innovation can result when individuals and groups generate many ideas, are able to dig deeper into those ideas, are willing and able to listen to their own inner voice, and have the motivation, openness, and courage to explore new and unusual ideas.

The first category, generating ideas, includes those characteristics most often associated with divergent, or creative, thinking (see Table 1). They include characteristics associated with fluency, flexibility, originality, elaboration, and metaphorical thinking. The ability to generate a lot of original ideas was a strength that Michael brought to the group. Often he successfully led the group in generating many ideas and engaged them in creative thinking so that many novel ideas were produced. The group's initial ideas tended to be rooted in their current thinking and approaches. As more ideas were produced, they became more original and unusual. Ideas began to emerge from different perspectives, looking

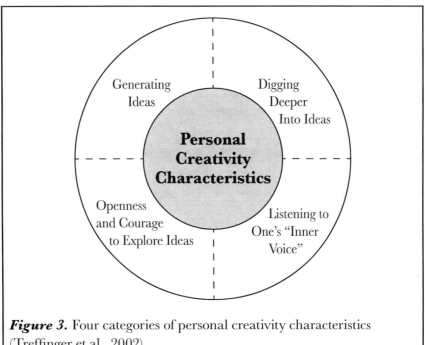

Figure 3. Four categories of personal creativity characteristics (Treffinger et al., 2002).

at the challenge in unexpected ways from unexpected viewpoints. This often resulted in unexpected possibilities. Although he wasn't aware of it, Michael would also employ metaphorical thinking. Metaphorical thinking is useful in understanding how different things are alike and building unexpected connections into new possibilities. Following Cheryl's lead, the group began to look more closely at the work that each of the 12 members had submitted to the group, choosing the best ideas from each and combining them with the original story idea. In this way, the group's thinking expanded and the story became richer, more detailed, and more interesting.

When we dig deeper into ideas (the second category), we engage in what is usually called convergent, or critical, thinking. Behaviors in this category include analyzing, synthesizing, reorganizing, redefining, evaluating, and finding relationships. Keep in mind that creative thinking is only half of the thinking needed for creative productivity. Critical, focused thinking and the ability to analyze ideas are also necessary. This was an area of strength for Lucy. She often displayed characteristics associated

Table 1

Four Categories of Creative Characteristics

Generating Ideas	Digging Deeper Into Ideas	Openness and Courage to Explore Ideas	Listening to One's Inner Voice
Fluency	Analyzing	Problem sensitivity	Sees self as creative
Flexibility	Synthesizing	Aesthetic sensitivity	Sense of purpose
Originality	Reorganizing	Aesthetic interests	Self-confident
Elaboration	Redefining	High levels of curiosity	Persistent
Metaphorical thinking	Desire to resolve ambiguity	Sense of humor	Needs autonomy
	Evaluating	Facility producing humor	Self-disciplined/ self-directed
	Seeing relationships	Playfulness	Independence of thought
	Desire to bring order to disorder	Capacity for fantasy or imagination	Task-oriented
	Preferring complexity	Risk taking (or thrill seeking)	Independent judgment/action
	Understanding complexity	Tolerance for ambiguity	Courage/ Nonconformity
		Tenacious, uninhibited, often spontaneous in expressing opinion	Does not fear being different, argumentative, stubborn, uncooperative, unconventional
		Open to feelings and emotions	Needs alone time, reflective thinking
		Emotional sensitivity	Rejects stereotypes
		Adaptable to current realities	Low level sociability, social skills
		Intuitive	Energetic
		Willingness to grow	Willing to work hard
		Critically examines authoritarian assertions	Intense concentration and absorption in work (absent-minded)
		Integrates personal dichotomies (selfish/ unselfish; extroverted/ introverted)	

Note. Adapted from Treffinger et al. (2002).

with digging deeper, including a desire to resolve ambiguity, to make the complex simple, and to bring order from disorder.

Openness and courage to explore ideas relates to problem and aesthetic sensitivity, curiosity, sense of humor, playfulness, imagination, and the ability to fantasize. Also in this category are openness to experience, tolerance for ambiguity, risk taking, tenacity, sensitivity, intuition, adaptability, and willingness to grow. The members of the writing group enjoyed many of these traits to some degree. Their curiosity and sense of humor seemed endless, as was Michael's tolerance for ambiguity and risk taking.

Often, the courage to explore involves critical examination of authoritarian assertions, questioning both why and how. Success is associated with those who question their own assumptions and assertions as well as those of others in authority. Openness and courage to explore also involves the need to integrate dichotomies or inconsistencies within one's own personality, such as striving to produce a great flow of novel ideas while at the same time being a person concerned with the quality of ideas and task completion. To attain creative productivity and to innovate successfully, depending on the demands of the situation and task or challenge at hand, requires the ability to balance (or juggle) such complex tensions.

Finally, listening to one's "inner voice" involves a person's level of motivation, self-confidence, and persistence. Again, this is a trait displayed by many of the writers while working in the group. Innovative and creatively productive individuals have a strong desire to create and believe that they are creative. Their self-confidence, self-efficacy, sense of purpose, and passion drive them forward. They understand their own strengths and work hard in the conviction that their goals are worthwhile. They focus on a subject or problem to the exclusion of most distractions, loosing sight of time, place, personal discomfort, and the social expectations of others. Such intense behaviors are the basis for the stereotype of the absented-minded professor. Considering Michael's lack of interest in any detail that he felt unimportant, including his handwriting or the presentation of his work, he may have been a young version of this stereotype. On the other hand, Lucy seemed to be highly motivated by details and doggedly pursued them.

Knowledge, Intelligence, and Metacognition

Among the characteristics that influence an individual's ability to be creatively productive are knowledge, intelligence, and metacognitive skills. We use the term knowledge to refer to content, understandings, information, and skills that a person has acquired through instruction or experience and retains in his or her memory. Intelligence involves one's aptitude or potential to acquire, organize, and apply knowledge. Metacognition is an active, ongoing, or continuous process of monitoring, managing, and modifying one's thinking. View it as "thinking about your thinking while you are thinking," or a process of constantly managing and directing your cognitive efforts.

Before going on, we need to remember that intelligence is not fixed and does not directly determine one's level of creative productivity or life success. Intelligence is influenced by factors such as brain development, domain, family background, educational experience, social environment, and life experience (Woolfolk, 2010). Although helpful, intelligence is often not as important as some other factors such as motivation and persistence.

Knowledge (both general and domain specific), intelligence, and metacognition are all important contributors to creative achievement and innovation. An ample store of knowledge gives people a rich array of possibilities on which to draw in new situations and when encountering opportunities and challenges. Intelligence enables people to access, organize, and apply their thinking; recognize and formulate patterns and relationships; understand or forecast the implications or consequences of possible actions; or envision new questions and connections for an opportunity or challenge at hand. After looking at the lives of seven highly creative individuals, Gardner (1993a) concluded that although they had characteristics that differentiated their careers from one another, their backgrounds shared several similarities, including the fact that in each case about 10 years of experience, learning, and training in their area of interest were needed before they were ready to make their creative breakthroughs.

Again, these were individuals who were very creatively productive and whose innovations changed the paradigm in their domain. Not everyone is able to reach that level of creativity. However, their output can be just as impressive when put into context. The students in the playwriting group did not have the experience or the knowledge required to change paradigms, but they had the intelligence needed to understand how stories are written and to create a unique piece that was ultimately produced and enjoyed by an audience.

Knowledge and intelligence can also become blocks or barriers to creativity if the individual is closed to new information or situations that do not conform to previous understandings. Openness, willingness to explore, and the willingness to question even one's own assumptions are characteristics of creativity that, in concert with knowledge and intelligence, enable people to be open and flexible or dynamic in the ways in which they address new situations.

To innovate and become creatively productive also requires individuals to be able to manage their thinking and to observe their own behavior as they move toward their objective and make adjustments based on feedback from the real world. Metacognition—applying procedural and self-regulatory knowledge—can be improved with training and practice and through the deliberate use of tools that allow people to think strategically, to be attuned to and select environmental cues and bits of information, and to combine cues and information with ideas drawn from long-term memory in ways that are interesting and possibly useful (Runco, 2003a; Woolfolk, 2010). Arthur Costa (1984), a long-time leading educational researcher and trainer, viewed metacognition as an essential element of effective, powerful thinking. Isaksen et al. (2011) emphasized the importance of metacognition (and "planning your approach") in managing change and solving problems creatively. They described the need for problem solvers to keep track of their thinking while it is happening, to manage choices, and to modify their approach as necessary to optimize their results. In that context, metacognition for creativity and innovation includes appraising the task or challenge thoroughly; considering the commitments, constraints, and conditions under which you will be working; taking into account the people who are or will be involved as the effort moves forward; and being deliberate in your choices regarding methods and tools.

Style: Discovering Your Creative Self

Let's now turn to the question of style, especially in terms of understanding your own approach to creativity and the approaches that others with whom you might be working bring to the table. Based on our developing understanding of problem-solving style, we believe that when different individuals are confronted with a problem, they may act very differently. This results in different actions and experiences that lead individuals to make different choices. When we consider Cheryl, Michael, and Lucy, we see three individuals with very different styles as they approached the challenge of writing a play in a group comprised of their peers.

Much of our current understanding of style grew out of the work of Carl Jung (1923, 1971). He defined two opposing functions on how people prefer to interact with the world: introversion and extraversion. Two other functions, sensation and intuition, were related to perception and how we gather information. In addition, two judging functions influence decision making: thinking and feeling. Katherine Cook Briggs and her daughter Isabel Briggs Myers expanded Jung's work, adding one more dimension that included two other functions: judging and perceiving (Martin, 1997). Their work has been important in helping individuals understand valuable differences, strengths, and areas for potential growth; why others may differ from them; and how to maximize the benefits of those differences (Lawrence, 1997, 2009).

In that a certain level of knowledge is a prerequisite for creative productivity, learning styles is an important consideration. Taking many definitions of learning styles together (e.g., Dunn & Dunn, 1978; Gregorc, 1985; Hilgersom-Volk, 1987; Kolb, 1981), we view them as the unique ways individuals perceive, take in, process, and apply information. Rita and Kenneth Dunn (1978) developed a learning styles model that included 21 elements arranged in five categories: environmental, emotional, sociological, physical, and psychological. In addition to elements shared by other models like preferences for kinesthetic, visual, auditory, and tactile learning and analytic/global and reflective/impulsive behavior, the Dunns discussed the amount of light, the presence or absence of sound, and the presence or absence of structure and authority. An important aspect of their work was that each element impacted different learners with different levels of intensity. For instance, some individuals are not influenced by structure. Whether or not it is present, they will learn with the same level of efficiency and effectiveness. For those, the element of structure is neutral. If a person is able to learn without structure, but can learn more effectively if structure is present, we can say that the individual has a preference for structure. For some, however, if the presence of imposed structure or the lack of imposed structure prevents learning, then structure is said to be a factor of their style. To Michael, structure was an annoyance. Whenever he could, he would ignore it. When circumstances forced him to follow a set structure, he would give it the least attention possible. Lucy, on the other hand, found that structure was important in guiding her efforts. She expected that each challenge would include some structure, and when that was not the case, she would develop her own structure before proceeding.

Selby, Treffinger, and Isaksen (2007a, 2007b) drew widely on research and theory in the areas of learning styles and cognitive styles (Cattell, Eber, & Tatsuoka, 1970; Guilford, 1980, 1986; Kirton, 1961, 1976, 1987; Martinsen & Kaufmann, 1999; Witkin & Goodenough, 1981), as well as research, theory, and field experience with instruction, training, and application in the areas of creativity, creative problem solving, and creative productivity (Guilford, 1986; Isaksen, 1987a; Schoonover, 1996; Selby, 1997; Sternberg & Lubart, 1995), to develop a model of problem-solving style. This model looks at three discrete dimensions of problem-solving style: Orientation to Change, Manner of Processing, and Ways of Deciding, which influence how individuals behave when solving problems and/or managing change. Each dimension involves two styles that describe differences in the ways people plan and carry out activities, such as gaining clarity about a situation, gathering and selecting data, generating ideas, focusing their thinking, and selecting and implementing solutions (Treffinger, Selby, Isaksen, & Crumel, 2007). Table 2 lists some of the preferences identified with the six styles associated with this model. Each style represents strengths that may contribute to the problem-solving process. Each carries with it areas that may be considered weaknesses or blind spots. The more aware individuals are of their own style characteristics, the more effective they are in solving problems or managing change, whether working alone or in a group.

As you look at Table 2, think about the three students and the play-writing group as a whole. Michael was always seeking novelty and could be counted on to generate many original ideas, sometimes to the annoyance of others or in disregard for decisions that had already been agreed to. The fact that there was a deadline for the script mattered less to him than the fun he had with his new idea. He was eager to share this idea

Table 2

Three Dimensions and Six Styles of Problem Solving

Orientation to Change		Manner of Processing		Ways of Deciding	
Explorers May:	Developers May:	Externals May:	Internals May:	Person-Oriented May:	Task-Oriented May:
• Seek novelty • Generate many new, original options • Be spontaneous • Envision the big picture • Prefer a flexible structure • Be individualistic • Trust their own judgment • Prefer generating over focusing • Be seen as unconventional • Like to stretch reality • Seem unconcerned with rules and deadlines	• Look for gradual change • Generate a few workable options • Be methodical • Understand the details • Prefer a clear structure • Be careful and precise • Be comfortable with the guidance of authority • Prefer focusing activities • Be seen as efficient • Like to minimize risk • Seek, accept, and employ rules and deadlines to organize work	• Gain energy from sharing ideas • Prefer social processing of information • Be engaged by the outer environment • Learn and work in a variety of ways and settings • Enjoy building on the ideas of others • Share thoughts and ideas early in process • Press for quick action • Seek a lot of input before closure	• Draw energy from reflection • Prefer quiet for private processing • Become engrossed with inner events and ideas • Learn and work on one approach at a time • Share thoughts and options after they are worked out • Engage in one task at a time • Weigh options carefully and thoroughly • Act after thorough analysis and consideration	• Look first to concerns for harmony and relationships • Consider first the human impact of problems and challenges • Be sensitive and caring when responding to individuals about their ideas • Prefer more informal work environments • Act on what they feel is right about and for people • Consider the personal impact of decisions • Work to ease group conflicts	• Look first to quality of outcomes or results • Consider first rigor and objective analysis • Keep people and their ideas separate and respond to ideas not individuals • Prefer more formal work environments • Look first at what is lacking or needs improvement • Base decisions on facts and what is rational • Disregard others' feelings in tense situations

Note. Adapted from Treffinger et al. (2007).

with others and couldn't understand why they did not see the logic of his new approach to the challenge. Lucy was also willing to share her thoughts and was considered the most social member of the group. She had methodically and efficiently brought the whole project to a conclusion. Like Michael, she couldn't understand why others didn't see the logic of her structure and her solution to the challenge. Cheryl listened quietly to the whole discussion for some time before making her suggestion to use some of Michael's ideas and Lucy's structure combined with other strong suggestions. She seemed very pleased when consensus was reached and the group was ready to get back to work.

Implications for Practice

Many personal characteristics associated with creativity and innovation can be enhanced through instruction and training and can be sharpened through self-analysis and understanding. The last six decades have seen the development of many robust tools that can extend our natural abilities to generate ideas and focus our thinking. These tools will be discussed in more depth in Chapter 15. Training in the tools and processes associated with the creative and analytical skills needed for creative problem solving can result in increased creative productivity by children and adults, as well as individuals and teams (Sternberg & Lubart, 1995; Sternberg, Jarvin, & Grigorenko, 2009; Torrance, 1987, 1995; Treffinger & Selby, 1993).

Elements of style may be more stable and less influenced by instruction, but our behavior can be modified to meet specific situations. This becomes more possible, more effective, and less stressful when we are aware of our own style and the preferences of those around us. In planning creativity instruction, teachers or trainers can differentiate their lesson based on both the levels and styles of their students. With those students whose creative characteristics are yet to be observed, instruction should focus on building basic understanding of creative tools and processes, as well as content knowledge in areas of interest. Learners whose potential is starting to emerge need opportunities to practice applying those creative tools and processes so as to build competence and confidence in their use and application. Some students need more advanced opportunities, as they are more able to express and apply their creative strengths in addressing challenges that are closer to real life. Those few students who excel in being able to employ observable strengths in all four categories can be expected to be creatively productive, exhibiting the self-direction and self-regulation of professionals in the field.

Taking the Chapter Forward

- Think about the most creative person you know. What characteristics set that person apart from others in innovation or creative productivity? What might you do to develop and hone the same behaviors to enhance your effectiveness when solving problems or managing change? Think also about your own style. In what ways are you most effective when solving problems? When you were a child or adolescent, did anyone (e.g.,. teachers, parents) ever talk with you about creativity? Did you think of yourself at all as being creative?

- Use the information in this chapter to consider the characteristics of your students. What characteristics do they display that are associated with their level of creativity? What seem to be their style preferences? Discuss with them their own understanding of their characteristics and preferences. What insights did you gain about the class? Consider how these insights might enable you to enhance your efforts (and their own) to recognize and nurture your students' creative potential. What would it mean for students to be innovative? (Do you believe that innovation is only an adult behavior?)

- You might also discuss the concepts presented in this chapter with your family members and your coworkers. Ask them about their views on the personal characteristics related to creativity and innovation. How do the views about characteristics differ from person to person? How do issues such as learning or style preferences fit into their understanding? Consider how these insights might be used as you seek to nurture the creative productivity of groups with whom you work.

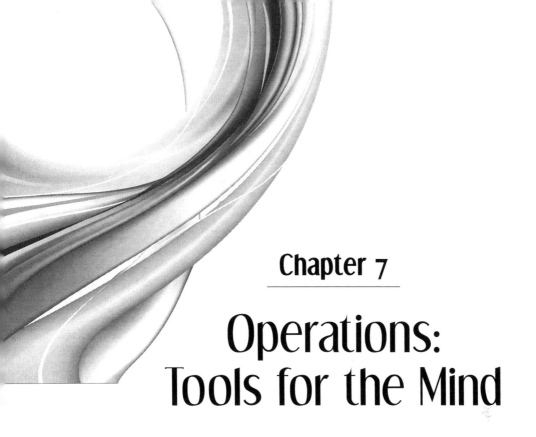

Chapter 7

Operations:
Tools for the Mind

After reading this chapter, you will be able to describe the nature and importance of operations—a person's command of appropriate methods, tools, strategies, or techniques that can be used to deal creatively with any task (e.g., a job, an assignment) or problem (e.g., an open-ended opportunity or challenge). You will also be able to describe a systematic instructional model for enabling students to learn and apply many operations.

Learning and Applying Operations

Instruction to guide students of any age in learning and applying the mental operations that support creativity and innovation involves three important goals. Connell (1991) identified those goals—the "three Cs"—as follows:

○ *Competence*: Learners know and are able to use many specific methods and strategies for generating and analyzing ideas, solving problems, and making decisions.

○ *Confidence*: Learners believe in themselves and their ability to be successful and creative.

○ *Commitment*: Learners accept creative challenges willingly and actively seek opportunities to use or apply their skills to new challenges.

Operations involve the degree to which one can choose, apply, and manage specific tools for creative work. These include tools for generating options, focusing options, and making decisions, as well as structured methods for finding, defining, and solving problems. Although it is both desirable and effective to have a rich array of possibilities, creative thinking is not sufficient by itself for productivity or action. One must also be able to sort, analyze, and choose among those ideas (i.e., use critical thinking). The operations component in the COCO model also includes the ability to use more complex processes for innovation or solving problems, such as Creative Problem Solving (CPS; Isaksen et al., 2011; Treffinger et al., 2006).

The operations component also involves thinking about your own thinking, or the use of metacognitive skills. These skills include understanding the language and vocabulary that accompanies methods and tools, monitoring your own creative efforts, and communicating your thinking to others. They also involve self-assessment of progress and needs while working on a problem, searching your repertoire of tools and methods, deciding which tools to use at any time, and adjusting or changing course as needed. Metacognitive skills are important in helping you move from the tentative, hesitant efforts of the novice to the confident, assured behavior of the expert.

The operations component of the COCO model suggests that innovation and creative productivity involves what you are able to *learn to do* as much as (or more than) who you are or what your traits or level of ability might be assumed to be.

Figure 4 presents a model that we use to organize our thinking about teaching and learning for creativity. The outer layers of the model highlight three important topics we have already discussed: the context or environment, metacognitive skills, and personal characteristics. In the circle in the center of the model, you see three essential dimensions of teaching and learning for creativity: foundations, realistic tasks, and real-life opportunities and challenges. They're arranged in circular fashion because they are not always approached in a fixed sequence as you implement the model. There might be times when you will begin with the foundational tools, practice them with sample tasks, and then extend them into real-life applications. However, in other circumstances, working on a real-life problem clarifies the need for new foundations, tools, or skills, or engaging a group in a practice task leads to real-life challenges or to the need to learn new basic tools. For simplicity of presentation, however, we will summarize each of the three dimensions, beginning with foundations.

Foundations

The foundation for creativity instruction involves learning and using a number of basic tools for generating or focusing options and for process management. What is a tool? Some everyday tools might include a hammer, saw, screwdriver, computer, sewing machine, and blender. With those basic concepts in mind, think about these questions and make note of your responses:

- Why do people need and use tools?
- What does any tool have or do and in what ways does that help us?

Some common responses to these questions are:

- makes work easier or more efficient,
- extends our physical capabilities, and
- makes some jobs possible that otherwise might be impossible (or nearly so).

The tools we'll emphasize and use in this book are what we call "tools for the mind," or thinking tools.

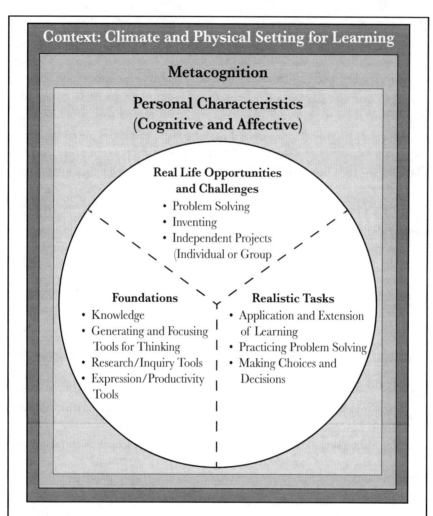

Figure 4. Model for teaching and learning productive thinking. Adapted from Treffinger and Feldhusen (1998) and Treffinger et al. (2006).

By the way, you will often find that people use the terms *tool*, *strategy*, and *technique* interchangeably, as though the words are synonyms. We believe they differ in meaning and implications (Treffinger, 1997). We use the word strategy to represent a deliberate plan or decision for selecting and applying tools. Your strategy involves questions such as:

♦ What tools might it be wise and helpful to select for this task? Why?

♦ In what order or sequence might I apply the tools I've selected? Why?

♦ If that doesn't do what I expect, what other tool(s) might I choose and apply? Why?

We use the word technique to describe our plans and decisions about how to modify or personalize any of the tools we choose and apply or the ways we carry out tools with a group. For example, we might consider:

♦ For this task, should I try this tool (or these tools) by myself, or should I use a group to help me?

♦ How might it be most interesting and productive to use this tool? (For example, if we decide to use the brainstorming tool with a group, will we write everyone's ideas down on a large sheet of chart paper or use a variation such as Brainstorming with Post-it® Notes or Brainwriting? You'll learn more about these variations as you continue reading this book.)

There are many ways for you to work with the foundational tools we present in this book. There has been debate for many years regarding direct versus content-embedded teaching of thinking skills (see, for example, Beyer, 1985; Costa, 1991; de Bono, 1983; Nickerson, Perkins, & Smith, 1985; Swartz & Parks, 1994). We believe that both direct and content-embedded instruction can be valuable. Many of the tools can be learned quickly and easily through the use of contrived exercises or activities that draw upon the common, everyday experiences familiar to most people. These direct instructional efforts may not represent the person's actual context for applying and using the tools—the domain or content area in which the person works—but they often help people recognize that the tools can be applied in a variety of different contexts. Direct instruction can always be followed, or even accompanied by, deliberate efforts to practice and apply the tools in context-relevant applications. Many published programs and materials can also be used to support direct instruction in the foundation tools; we will describe a number of those in Chapters 16–18. You probably already engage your students in many kinds of activities in which they could apply the basic tools for creative and critical thinking in our model.

A school district received a grant to develop video segments using puppetry to illustrate and teach basic thinking tools to elementary school students. To make the project more enjoyable, the development team also created a "Masked Marauder" character who delivered each tool's video to classrooms, playing it for the students (with the teachers also observing, of course) and answering questions. It proved to be a very original method of delivering tools to the students and professional development to the teachers—as well as enjoyment for the developers!

Tables 3 and 4 summarize some words and phrases that might appear in objectives or in instructional activities in your classroom that indicate opportunities for creative and critical thinking (and for using the basic tools in this book). These words and phrases may also be helpful for you in constructing and posing open-ended questions that extend beyond recognition and recall and challenge students to think creatively and critically.

Table 5 summarizes the 10 tools that make up our basic toolbox for thinkers. We will deal with these five generating tools and five focusing tools in greater depth in Chapter 15.

You may discover that an Internet search on creativity will yield many sites that present some variation of several of these tools. Given that profusion of information, you may wonder what, if anything, makes this set unique and important or what differentiates our approach from that material. Table 6 presents seven key points in our response to that question.

Table 3

Words and Phrases in Creative Thinking Objectives

The student will be able to:
- Produce many possible ideas for . . . (ways to . . .) or produce at least three (five) . . .
- Identify changes that might . . .
- Transform . . .
- Make predictions about . . .
- Hypothesize . . .
- Identify connections or relationships between . . . (among . . .)
- Describe possible causes of . . .
- State possible consequences of . . .
- Represent [any concept] in a variety of ways (modes; formats)
- Describe what might happen if . . .
- Identify unusual connections between . . .
- Design an original . . .
- Adapt or modify . . .
- Elaborate on or add details to . . .
- Identify ways to change . . .
- Explore ways to increase the efficiency or effectiveness of . . .
- Make an original model or representation of . . .
- Describe ways to simplify, eliminate, reverse, or rearrange . . .
- Propose new ways to combine or synthesize
- Substitute, use, or do in a different way . . .

Realistic Tasks

In the realistic dimension of our model, the primary goals involve learning and practicing a systematic approach to solving problems, drawing on both creative and critical thinking skills (Isaksen et al., 2011; Treffinger et al., 2006). Realistic experiences, such as packaged practice problems, help to expand and build upon the foundation tools.

The realistic dimension sometimes involves the use of contrived practice problems or exercises for any of the CPS components or stages. They may take the form of simulations, case studies, video clips or dramatizations of brief scenarios, or printed exercises. Realistic practice problems are intended to use content that will be of interest to the students, even though it is not of direct personal importance or consequence. The goal is to provide problems that are sufficiently engaging to be motivating for the group, but not so intensely involving that the students' investment in solving the problem makes it difficult for them to learn and practice

Table 4

Words and Phrases in Critical Thinking Objectives

The student will be able to:
- Analyze . . . (identify the key parts of . . .)
- Compare two (or more) . . .
- Contrast . . .
- Justify or evaluate (using internal or external criteria) . . .
- Rank or prioritize several options
- Group or cluster various options
- Organize and present data
- Identify pluses and minuses of . . .
- Refine, improve, develop, or strengthen . . .
- Substantiate or document . . .
- Construct, present, and defend . . .
- Verify . . .
- Deduce (make deductions) . . .
- Make and support inferences (infer) . . .
- Distinguish or differentiate among . . .
- Assess . . .
- Make and defend a decision to . . .
- Describe a classification system or scheme for . . .
- Describe the unique features of . . .
- Summarize . . .
- Recognize fallacies, flaws, or propaganda . . .

appropriate CPS tools. No one expects that anyone will actually use or do anything with the solutions that are created, because the problems are imaginary. Thus, we describe them as realistic problems, rather than as real problems.

Several published collections of practice problems provide brief sample situations that you can use to provide opportunities for students to apply CPS methods and tools in an enjoyable and engaging context while working within the constraints of the typical classroom setting. A number of national and international programs for students spanning a variety of ages from the elementary school through college levels also engage students in more extensive experiences for learning and applying CPS methods and tools. We'll discuss those in Chapter 17.

Table 5

The Creative Problem Solver's Basic Toolbox

Tools for Generating Options	Tools for Focusing Options
Brainstorming and its variations: Generating many, varied, or unusual options for an open-ended task or question. (Variations include Brainwriting and Brainstorming with Post-it® Notes.)	**Hits and Hot Spots:** Selecting promising or intriguing possibilities (identifying "hits") and clustering, categorizing, organizing, or compressing them in meaningful ways (finding "hot spots").
Force-Fitting: Using objects or words that seem unrelated to the task or problem or to each other to create new possibilities or connections.	**ALoU:** Using a deliberate, constructive approach to strengthening or improving options, by considering Advantages, Limitations (and how to overcome them), and Unique features.
Attribute Listing: Using the core elements or attributes of a task or challenge as a springboard for generating novel directions or improvements.	**Paired Comparison Analysis (PCA):** Setting priorities or ranking options through a systematic analysis of all possible combinations.
SCAMPER: Applying a checklist of action words or phrases ("idea-spurring questions") to evoke or trigger new or varied possibilities.	**Sequencing: S-M-L:** Organizing and focusing options by considering short-, medium-, or long-term actions.
Morphological Matrix: An analytical tool for identifying the key parameters of a task, generating possibilities for each parameter, and then investigating possible combinations (mixing and matching).	**Evaluation Matrix:** Using specific criteria in a systematic manner to evaluate several options or possibilities to guide judgment and selection of options.

Note. Adapted from Treffinger et al. (2006) and Treffinger and Nassab (2011a, 2011b).

Table 6

What's Unique and Powerful About Our Basic Toolbox?

Organization and Balanced Structure
- Emphasis on the use of generating and focusing in harmony
- Integrated with our definitions and guidelines
- Link between creative and critical thinking tools and defined roles for each

Purposeful and Instructionally Relevant
- Clarity regarding the value and benefits to guide selection and use of tools
- Understanding of style dynamics when selecting and using tools
- Not just a playful "grab-bag" of isolated activities
- Tool set supports intentional process decisions

Robust and Broadly Applicable
- Applicable across ages, cultures, and platforms (business, education, nonprofits)
- Applicable across content or curriculum areas
- Accompanied by an array of supporting resources

Systematic and Integrated With Problem Solving
- May be used by individual problem solvers, pairs, teams, or large groups
- Explicit role for generating and focusing in each Creative Problem Solving (CPS) component and stage

Carefully Presented Based on Sound Research
- Commitment to accuracy and historical context
- Supported by an extensive body of research and development
- Research base may be invisible to end user, but still important
- Striving to attain and maintain precise, concise, consistent language (e.g., is brainstorming a tool, technique, strategy, method, process?)

Readily Learned, Mastered, and Applied
- Not so difficult as to be discouraging or frustrating
- Not superficial ("mindless fun")
- Challenging but rewarding
- Applicable in developmentally varied but appropriate ways

Real-Life Opportunities and Challenges

No one learns CPS simply as an interesting academic exercise or just for the opportunity to do practice problems that are contrived and provided by a teacher, trainer, or workshop leader. Each of the students introduced in Chapter 1 was eventually able to meet the challenge of real-life opportunities. William addressed his challenge by first becoming knowledgeable about the band literature and then drawing from that knowledge to write interesting arrangements that were performed in public. Before her team began working on its research project, Sue's teacher grounded the students in the problem-solving process and tools. This allowed them to tackle open-ended challenges and produce a promising medical process. Eric and his friend Jimmy needed a lot of instruction in the process and the use of the tools for generating and focusing. By learning and applying these tools while engaged in a meaningful task, they were able to take their newly found skills with them to the next grade and continue to produce successful presentations and publish articles in the local newspaper.

The reason most people learn CPS is to increase their ability to think productively (creatively and critically) in situations that really matter in their life and work. Unlike the contrived practice problems sometimes employed in the realistic dimension, real problems are the authentic opportunities, challenges, and concerns people encounter in real life. Real problems are situations that you really care about; you feel strongly about them, and you want to be able to solve them. You intend, without any doubt, to put the solutions to work and carry out your results. Working on real problems—not just realistic exercises—is the eventual goal of any instructional or training program in CPS.

Taking the Chapter Forward

o Try this exercise. Have you ever ridden in an airplane? Consider the complex skills that the crew members in the plane's cockpit have mastered. How might the model in this chapter have applied to their learning of that complex set of skills? If the "real deal" is being in the cockpit of that flight you were on, what might have been some of the realistic tasks that crew experienced before they took your plane (or any plane) up into the sky? What were the some of the foundational skills they needed?

Level	Example
Real-Life Opportunities and Challenges	Flying a real airplane
Realistic Tasks	
Foundations	

o   Make a list of some complex skills at which you are quite pro-
    ficient today. How might you describe the three levels in this
    model as they would pertain to those skills?

o   Next, think about some essential skills that we expect all students
    to learn. What are some basic academic skills that schools teach
    to all students? How do we provide opportunities for them to
    grow in their mastery of those skills by practicing? What kinds
    of practice activities or experiences do we use in the classroom?

Chapter 8

Context

After reading this chapter, you should be able to identify and describe several factors that make your school or classroom a "best" learning place—factors that stimulate or inhibit creativity and innovation in a variety of situations. You will understand nine specific climate factors and describe ways your school or classroom takes these factors into account in seeking to establish and maintain a climate that supports creativity by staff and students alike.

What Is Context?

To put this part of the model into a personal context, think about where your best ideas come from or think about where you were when you did your best thinking about a challenge or opportunity you faced. Where were you when you had your best or breakthrough idea? Were you at work, at school, at the gym, or someplace else? Were you driving, sleeping, daydreaming, raking leaves, or washing dishes? Now think about the factors that helped or hindered your creative efforts. When people have been asked to describe their experiences with environments that tend to limit good ideas, they often report too much pressure, not enough time to think, lack of support, or arbitrary pressures to conform. In negative environments, ideas are often shot down very quickly, harshly, and consistently. Unfortunately, this probably sounds familiar. Try to think also about environments that supported or facilitated good ideas. Perhaps the climate felt open and supportive—maybe even fun.

Context includes people, process, procedures, and places; it surrounds us at home and at work and influences our feelings, attitudes, and actions. Context includes internal and external factors that encourage or block creativity (Isaksen, 2007). For schools, the *internal* factors include intrinsic motivation, level of confidence, levels of trust and openness, and feelings members of a group might have for each other and the school, as well as the perception by members of how valued they are by others in the group. *External* factors might include the local, state, and national government; the larger political and social system; the surrounding community and its people and organizations; and a variety of technologies. Within a classroom, the context includes teachers, students, physical facilities and equipment, and a variety of outside factors, such as parents, administrators, community resource people and groups, the curriculum, local attitudes and support, and official policies and expectations. Researchers often distinguish between culture (i.e., the stable, long-established values, beliefs, procedures, and practices that guide and direct us in our setting) and climate (i.e., the ways people perceive and respond to the context in which they are operating). This chapter examines several important factors that influence the context—and particularly the climate, which you can establish and maintain—to value and nurture creativity and innovation.

Creative Climate in School

Several different lines of research have shown that climate can affect many people in schools and the effectiveness of their work. For example, Kuperminc, Leadbeater, Emmons, and Blatt (1997) reported that positive school climate was associated with fewer behavioral and emotional problems for students. Other research on school climate has shown that a positive school climate can significantly influence student success in high-risk urban environments (Haynes & Comer, 1993) and can lead to positive social interactions, healthy emotional development, increases in achievement, and prevention and reduction of antisocial behavior (Haynes, 1998;

Kuperminc et al., 1997; Marshall, 2004). Much recent work on school climate has focused on its relationship to bullying or gender issues. More specifically, however, in this chapter, we're concerned with the climate for creativity and innovation in education. This more specific understanding of climate has also been studied in relation to problem solving and talent development with at-risk adolescents (McCluskey, 2000), as well as in educational leadership for innovation and effective schools (McCluskey, 2008) and the conduciveness of classroom climates for student creativity in the United States and Canada (Treffinger, Isaksen, & Dorval, 2011) or in international settings (Klimoviene, Urboniene, & Barzdziukiene, 2010; McLellan & Nicholl, 2008).

Göran Ekvall, an industrial psychologist in Sweden, conducted early research and development on climate dimensions that influence creativity. He observed differences in the working atmosphere of different organizations and their effects on idea generation. Ekvall (1983) developed an instrument to assess an organization's climate for creativity. Ekvall's original work was extended by Isaksen and a number of his associates, leading to the development of a revised instrument based on nine verified and refined factors from the original 10 postulated by Ekvall. The instrument is the Situational Outlook Questionnaire (SOQ; Isaksen, 2007; Isaksen & Ekvall, 2007; Lauer, 1994); it provides a tool for assessing the nine specific dimensions of an organization's climate for creativity. Treffinger et al. (2011) discussed these nine factors specifically in relation to their potential extension and application to educational settings; an earlier form of the SOQ has been used in some educational settings (e.g., by school improvement planning teams considering the school's climate for creativity rather than the specific classroom context). We believe that it is reasonable to hypothesize that, in some form, the same nine general factors may be at work in classrooms.

As you read about each factor, think about your initial list of what helped or hindered your best ideas. Your list will very likely contain some of these factors. The same factors that are important for a positive workplace environment are likely to be important for creativity and innovation in education. In education, we might consider two levels of climate: a macro-level, in which we would look at the school or even at the school district climate, and a micro-level, in which we might look at the climate of an individual classroom and its impact on students and teachers and their interactions. McLellan and Nicholl (2008) noted that classrooms in the same school may have different climates or learning environments. As we discuss learning environments, we include teacher collaboration in teams for professional learning communities (PLCs). These learning communities can be an incredibly important influence on classroom climate and one of the most effective ways to improve student learning (Honawar, 2008).

Importance of Understanding the Creative Climate

Many factors influence the culture and climate of a school or school district. In addition to a variety of levels of governmental systems and requirements, there are also local influences (e.g., school board policies) or even school-level influences (e.g., administrative policies and decisions, parental influence). All of these influences eventually impact the classroom in both direct and subtle ways.

The context of your classroom involves the influences of many people and systems. Any one individual might not easily change these influences within the school, but the climate within your classroom is something you can manage for your own benefit as well as for your students and their learning. If you work with other teachers to generate ideas to improve student learning, you will no longer be working in isolation. You will be part of a team or PLC that can support you as you work with your students. As you read about the nine factors, think about some of the students discussed throughout this text and the ways in which their teachers and schools provided a climate in which they felt comfortable and encouraged to pursue their interest, develop their potential, and meet some meaningful challenges. Ask yourself which of these factors was being addressed and how you might include these factors in your classroom or curriculum.

Collaborating with other teachers may help you to include these factors to benefit your classroom. The irony is that we expect our students to collaborate on activities or to work as part of a team, but teachers still mostly work in isolation. This is a very 19th-century idea in a 21st-century setting. Your classroom may already be an example of the best learning experience for each of your students. McLellan and Nicholl (2008) found, however, that many teachers they interviewed in design and technology classes in the United Kingdom were limited in their awareness of the impact and importance of the classroom climate and their role in establishing and maintaining a climate conducive to creativity. Often they perceived the limitations on creativity in the students' work as arising from the students and their desire not to be challenged outside their personal comfort levels. Only a small number of the teachers they interviewed recognized that their choices, decisions, and interactions with the students might contribute in important ways to creativity. These researchers concluded that efforts were needed to establish a more conducive culture in the school to value and support creativity, and also that teachers needed to recognize and respond to the challenge of addressing a constructive climate for creativity in their classrooms. Three factors seemed to be of particular importance: challenge, freedom, and idea support (McLellan & Nicholl, 2008). Students in design classes felt that much of their assigned work lacked challenge and freedom, and that they did not receive support for their ideas. In another study, in a different country and a different teaching context, researchers also found that it was important for teachers to understand and respond to specific climate factors in order to be successful in promoting students' creativity (Klimoviene et al., 2010).

Understanding climate for creativity is important for you as an educator because it:

- can help you to understand more clearly how you perceive the environment (it makes the invisible a little more visible),
- may help you to identify and become more involved in shaping the climate within which you work (in your classroom and in your school), and
- may allow you to reduce certain negative aspects and focus upon the more positive aspects of your perceptions of the working climate (also at both the classroom and the school levels).

For the school, PLC, or team level, understanding climate is important as it helps:

- promote honest communication among staff or team members,
- uncover negative perceptions of other staff or team members and promote effective problem solving to overcome these obstacles to productive group functioning, and

○ discover and build upon unexpected or unknown strengths.

At the school or district level, understanding climate may:

○ help to determine the appropriateness of the climate to the success of the school and the district within the local area or community (how well does the climate fit the tasks or purposes of the district and its role in the community?);

○ help to determine the appropriateness of the climate to the well-being of the people of the school or district (how well does the climate match the needs of the human resources within the school or district?), and

○ allow the school or district to enhance or improve its structure and thus create a more productive and successful environment for students, staff, and community to build upon those structures that seem to be working well and modifying others (what structures may help promote creativity and better meet the needs of your school or district?).

Nine Specific Climate Factors

Challenge and Involvement

When challenge and involvement are present, students are interested and curious. They are motivated to learn and eager to explore. However, when challenge and involvement are missing from a classroom, students will feel apathetic and alienated toward school, their classroom, or learning in general. The goals may be too high for some and too low for others. It is not possible for your students to be involved at every level of classroom operation, but there are still plenty of areas where they can be involved. You can also create a sense of a shared vision within your classroom so that the students will see the classroom as *their* classroom, not just *your* classroom. An example of this is a fourth-grade teacher who had his class help him generate ideas for organizing the books and other resources in their classroom. This was done at the beginning of the year, and it helped the teacher to get to know the students better. As the solutions were put into action, it also helped the students to become better acquainted with each other and the teacher and to gain a sense of ownership for the resources within the classroom.

Challenge your students by providing appropriate tools for generating ideas and focusing. You can also stimulate your students' curiosity with open-ended activities that encourage exploration and questions. For example, as they read or research different concepts, encourage them to ask who, what, when, why (and why else), and how (and how else). Encourage students to solve real and realistic problems individually, in groups, or as a class. Engage your students with a variety of activities, projects, and learning centers.

Freedom

When freedom is present, opportunities are provided for goal setting, independence, and self-directed learning. There is variety in routine, procedures, and ways of demonstrating accomplishments. But, when it is missing, students tend to work within strict rules, and the teacher prescribes the goals and objectives with very little room for flexibility.

Each person has his or her preference for learning new material or working on a task. Not all of us can work effectively in desks anchored to the floor in neat rows. Some of us prefer to work in groups, whereas others may prefer to work alone. Work with your students to help them understand and appreciate their own and others' unique learning style preferences. Your students will gain ownership of their projects and assignments through contracts or learning agreements where they learn to manage their individual or group learning goals and activities. Isaksen, Treffinger, and Dorval (2000) listed specific strategies to help you and your students:

- Teach process skills and procedures for finding and using resources and equipment.
- Provide for and guide group collaboration in planning schedules, deadlines, and procedures.
- Use project teams or small groups for problem-solving projects.
- Use student record-keeping forms, class meetings, and team or individual conferencing to help students to organize their work, manage their own activities, and learn to handle greater freedom in a responsible way.

Trust and Openness

Ideally it is better to work where people are open and frank with each other and can count on each other for support. Effective learning communities take time to build collegiality based on trust and openness. It is much better and easier to work where respect and open communication exist. When trust and openness are missing in a classroom or in a team environment, people become suspicious and guarded. For example, students may say they agree or understand when they do not. Your classroom can be a safe place for unusual ideas and opinions. It can also be a place where students know that credit is given where it is due. We should model these actions so that our students will become adults who also provide a safe, supportive workplace or classroom. For example, as your students ask the who, what, when, why, and how questions, encourage them to explore other resources to find answers.

Idea Time

Besides having a safe and supportive place to explore ideas, we all need time to generate and develop ideas. Teachers need a safe and supportive climate in order to develop curriculum activities that will enhance learning for their students. Professional learning communities can provide the safety and support that teachers need for quality idea time. When there is sufficient idea time in a classroom, time and possibilities exist to pursue meaningful learning projects and to go beyond recall and drill. Students will have time to explore new topics. When idea time is missing, however, every moment is filled with prescribed activities with a heavy emphasis on covering the material.

Think about ways in which you might support your students with productive idea time. When assignments are constructed, do you provide choices for different ways in which they can be completed? For example, you could allow students to choose whether they want to work in a small group or work alone. Also, think about the different ways in which the final product might be presented and suggest different options, including the choice for the student to develop his or her own way of presenting the product. You can still use a rubric that clearly states your expectations for the assignment, which is very important for those who need some parameters in order to begin generating ideas. Idea time is also about having *enough* time to explore and develop ideas. Provide a realistic time frame and perhaps involve your students to develop this with short-, medium-, and long-term goals within a time frame.

Playfulness and Humor

Laughter and learning are comfortable companions. People are better able to absorb information when they are relaxed. If they can relate the information to something humorous, they might be more likely to remember it later. When playfulness and humor are present, there is more spontaneity and ease within the classroom. There is a good balance between working hard and allowing students to enjoy what they do. When this factor is missing, the atmosphere is grave and serious. Jokes and laughter are seen as improper and intolerable.

Your classroom does not need to be a stand-up comedy club, but it can be a place where humor can find an appropriate place and time. A sense of play and a good sense of humor can help put students at ease with a new subject that might be difficult to absorb. It can also help to engage students and hold their attention. Two of this book's authors observed a science teacher work with nearly 40 students in a small classroom as the students worked in groups to figure out the mystery object in their group's box (a small juice container). He challenged the students to ask questions and explore options to help them discover ways to identify the mystery object, and he allowed a sense of play as they worked within their groups. As each group responded with its ideas, he used humor to encourage them to think deeper and wider about the process of exploration. There was a lot of laughter, but there was also a great sense of engagement in the learning process.

Conflict (Low)

In high-conflict situations, students may express their dislike and hatred easily and vehemently; there may be problems with physical or verbal aggression. However, in low-conflict situations, people react in a more mature manner and accept and deal effectively with diversity. There are, unfortunately, classrooms where there is high-conflict atmosphere, and learning of any sort would have a hard time taking root when everyone (including the teacher) feels threatened.

Idea Support

When idea support is present, ideas and suggestions are supported and encouraged. Students and teachers demonstrate respect for each other and their ideas, and there is active listening and discussion. When there is no evidence of idea support, new ideas are responded to with an automatic "no." People will find fault with these new ideas and block them with "idea killers." If you have ever been part of an idea-generating session where someone suggests that your group brainstorm, what happens during the session? Quite often there is one or two in the group who want to dissect ideas as they are generated. This tends to put a halt to productive idea generating. You can best support, and model that support, by using the guidelines for generating options, which includes deferring judgment, free wheeling, and generating as many ideas as possible, to build and expand on other ideas. The other side of this coin is using affirmative judgment when critical thinking or idea-focusing activities are called for. Although judgments must be made, you can lead students to seek the best ideas by improving them and building them up, and as you do so, other ideas can be set aside for possible use at another time.

Debate

When debate is present, ideas are generated, judgment is deferred, and diverse perspectives are shared with plenty of time to reflect. Participants in a healthy atmosphere of debate respect conflicting ideas and will explore the situation from different perspectives in an affirmative and constructive manner. When healthy debate is missing, only one right answer or a single correct position is expected from everyone for each task or issue without question. Conflicting ideas and perspectives may be rejected, and debates can escalate into conflicts.

The reality of any group is that everyone will not always be of one mind on any issue the group may take up; fair-minded people working in good faith may view issues differently. Rather than resolving such differences through conflict, power, or arbitrary imposition of one viewpoint on all opposing views, debate offers a way to have a full, open airing of issues and viewpoints leading toward a constructive outcome or decision—a situation in which individuals can disagree on their conclusions in a respectful, supportive way. Educators can ensure that all views are respectfully attended to and that speakers do not interrupt each other, and can remind students that choices eventually must be made. Students whose views are not implemented must understand that this is not a personal rejection, but an effort to find a solution that will benefit the whole group. Sorting, sifting, combining, and evaluating ideas should involve affirmative judgment and constructive learning opportunities.

Risk Taking

Some people find it easier than others to accept ideas and solutions when the outcome is unknown. At the same time, it is also easier for some to work with disorder and chaos than it is for others. When risk taking is present, there is a willingness to attempt challenging tasks and a tolerance for ambiguity. People feel safe in expressing themselves. But when this factor is not present in a classroom, students tend to stay on the safe side and will only select the tasks that they perceive as easy or familiar.

Although rules and guidelines are important, sometimes the best way to encourage productive thinking and problem solving is to tolerate a certain amount of chaos and ambiguity. Order will emerge with careful guidance and support. For people who prefer incremental change, this can be challenging. Likewise, for those who prefer huge leaps, it is a challenge to take smaller steps.

An example of risk taking is the veteran sixth-grade teacher who decided to use Creative Problem Solving (CPS) to help his students explore their group's assigned country as part of the geography unit. He allowed each group to decide which country they would study and how they would present the information. He was quite skeptical about allowing this much freedom on this assignment, but he persevered. In the end, the teacher said his students learned far more than they would have with a standard geography activity of memorizing the details of each country. The teacher said the project presentations were exciting and informative and went way beyond his expectations.

What You Can Do

A healthy climate that promotes creativity and innovation in the class is more than a feel-good option. Students are not one-size-fits-all learners, yet teachers today are often expected to teach the same thing to everyone—with zero-tolerance policies thrown in for good measure. At the end, students are tested using approaches that remind us of Henry Giroux's (2010) depiction of much testing as "formulas that may be useful for measuring the heights of trees but little else" (para. 5). If you are part of a PLC, look at the nine climate factors and consider how well your learning community is functioning. Although each learning community is very different, there are common elements that are shared. Lieberman and Miller (2011) listed eight common elements that are also reflected in the nine climate factors just discussed. Successful learning communities:

- meet regularly and invest in the time to build relationships based on trust and openness;
- work hard to develop a clear purpose and collective focus on problems of practice;
- create routines and rituals that support honesty and disclosure;
- engage in observation, problem solving, mutual support, advice giving, and peer teaching and learning;
- organize and focus on activities that enhance learning for adults and students in the school;
- use collaborative inquiry to stimulate evidence-informed conversation;
- develop a theory of action; and
- develop a core set of strategies to connect their learning to student learning.

Fostering creativity and innovation requires perspectives about education that are richer, more exciting, and more engaging, and building such perspectives requires efforts to establish and maintain a constructive climate at the classroom level, at the school and school district levels, and throughout the broader community. How can you accomplish that? Begin with things you believe you can implement now. Here are some suggestions:

- Show the value of understanding individual style differences and points of view through activities, tasks, or other ways to demonstrate what it means to be different. Respect an individual's need to work alone or in groups. Encourage self-initiated projects or activities.

- Provide choices in the ways in which projects and tasks might be done. Encourage unique approaches by providing resources and room rather than controls and limitations. Involve students in goal setting and decision making. Provide an appropriate amount of time for tasks, and provide the right amount of work in a realistic time frame.

- Facilitate the learning and application of specific and deliberate creative problem-solving techniques and skills, including tools for generating ideas and focusing.

- Establish an open and safe atmosphere by respecting, supporting, and reinforcing unusual ideas during generating and focusing sessions. Communicate your confidence in your students' abilities, and turn mistakes into positives through affirmative feedback and judgment.

- Remain flexible and model a tolerance for some complexity and disorder, at least for a short period. Demonstrate ways of bringing order out of chaos through the use of strategies for clear goal setting and organization.

- Create a climate of mutual respect and acceptance among students and you so that they will share, develop, and learn cooperatively. Encourage interpersonal trust and teamwork through team-building activities and conflict resolution skills.

- Maintain high but attainable standards and expectations that call for creative and critical thinking and learning; model the thinking tools in your own thinking and invite participation in realistic and real challenges. Provide space, time, resources, and—most of all—questioning to encourage students to go beyond recognition and recall.

- Become a talent spotter. Encourage and challenge students to solve problems and work on new tasks in new ways. Keep asking questions! Allow time for reflection so that students can develop their ideas. Use questioning strategies to help students clarify their reasoning and polish their ideas.

- Model active listening and avoid control of every element, step, or decision in a task or project. As you listen, acknowledge the messages. Allow yourself and others to laugh and enjoy the moment.

This will help a warm, supportive atmosphere to develop and will encourage students to play with possibilities.

You probably do many of these things already and, if so, you have a head start. The specific Creative Problem Solving process and the generating and focusing tools will help you as you move forward. Understanding the diversity of context, celebrating our differences, and teaching the CPS process and tools will help your classroom climate become the place to which your students will want to come early and stay late . . . and you will, too!

Taking the Chapter Forward

o Think about the things that encourage your creativity. List them. Now think about the things that block or are barriers to your creativity. How might you break down or overcome these blocks and barriers?

o Using the information from this chapter, how might you construct an optimum climate for creativity in your classroom? How many of the nine factors that support a creative climate do you already incorporate positively in your classroom? What might you improve or add? List some steps you might take within the next 24 hours. Consider posing these questions to your students, too, and discussing their responses.

o Finally, think about the climate of your school in relation to the factors that encourage (or inhibit) creativity among the staff or the students. Examine the nine climate factors again, and rate your school from 1 (*low*) to 10 (*high*) on each of them. Which factors are highest? Lowest? Where is more effort needed?

Chapter 9

Outcomes

In this chapter, we will consider the factors that influence the outcomes of your creative efforts. People use different approaches to judge whether or not an outcome or product is indeed creative. We will discuss some of those approaches along with three categories used for identifying outcomes as creative. How we go about assessing products and outcomes is important to how we act as consumers, but more importantly how we behave as educators and trainers. Our own opinions as to what determines a creative outcome influences our reaction to our students' products and whether that reaction will be encouraging or one that deflates a promising idea before it ever leaves the ground.

What Makes Outcomes or Products Creative?

Consider, if you will, the three different products illustrated in Figure 5: a fully loaded Swiss Army Knife, a wrist watch with TV/DVD remote capabilities, and eyeglasses with electric wipers. Are these products cre-

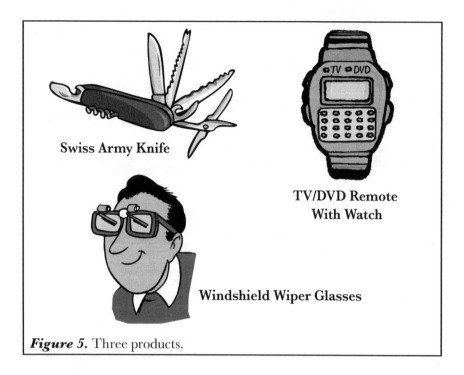

Figure 5. Three products.

ative? Why or why not? What goes into making a determination that a product or outcome is creative? What criteria do you use?

Creativity and innovation are often assessed in light of the products or outcomes that result from the creative act. By outcomes, we mean the results of creative endeavors. Although innovation is often defined in terms of the success of its outcomes, we believe that the people, processes, and context that contribute to innovation should not be overlooked. Creative productivity and innovation grow from our imagination, which is based on life experiences. This often sets up an interesting cycle where real-life experiences lead to imaginative thoughts, which are manifested in behaviors that result in a creative outcome that changes reality. Thus, outcomes become an important element in renewing the creative cycle (Eckhoff & Urbach, 2008). Outcomes include products, performances, ideas, concepts, theories, inventions, songs, works of art, and even changes in personal or group behavior in terms of novelty, usefulness, and style.

How do we know if an outcome is creative or not? The assessment of outcomes has a subjective element to it; it relies on the types of products, performances, or ideas that an individual judges to be creative. Those judgments are influenced by several factors. At least in part, they are often influenced by an individual's problem-solving style (Treffinger et al., 2007). Cultural setting can also play a role, as an outcome considered highly creative in one culture may be completely ignored in another. A newly designed fishhook may receive little interest among desert nomads, but may be highly valued by fishermen on the coast of Maine.

Some of those who study creativity put great emphasis on public acceptance. They argue that a product's level of creativity might not be recognized at first, but if it is not eventually found to be acceptable in some cultural context, then it is not creative (Metzl & Morrell, 2008). Others base their work on the assumption that success in the marketplace is the strongest indicator of creativity (Craft, 2008). According to Csikszentmihalyi (1997), in order to be creative, the novelty demonstrated in an outcome must be accepted and then adopted by those in the appropriate field. This might call to question the life of someone like Van Gogh, whose works were not at all well received by the marketplace nor by those who dominated his field while he lived. Then he died, and the rest, as they say, is history. Does this mean that Van Gogh was not creative when he lived, but became creative after he died? Obviously, this line of argument could become a bit silly.

Nevertheless, it is difficult to separate creative individuals from their products and from the outcomes they produce, as well as their acceptance as useful by someone. And so, the study of creative products and innovation becomes central to the study of creativity itself (Isaksen, 1987b). How can we know it is there unless we observe it? MacKinnon (1987) argued that the analysis of products is "the bedrock of all studies of creativity" (p. 120). However, the feeling remains that there must be something more than public acceptance.

There are numerous other approaches to assessing the degree to which an outcome is or is not creative (Kaufman & Beghetto, 2009). These include self-assessments ("I did this and I feel it is creative"), assessments by laypersons ("I'm no expert but this looks creative to me") based on the premise that most people know something that is creative when they see it, and assessments by experts ("This is my field and, based on all of my experience, this product is really creative"). In corporate settings, the creative level of teams, or their level of innovative effectiveness, is often assessed on the basis of total output (Hulsheger, Anderson, & Salgado,

2009). In these cases, a supervisor will rate a team's level of success based on total numbers of suggestions and possibly the number of new products or patents that result from those suggestions.

Then there is the matter of degree. How much creativity does the outcome reflect? This is the issue of Big C and little c that we introduced in Chapter 3. Is this an outcome that changes everything, that creates a long-term paradigm shift or a major innovation in a field? Does it, as Csikszentmihalyi (1997) suggested, completely change a domain or bring about a new one? Outcomes in this category are considered Big C. On the other hand, if this is an outcome that makes a small incremental change—one that may go completely unnoticed by anyone but the creator—this is little c. These are the two extremes on a continuum. All of the human behavior that we might consider creative results in outcomes somewhere between these two extremes. There are thousands of journal articles written by highly trained and experienced researchers and theorists in a variety of academic domains, works of art in galleries around the world, new music pieces, letters to the editor of the local paper, and improvements in the way things are done, none of which come close to being the Big C variety of creativity (Kaufman & Beghetto, 2009).

The playwriting team that we met in Chapter 6 had their work performed in front of their community over a 3-day period. Teachers, parents, relatives, community members, and their fellow students all remarked on the high level of creativity that was demonstrated by the production. Yet, no paradigms were shifted; no new trends in theater were established. Although most of us (including Csikszentmihalyi) would agree that a new medical procedure, such as the one developed by Sue and her friends, was a creative outcome, what about Eric's presentations and articles or William's improvisations and arrangements? Every day, people in every walk of life engage in little c processes that collectively result in a significant impact. Indeed, at Toyota, millions of new ideas are implemented each year. In most cases, ordinary workers generate these ideas. Over the long term, it is often these incremental changes that build the foundation for a paradigm shifting big C innovation in one domain or another (Maddux, Leung, Chiu, & Galinsky, 2009).

So, how are you to decide? Besemer and Treffinger (1981) suggested three major sets of criteria against which we might assess creativity: novelty, resolution, and elaboration and synthesis. They began by pointing out that we should not confuse criteria for assessing the creative person with criteria for assessing creative products. Still, in order to identify a person as creative, we need to at least consider the outcomes that the individual's efforts have produced. Based on a wide review of the literature, Besemer and Treffinger developed the three sets of criteria, providing us a sound yardstick with which to measure any outcome and its level of creativity. Let us look at each of these sets of criteria in detail. The original three sets of criteria were restructured and refined through later research (Besemer, 2006; Besemer & O'Quin, 1986, 1987, 1993; O'Quin & Besemer, 1989).

Novelty

When considering novelty, we look at the extent to which an outcome demonstrates newness. Is this outcome a new process, technique, material, concept, or product? To what extent is it unique in its field? Will this outcome influence future creative efforts in or out of its recognized domain? Among the general criteria included in this set are: originality, the product's germinal quality, and its transformational aspects.

Originality is often considered the prime criterion for assessing creativity. An original outcome is not commonly found or observed in the everyday course of things. It is statistically unusual and clearly stands out from what would normally be expected. With students, originality might be considered in light of the frequency with which you would expect a specific outcome given the age, culture, and life experience of the child. We also need to consider the various aspects of the outcome. Some aspects may be original, others more common, but still the overall result might be considered creative. A higher level of originality is ascribed to outcomes with more uncommon or new aspects.

The germinal qualities of an outcome refer to how likely it is that other creative products will develop directly from this outcome. The more an outcome can be generalized to other fields or lead to the creation of other new approaches or products, the more this aspect of creativity is recognized.

A transformational outcome may be startling in its "newness." This element looks at the extent to which the outcome forces people to shift their thinking or look at things in a totally new and different way ("Things won't be the same anymore because of this!"). Highly transformational outcomes bring about complete paradigm shifts in a domain or in an entire culture. A transformational outcome might challenge tradition, do away with the restraints of convention, and produce a radical change in thinking or the way things are done from that point in time.

Resolution

Resolution refers to the extent that the outcome seems to be correct, complete, or right. How clearly does the outcome meet and/or fill the need that it was intended to address? The basic questions in terms of resolution are: "Did this work the way we expected?" "Did this do the job and address our challenge?" "Did this get us from our current reality safely to our desired future?" The general criteria in this set include: adequate, appropriate, logical, useful, and valuable.

An outcome is adequate to the degree that it answers the needs of the situation. Adequacy is judged by the ability of the outcome to meet enough of the needs established by the initial challenge so that the effort can be considered successful by the individual problem solver. Does the product perform the desired function to an acceptable degree?

To judge if the outcome is appropriate, we consider the degree to which the outcome fits the situation or challenge. Given the context, does the solution make sense? Does it have some social relevance?

A product can be said to be logical if it follows the accepted and understood rules in the domain or the reality in which it has been carried out. In other words, given the facts, the reality of the context, and the creative efforts being made, does this outcome logically follow? It still needs an element of originality, but at the same time it should make sense. You might note here that there is some overlap among these sets of criteria.

Usefulness is the extent to which the applications of the outcome are practical and clear. Usefulness takes a broad look at an outcome's application. A new product's design may make someone's job easier, while a new work of art may stimulate thought, spark a conversation, or bring about an emotional response. The question then becomes, "Useful to whom and in what setting?"

An outcome is valuable if those who use, listen to, view, or consume it deem it worthy. This is a highly subjective criterion. Again, we need to consider the value of an outcome broadly. Value has characteristics that are both intrinsic and extrinsic. There are also short- and long-term considerations, as well as overall costs/benefits. A teacher may spend weeks developing an instructional approach designed to help just one student overcome a reading problem. If the approach is successful, was it worth the time and effort? The answer to this might depend on who you asked, what other teaching duties were set aside in order to work on this one challenge, and the long-term benefit to the student and the teacher.

Elaboration and Synthesis

This set of criteria takes in the degree to which the outcome brings together diverse and unlike elements and refines them into a new coherent whole. Here we might think of the impact of style on the way the assessment of criteria is undertaken and experienced. As with some of those above, the criteria below often reflect a degree of bias. It is in this area that we often depend on experts or very clear definitions to tell us if the criteria have been well met. This set considers packaging and presentation, along with the manipulation of the various elements of the outcome and whether it might be said to have been well done. The general criteria in this set include: attractiveness, complexity, elegance, expressiveness, organic qualities, and if the outcome is well-crafted.

An outcome might be attractive by being pleasing to the senses or by drawing people to it in some other way. To what extent does the product command the attention of and appeal to the intended audience or user? This criterion may consider beauty and appearance, but may also look at the degree of surprise or delight. Humor, enjoyment, entertainment, and/or pleasure might also be appropriate considerations. Especially when considering this element, we need to remember that beauty is in the eye of the beholder.

A complex outcome contains many elements at one or more levels. This complexity should not be just busy, but also add direction to a work in a way so that the complexity is brought under control to the point where it seems almost simple. This criterion is closely related to the next.

Elegance is expressed in a refined, understated way that suggests harmony and subtlety. This is often seen as a criterion for judging highly creative outcomes. In science and mathematics, elegant solutions may be described a being a simple, direct, pleasingly ingenious approach that addresses all of the pertinent facts.

An expressive outcome promotes communication or makes the solution easy to understand. In the arts, the effective use of the various elements in a piece may be considered. In products, we might assess the degree to which a new device invites user interaction with it.

The organic qualities of a work refer to the degree of completeness or wholeness found in the outcome. Products are often assessed in terms of their organizational unity. How well do the individual aspects of the product work together while fully addressing the product's underlying purpose? Does the outcome hold together? Does it show balance and proportion? Does it manage to bring order from a state of disorder?

A well-crafted outcome has been deliberately worked and reworked and developed to the highest possible level for a particular point in time. Outcomes that reflect care and attention to detail are assessed as being well-crafted.

In using these sets of criteria, we need to understand that not all of them will apply to all outcomes and that when they do apply, they will do so at different levels of strength and impact. Indeed, it is the extremely rare work that would be highly rated on each criterion in each of the three sets. That said, if we are to consider an outcome to be creative, there should be some obvious degree of novelty, resolution, and elaboration and synthesis.

Building on the work above, the Creative Product Sematic Scale was developed to aide in identifying the degree to which a creative product or work addresses each criteria (Besemer, 2006; O'Quin & Besemer, 1989). Other less extensive scales are also available. Balchin (2009) suggested, for example, a set of criteria that shows some overlap with Besemer's work, including uniqueness in place of novelty and effectiveness, which seems to fall under resolution. But, he also considered some additional factors such as risk taking. This criterion asks: "Is it a bold attempt? How ambitious is it? Is there a clear challenge taken on?" (Balchin, 2009, p. 207).

This last criterion taken along with the others above might be helpful when considering the work of students in the classroom. The changing reality in the world requires us to refocus our efforts on more authentic assessments. These are assessments that consider students' accomplishments in applying their acquired skills and knowledge in real-life situations or situations that are as close to real life as possible (Treffinger, 2003a). Student products such as community service projects, portfolios, writing examples, and works of art can be assessed using rubrics based on appropriate criteria reviewed in this chapter along with relevant content-based criteria. Doing so might help students realize that they too have creative potential.

Now that you have finished reading about these specific product criteria, go back to the example in Figure 5 and reconsider the three products illustrated there. If you had read about the three sets of criteria before judging whether or not these three products were creative, would the task of assessing them have been easier? Might your results have differed? Which of the criteria apply to the three products? Ask yourself the question: "Might these products each be creative in different ways?" Based on your new understanding, what is your conclusion? Find some products in your everyday life that you consider especially creative, and ask a friend to rate each product based on his or her own criteria. Compare your views with your friend's. When looking at your own work, try to think of the outcomes you produce in terms of the three sets of criteria discussed in this chapter.

Remember, although each of the three sets might be represented, each will be represented at different levels—and sometimes one factor may be so strong that the others really don't matter very much at all.

Finally, think about the role that style plays in both the kind of outcomes we seek and the kind of outcomes we find pleasing or creative. Looking back at Table 2, you will see that Explorers look for and are excited by outcomes that are new, break new ground, and bring about change. Developers, on the other hand, seek and are more comfortable with outcomes that make things better, that represent incremental change. Think about how those differences might lead people to react differently to the creativity of each of the three products in Figure 5.

Taking the Chapter Forward

○ Have you ever said to your students, "I want you to be creative in what you do" for a particular assignment or project? What did you mean by asking them to be creative, and what kinds of product(s) might they have turned in that would have satisfied that they had met your challenge successfully? Are you confident that they understood what you were asking them to do or that they understood the "be creative" instruction the same way you did? Think about some specific ways to ensure that you and your students might be effective or on the same page in understanding and responding to requests for creativity in their products.

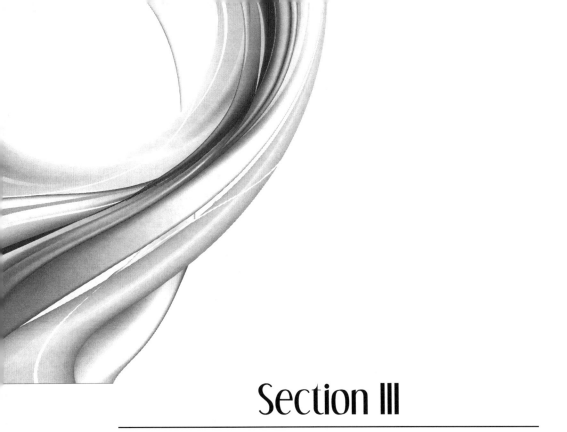

Section III

Identifying and Measuring Creativity

Chapter 10

Foundations of Creativity Assessment

After reading this chapter, you will understand the need for creativity assessment, and you will be able to define and appropriately apply the terms *testing*, *measurement*, and *assessment*. In addition, you will be able to define and distinguish between formal and informal data sources, objective and subjective data, qualitative and quantitative approaches to data gathering, traditional and authentic assessment, and validity and reliability.

Why Do We Need Creativity Assessment?

Elsewhere in this text we indicate support in the literature for the view that all healthy individuals, including children, have creative abilities and have the potential to be creatively productive. You might ask, "If that is so, why do we need creativity tests and assessments?" Even though we accept that creativity is a human survival trait, several questions still need to be answered if we are going to guide all people—and especially our students—to reach their full potential. These questions include:

o   In what domains or content areas is the individual's creative potential greatest?

o   What is the individual's style of creative problem solving?

o   What is the individual's current level of problem-solving ability?

o   Based on the data, what predictions can be made concerning a group's or an individual's eventual level of creative productivity?

o   What strengths might be cultivated and built upon to enable the individual to reach his or her potential in terms of creative productivity?

o   What instructional approaches would be most appropriate to enable the individual to reach his or her creative potential in areas of strength and in life in general?

o   What impact has creativity instruction had on a group's or individual's level of creative productivity? Has there been growth over time? What adjustments need to be made in our instructional approach?

o   What do assessment data tell us about the need for future research and the advancement of theory?

The goal of creativity assessment, as with all educational assessment, should be to inform instruction. Assessment data are most effective when they form the foundation of an instructional program designed to help groups and individuals grow and obtain the knowledge and skills that will enhance their natural ability.

Thinking back to our student examples in Chapter 1, we noted that Sue's interests and abilities were likely to be apparent to anyone who engaged her in conversation for any length of time. But, can we be sure that the instructional approaches taken by her teacher were the most effective for her style? William was obviously creative in music, but were there other areas in the curriculum in which growth might have been nurtured? What would have been the outcome if his teachers were more aware of his talents and if they were working from an overall profile of his interests and strengths? Before the school recognized his interest in the Civil War, Eric had shown some potential at home. If assessment had been an ongoing practice in his school and district, might his potential been recognized sooner? Would such recognition earlier on have contributed to an instructional approach that reduced his boredom and provided him with positive outlets and opportunities for interaction with his peers? Would he have been viewed less as someone to be tolerated and more as someone to be encouraged? In addition, from our experience, we are confident that if Cheryl, Lucy, Michael, and the others on their team had had knowledge of their problem-solving styles and an understanding of the different strengths that each brought to the project, the conflict described in Chapter 6 would have been reduced, and the group's overall effectiveness might have been increased.

Some Assessment Basics

Before we continue our discussion of assessment, we should be certain that the definitions, use, and distinctions among certain terms associated with assessment are clear. It will also be helpful if you understand how some of these terms are applied specifically in the assessment of creativity.

Qualitative and Quantitative

Assessment involves the collection of data from several sources. These data will fall into two categories: quantitative and qualitative. Quantitative often refers to data that are number-based and that are easily subject to statistical procedures. They are typically derived from tests, surveys, checklists, and self-report inventories and rating scales that provide scores that describe identifiable attributes, characteristics, or objectives. The results of quantitative analysis are often expressed in terms of percentiles, averages, or means. In the collection of these data, efforts are made to develop test items and procedures that control or eliminate bias and reduce error. Quantitative measures are intended to provide objective answers to questions about cause and effect, relationships, differences, the degree to which a trait exists, or how much of a particular characteristic an individual displays as compared to others.

The question on a test of divergent thinking is an example of quantitative data on creativity assessment. After asking students, for example, to "List as many things as possible that you might see inside an elementary school," counting the total number of responses (a measure of ideational fluency) for each student involves using quantitative data. (Treffinger, 2003a, p. 62)

Qualitative data provide insights into context and meaning and are gathered in more natural settings. Qualitative methods include observations, the collection of biographical information, case studies, ethnographic studies, and the collection and analysis of anecdotal records. Qualitative data provide the basis for in-depth discussion, often exploring possible biases, values, and context issues in an effort to gain a deeper understanding or to discern meaning so as to develop hypotheses. Qualitative data can provide insight into the circumstances that precede certain behaviors or why those behaviors occur when they do. In a school setting, examples of a student's curiosity and problem-solving skills might be gathered in the classroom, lunchroom, and playground or during afterschool activities. "An observer's description and analysis of a child's curiosity and creativity, as expressed in spontaneous exploratory behavior in a typical school setting, is an example of the use of qualitative data concerning creativity" (Treffinger, 2003a, p. 61).

Measurement, Testing, and Assessment

Three words—measurement, testing, and assessment—are often used interchangeably. In fact, each has a different meaning as applied to the collection and analysis of data and to the application of data-driven understandings and conclusions.

Measurements determine the amount, level, or degree of something. They are usually associated with quantitative data gathering. Measurements are usually made in reference to some standard or predetermined scale and, in educational and instructional settings, might be used to compare levels of proficiency, performance, or potential in a specific domain or in terms of a specific characteristic. As a verb, measurement refers to the act of measuring something, usually some instrument or testing procedure to gather information or data that might be compared with some reference point or might be analyzed statistically, as in the human sciences. In evaluating creativity-related instruction or training, we might want to gather test scores before and after instruction to measure the effectiveness of the instruction on the students' creative thinking, skills, and productivity or compare the gains made by a group of creativity students with a control group (Treffinger, 2003a).

In educational terms, a test is a tool or procedure used to develop data relating to proficiency, achievement, performance, or potential. Tests are usually designed to gather data in one specific domain or about a specific characteristic. As a verb, the word *test* has to do with the steps taken to gather data required to make judgments about or to evaluate an individual's strengths, proficiencies, or knowledge. Tests provide quantitative data that can be compared with data gathered from similar or matched sources or that can be combined with data from other sources in order to form a more complete picture of participating individuals.

An assessment is used to evaluate or estimate the nature or quality of something and usually results from data that describe different aspects of a complex construct, allowing for an overall understanding of that construct. An assessment may draw on data from tests, observations, surveys, interviews, rating scales, and checklists. Assessment

> is a process of appraisal or taking stock of an individual (or a group) by drawing together information from a number of sources and attempting to organize and synthesize those data in a meaningful way in relation to a specific purpose, goal, or task. (Treffinger, 2003a, p. 62)

Creativity assessment involves efforts to gather data that will enable us to identify or evaluate characteristics associated with creative productivity, potential, or level of readiness for a specific instructional approach. A comprehensive creativity assessment will very likely include both quantitative and qualitative data derived from varied sources such as the administration of formal tests, informal observations, surveys, interviews, rating scales, and checklists. Such an assessment might include observations of "cognitive abilities, learning styles, work habits, attitudes, self-efficacy, interests, and major personality characteristics, as well as the familial, community, and educational background" (Kirschenbaum & Armstrong, 1999, p. 339).

Formal and Informal

Assessment data can be gathered using either formal or informal methods. Formal methods usually depend on a standardized instrument, whether it be a test, rating scale, or survey. The individual administering the instrument will do so in accordance with a predetermined procedure and carry out the analysis in the same way. The individuals responding to the instrument know that they are being evaluated and that their responses will be analyzed; generally, they expect feedback after the analysis is completed. Participants also know that the assessment follows procedures that are in accordance with some recognized and authorized format. Formal assessments are usually administered at a set time and place and, in the case of many tests, last for a specified period of time. In the classroom, both standardized and teacher-developed tests come under the formal heading. Summative assessments are usually formal in nature, but the results may also be used formatively.

Informal assessments may be made at any time and place where the behavior of the participant can be observed. The informal approach has an unofficial, relaxed, and possibly friendly feeling to it. In school, informal assessment may take the form of teacher questioning, probing deeper into a student's thinking, data from afterschool or classroom activities and discussion, and observations of behavior during unstructured time (such as lunch or recess). Feedback, when provided, is usually immediate. Informal assessments in the classroom are almost always formative (i.e., designed for use in guiding growth or improvement), with questions developing from the natural course of a lesson, the students' responses, and the content of the course. Questions are not predetermined and are often improvised to meet an immediate instructional need. Data gathered informally may be compiled over time, allowing a more complex picture of the participant to slowly develop. It tends to be subjective. This type of assessment allows insights into an individual's passion and depth of commitment when pursuing a particular domain or when forming an understanding of the ways in which the individual expresses his or her creative potential in real-life situations.

Objective and Subjective

Data collected as part of the assessment process may also be categorized as either objective or subjective. Quantitative data, data gathered formally, and data gathered using standardized tests are common examples of data that would be considered objective. If data are objective, it is assumed that they have not been influenced by feelings or opinions, but describe observable facts. If two or more individuals look at data collected using an objective approach, it is likely that they will arrive at the same or similar findings. Likewise, we might assume that objective conclusions have been reached logically, on the basis of facts, without bias or emotion. Subjective data are usually qualitative in nature. Feelings, opinions, and perceptions are often the very stuff of subjective data. The conclusions that follow depend on individual judgment.

In the real world in which we hope to encourage creative productivity, it is important to consider data that are gathered widely and are both quantitative *and* qualitative as well as objective *and* subjective. We also must understand that the line between each is not always so clear. If you have an emotional response to an event, that response is properly considered subjective. However, it is an observable fact that you had that response, and it may well be observed that that response impacts your behavior as you work through the creative process.

Traditional and Authentic

Many educators and researchers have contrasted traditional assessment with alternative approaches described most often as authentic or performance assessment (Hart, 1994; Mueller, 2011; Wiggins, 1989, 1993). Although traditional assessment can be understood in many ways, it is usually used to describe assessment tools and processes that rely on formal, quantitative resources such as tests. By contrast, authentic assessment focuses on more qualitative approaches that emphasize what students are able to do (or how they are able to use or apply) what they have learned. Although these approaches are sometimes treated as being opposed to one another, it is often true, and especially so in relation to complex challenges such as assessing creativity and problem solving, that an effective approach draws on both forms of assessment. As we discuss the role and development of the Creative Strengths Profile for students in Chapter 11, you will see how the profiling process can involve data from both traditional and authentic sources. In Chapter 12, we focus in greater detail on the student portfolio, which is a form of authentic assessment, and its uses in assessing creativity.

Validity and Reliability

Quality assessment tools or instruments are both valid and reliable. These are complex constructs, and you will usually depend on the published manual of an instrument, reviews in professional journals, or reviews in the *Mental Measurements Yearbook* (available in most reference libraries or online at http://www.unl.edu/buros/bimm/index.html) for unbiased and complete information about most published assessment tools.

Validity. Briefly, the validity of an instrument involves the key question: "What evidence supports the claim that this instrument actually measures what it purports to measure?" Establishing an instrument's validity is an ongoing process; it is not a matter of stating a single value or judgment about the instrument. Callahan, Lundberg, and Hunsaker (1993, p. 136) presented several important cautions, including:

- Do not rely solely on assessments of an instrument offered by its authors. Consider all available data and external reviews and evaluations whenever possible.
- Remember that instruments that yield good reliability data on heterogeneous groups may not be reliable for homogeneous groups.
- Tests are never simply valid or invalid.
- If predictive or construct validity evidence is not available but the instrument appears to have adequate content validity for use in your situation, consider using the instrument on a pilot basis to gather data.

Linn and Gronlund (1995, p. 49) posed five important cautions when using the term *validity* in relation to testing and assessment. These were:

- Validity refers to the appropriateness of the interpretation of the results of an assessment procedure for a given group of individuals, not to the procedure itself.
- Validity is a matter of degree; it does not exist on an all-or-none basis.

o   Validity is always specific to some particular use or interpretation.

o   Validity is a unitary concept [based on various kinds of evidence].

o   Validity involves an overall evaluative judgment. It requires an evaluation of the degree to which interpretations and uses of assessment results are justified by supporting evidence and in terms of the consequences of those interpretations and uses.

Documenting the validity of any creativity instrument can involve several different forms of evidence. First, there is evidence based on an analysis of the instrument's content. Is there a good match or fit between the instrument's actual content and the theory and definition of creativity upon which it is based? You will usually evaluate this evidence by reviewing the instrument's manual or other supporting publications that explain the instrument's theoretical or conceptual foundation, definition of creativity, and rationale and comparing that with the instrument's content.

Validity may also involve demonstrating relationships between one instrument and other established measures or criteria of creativity. If multiple instruments exist with comparable conceptions of creativity, you would expect the results among them to be similar for any person. If they are measuring the same construct, you wouldn't expect someone to score very high on one instrument but average or low on another instrument. You might expect, then, positive correlations between students' results on one instrument and ratings of the students' creativity by teachers, parents, peers, or others who have had opportunities to observe the students' performance in the same aspects of creativity. Other approaches to establishing the validity of an instrument involve the extent to which results on the instrument actually predict subsequent creative behavior or the existence of experimental studies that demonstrate the relationship between results on the instrument and behaviors or actions consistent with those results. Knowing a person's results on the instrument, for example, how accurately are we able to predict his or her actual creative accomplishments or products at a later time?

Reliability. The reliability of an instrument refers to the accuracy or consistency of the results it yields. Reliability is usually evaluated in two categories: stability and consistency.

Stability deals with the instrument's effectiveness in providing data that are steady or stable across reasonable intervals of time, so that changes in results reflect changes in performance, not merely inconsistent or inaccurate assessment. You would not trust a scale, for example, if it told you that you weighed 160 pounds first thing in the morning, but then an hour later told you that you weighed 270 pounds. Rather than concluding that you gained 110 pounds at the breakfast table, we hope you would conclude that something was wrong with the scale. Of course, if what the scale measures actually does change over time, you hope to be able to see those results, too. If your weight changes from 160 to 152 after a few weeks of diet and an exercise regimen, you may be justified in your efforts rather than throwing out a "faulty" scale.

Consistency involves determining the extent to which the parts (alternate forms, subtests, or items) provide an accurate and fair representation of the person's responses. This is usually presented as a correlation coefficient, such as the correlation between Form A and Form B of the same instrument, or as a coefficient of internal consistency, such as Cronbach's coefficient alpha, for example.

The reliability of a creativity instrument may be trickier than your bathroom scale, of course, or even trickier than a classroom test on content knowledge. As a very complex construct, creativity may be more challenging to measure than body weight or facts about our country's history. Creativity can be expressed in many and varied ways, not all of which may be appropriate to assess the same way or with the same tools. Creativity may not always be completely stable within any person over an extended period of time (creative producers often report an ebb and flow in their energy, inspiration, and productivity). Not everything one produces will be a masterpiece. Norris and Ennis (1989) also cautioned about the challenges of interpreting and applying technical information concerning measures of critical thinking; their observations are also pertinent to creativity assessment. They proposed:

> Reliabilities appear in test manuals as stark, apparently unambiguous numbers, quite different from the picture we have painted. . . . We have said that it is difficult to know what level of reported reliability is desirable in a technique for gathering information on critical thinking. To say otherwise would, in our view, be misleading. People gathering information on critical thinking must realize

the primitive state of the art. Good sense is demanded in judging the level of reliability needed for the use to which the information will be put. Clearly, the more individual-specific and important the use for the information, the greater the reliability needed. However, reliability in the sense of consistency is not enough. (Norris & Ennis, 1989, pp. 48–49)

Taking the Chapter Forward

o   Now that you are armed with an understanding of some basic terms associated with assessment, as well as some of the limitations of assessments and creativity assessments specifically, you should be able to move through the next two chapters readily. You might also want to supplement your study by looking into some of the professional journals dedicated to the study of creativity and creativity instruction. The discussion in this chapter will enable you to have a better understanding of the material published in journals. The creativity journals include:

➤   *Creativity Research Journal*,

➤   *The International Journal of Creativity and Problem Solving*,

➤   *The Journal of Creative Behavior*,

➤   *Journal of Creativity in Mental Health*, and

➤   *Psychology of Aesthetics, Creativity, and the Arts*.

You might also find related material in *Gifted Child Quarterly* and *Gifted Child Today*.

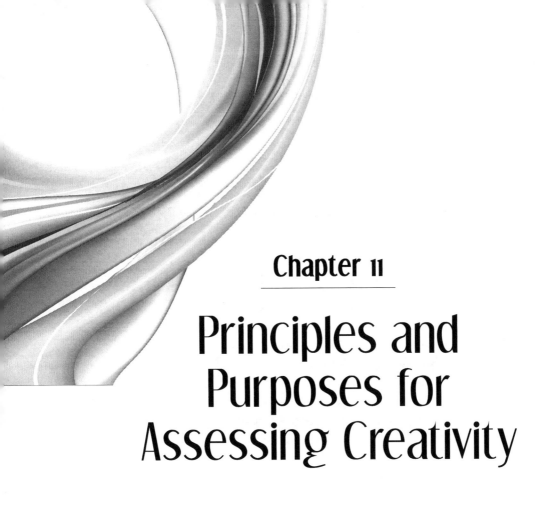

Chapter 11

Principles and Purposes for Assessing Creativity

After reading this chapter, you will be able to describe four important foundations for a practical approach to identifying creativity in your students. Our goals for this chapter are to guide you to designing and applying an approach that is data-driven, contemporary, and scientifically and educationally sound, as well as practical, realistic, and mindful of the constraints under which education actually takes place on a daily basis.

Constructing a Sound Approach

What do we mean by a sound, contemporary approach? Let's consider four basic principles underlying this type of approach to identifying creativity in education. They are:

- Know what constitutes a quality assessment tool and make a commitment to quality tools.
- Ask the right questions.
- Use multiple sources of data in an ongoing and dynamic model.
- Use assessment tools and results wisely and appropriately.

Know What Constitutes a Quality Assessment Tool and Make a Commitment to Quality Tools

Although we've sometimes heard people express the opinion that creativity can't be measured, the truth is that there are actually many tests, checklists, inventories, and rating scales that purport to do just that—we have more than 70 different instruments in our current collection. (You can view a list of them and read descriptions and reviews at http://www. creativelearning.com). An Internet search will yield many more that we didn't include in our database because they are very often lacking any evidence at all to support them. You can find everything from homemade rating scales to 2-minute "creative IQ" quizzes. We found one instrument that claimed to be scientifically validated, and when we followed that link, we learned what the claim meant: The author had given it to students in a college course, and they all assured him it measured what he said. There is old adage that is worth remembering: garbage in/garbage out.

You might consider two variables: an instrument's ease of use and the quality of the data it provides. Each of these is a continuum, but for convenience, let's look at the two "poles" of each one. Ease of use might be high (easy to use) or low (difficult to use), and quality of data might be rich (really informative) or poor (very little useful data). Table 7 illustrates the combinations this produces.

The risks of "fantasy land" and self-abuse seem apparent, although in the former case, you must use caution not to be taken in by appealing—but undocumented—claims (if it looks too good to be true, it probably is). So, the choices are usually between rigor and expedience. How much quality of data are you willing to sacrifice in order to gain greater economy or ease of use? Our position is clear: Making a commitment to quality will always be the best guiding principle for your efforts. Informal data may sometimes be useful to help you add insights to other efforts, but in general, we do not subscribe to the view that bad data are better

Table 7

An Instrument's Ease of Use Versus the Quality of Data

	High Ease of Use	Low Ease of Use
Yields rich data	"Fantasy Land": Expecting rich results with little or no investment of effort	Rigorous: Willing to make an investment of time and effort to obtain good data
Yields poor data	Expedience: Using quick, easy method knowing that it will not yield rich results	Self-abuse: Investing much time and effort and still not getting rich results

than no data at all. To obtain data you can justify and use with confidence in making instructional decisions, and to make any assessment process worth your time and effort (and your students' time and effort), seek and use tools that meet acceptable standards of validity, reliability, and appropriateness for your purposes and population. Although it may be complex and require time and careful study, we believe that commitment to quality is important. Attention to quality will yield accurate and useful data and will inform and guide effective instructional planning and implementation.

Ask the Right Questions

You have probably heard the old story about the person, late at night, searching under a street lamp for his keys. When asked, "Were you around here when you last had them?" the person replied, "No, I was over there [pointing to a dark area some distance away] but I am looking here because the light is so much better." Although it might not be much of a joke, we'll risk making it worse by saying that it does "illuminate" an important point about assessment. You won't get helpful answers if you aren't asking the right questions or looking in the right place.

Once you understand the basic terminology of assessment, you will have a foundation for asking the right questions and designing ways to get sensible, useful answers to them. It's not just about whether or not creativity tests are "any good" (although you can find a lot of discussion about that question, often generating more heat than light). It's not about deciding what test to use. It's most certainly not about using a score, or a set of scores, to set a cut-off point above which you might label some students creatively gifted (and thereby exclude everyone else from that special category). Finally, it's not about deciding whether a student is or is not a creative person; as you've already read, we believe that everyone has potential for creativity.

If your goal in assessing creativity is to gather data about students that will help you to provide effective, challenging instruction or perhaps to evaluate the effectiveness or impact of an instructional program, attend to the following guidelines:

- *Labels and categories are not important.* Your goal is not simply to classify students or separate them into groups such as high, average, or low. Instead, any assessment tools you use should provide information that informs you about the students' characteristics (or, in an evaluation, about a group's performance).

- *All students have the potential for creativity, but it may take many different forms of expression.* Keep in mind that the question "How are you creative?" is more informative than asking "How creative are you?" Consider many and varied ways in which your students may be at their creative best.

- *Seek the meaning, not just a number.* When you are examining any assessment tool, look beyond the numerical results or scores it will produce; look carefully at the data it will give you. What will it tell you about your students? Is that information consistent with your definition of creativity? Will that information be useful to you in planning, conducting, and evaluating instruction? Remember: If the data don't help you teach better, they're not worth gathering.

An approach known as Response to Intervention (RtI) has received a great deal of attention in education in recent years (see the special issue of *Gifted Child Today* magazine [Volume 32, Number 3, Summer 2009]). This approach emphasizes bringing together as much information as possible about a child's strengths and needs and then linking those data to sound (evidence-based) instructional approaches (Bender & Shores, 2007). Although its focus was originally on ensuring appropriate instruction for students with learning disabilities or special needs, its emphasis on using data to guide instructional decisions is also consistent with educational efforts to identify students' strengths and talents in order to ensure that instruction will be appropriate and challenging. Coleman and Hughes

(2009) argued that the "focus of RtI is on early intervention, the early provision of services that build on the child's strengths and address his or her learning needs" (p. 16). They emphasized that RtI "hinges on a collaborative approach to recognizing and responding to the needs of each child. This collaborative approach requires educators to think about the child first and match the supports and services to the child's strengths and needs" (p. 15).

Use Multiple Sources of Data in an Ongoing and Dynamic Model

You don't understand a person by looking at one picture. It's better to look at an album from which you can observe different views, angles, or perspectives and see how changes occur over time and circumstances. It's much the same when you are attempting to understand a person's creativity. There are different ways of looking at creativity, many ways of expressing and using one's creativity, and many changes in experiences, interests, and motivations that can lead to variations in one's creative efforts and accomplishments. It is inappropriate to expect that one source of data will provide a complete and unchanging description of an individual or of the individual's strengths and weaknesses. Creativity, creative problem solving, innovation, and managing change are all complex challenges and processes. They involve the development and use of many abilities and are impacted by a complex array of social, cognitive, personality, and situational factors.

In addition, people are not static or unchanging. They grow daily and over time are very likely to change in their interests, motivations, skills, and knowledge. For instance, there is evidence that fluency in generating ideas is influenced by experience (Runco & Acar, 2010). Therefore, we can expect that a person with a broader, richer base of life experience or with more practice generating ideas will tend to be able to attain a higher fluency score than someone with limited background and experience. To keep up with the changes that are constantly occurring in students' lives, then educators who are seeking to assess creativity need to gather data on an ongoing basis. Assessing creativity is more a matter of assembling an album (or perhaps putting together the pieces of a puzzle) than just taking one quick snapshot. The lesson is simple: Don't rely on just one instrument or source of data.

One positive piece of data can give you a great deal of valuable information. When you observe a student's imaginative or original behavior, that's certainly an indication of his or her creativity. But even then, it's an instance, not a pattern, and it's taking place in a specific setting or under certain circumstances; it's valuable data, but not a comprehensive assessment. By the same token, one negative piece of data may give you very little information about what might occur on a different task, in a different setting, or under different circumstances (e.g., varying motivation or incentives, a different content area or topic). It tells you what the person *did not* do, but not what the person *cannot* do; it is often said that "lack of evidence is not evidence of lack." Keep in mind also that people, children especially, are continually changing. They are in essence moving targets. Collecting data about where they are on a particular day does not necessarily tell where they will be a week, a month, or a year later. It is important, then, to have continuous data from multiple sources. Assessment is a dynamic process, not a static event in which you gather data once and put it away in a file drawer. As the data record for each individual (and for groups) continues to grow, your understanding deepens, and you become better able to develop appropriate instructional approaches and to recognize when you need to change course.

Treffinger et al. (2002) described four principal sources of data as ways to gather information about a person's creative abilities, strengths, skills, or potentials. Each of these four data sources has both advantages and limitations and may be useful in different ways or for specific assessment needs and circumstances. The four sources of data that might be considered in a comprehensive approach to assessing creativity are tests, rating scales, self-report data, and observations and product data (Treffinger et al., 2002).

Test data involve a person's responses to a structured set of tasks or questions, administered under controlled or standardized conditions, through which he or she demonstrates the ability to think or respond creatively. There is often a tendency among some people to trust test data because it is (or appears to be) objective, readily quantifiable, and comparable for all who respond by virtue of its standardized format. Other people argue that the very concept of a standardized test that can be scored objectively is a contradiction in terms.

Tests

The Torrance Tests of Creative Thinking (TTCT; Torrance, 2006), published by Scholastic Testing Service, Inc. (http://www.ststesting.com), are the most widely known and used tests of creative thinking. The TTCT include both a figural form (Thinking Creatively with Pictures) and a figural form (Thinking Creatively with Words), each of which involves multiple tasks. The figural form uses three picture-based exercises to assess fluency, elaboration, originality, resistance to premature closure, and abstractness of titles. The verbal form uses six word-based exercises to assess fluency, flexibility, and originality in thinking. The verbal exercises provide opportunities for the respondent to ask questions, identify possible causes and consequences of actions, improve products, and respond to "just suppose . . ." hypothetical situations.

Rating Scales

The second data source, rating scales, involves instruments that provide specific descriptions of creative qualities or behaviors rated by others (e.g., teachers, parents, supervisors, mentors, peers). The usefulness of rating data depends on several factors, including the rater's understanding of the characteristics or behavior to be rated, the opportunity of the rater to know or observe the person in situations in which that behavior might occur, and the rater's willingness to limit judgments to the specific characteristics being rated. Rating scales can provide helpful information efficiently, but if they are not properly used, may also be quite suspect in validity or reliability.

Rating scales typically present a number of items, each representing a particular trait or behavior associated with creativity (e.g., "When given an open-ended question, this person generates many responses"), accompanied by a rating scale such as a Likert scale (often a four- or five-point scale, such as *never, seldom, often,* or *always* or *strongly agree, agree, disagree,* or *strongly disagree*) or a quantitative rating (e.g., "rate the person from 1 [*low*] to 7 [*high*]"). Ryser's (2007) Profile of Creative Abilities (published by PRO-ED; http://www.proedinc.com) or the Scales for Rating Behavioral

Characteristics of Superior Students by Renzulli et al. (2004; published by Creative Learning Press; http://www.creativelearningpress.com) are examples of popular creativity rating scales.

Self-Report

Another source of data, self-report, involves the responses people give to questions about themselves and their behavior. Some researchers have argued, quite seriously, that the best way to determine whether or not people are creative is, in fact, simply to ask them! There are a number of attitude inventories, personal checklists, or biographical inventories that provide self-report data about creativity. These self-report inventories can be efficient to use, but there may often also be concerns about the completeness and accuracy of self-report information.

The Khatena-Torrance Creative Perception Inventory (Khatena & Torrance, 2006), or KTCPI, also published by Scholastic Testing Service (http://www.ststesting.com) includes two self-report checklists, Something About Myself (SAM) and What Kind of Person Are You? (WKOPAY). SAM measures six broad creative attributes as perceived by the individual about him- or herself: environmental sensitivity, initiative, self-strength, intellectuality, individuality, and artistry. WKOPAY assesses acceptance of authority, self-confidence, inquisitiveness, awareness of others, and disciplined imagination.

Observation and Product Data

Observations and product data are another source of data. One important way to obtain information about people's creativity is through their actual behavior: their creative products, performances, or accomplishments. You might obtain these data through records or first-hand observations in natural (real-life) settings or through the person's performance in constructed tasks that simulate or approximate the real-life settings but can be arranged and observed under controlled conditions. It might be useful to think of the former set as documentation of real-life creativity and the latter as demonstration of creativity under realistic or simulated conditions. In classroom settings, these data are often gathered through the use of rubrics. A rubric is a document that states criteria or expectations for successful performance on an assignment, task, or product. Rubrics typically include specific descriptions of performance at various levels of accuracy, completeness, or quality (e.g., using a four- or five-point range from *unsatisfactory* to *excellent*), although the number of categories and the specific labels and descriptions vary widely. In addition to providing evaluative data, rubrics can also guide learning by enabling students to understand expectations from the beginning of their work on a task. Some rubrics may be created by teachers or curriculum developers, but it is also common (and valuable as a learning tool) to engage students in discussing the nature and criteria of acceptable and excellent work and serving as co-creators of rubrics that will be used to assess their work (and to engage the students in assessing their own work and that of their peers). Observation and product data have credibility in real-life or realistic accomplishments and products. However, from an assessment perspective, they may be difficult to summarize and evaluate concisely and consistently and may make direct comparisons among individuals or across groups very complex. It may also be challenging to establish reliability between or among various observers.

An example of a basic rubric for assessing performance on a task involving use of the brainstorming tool for generating ideas might be:

3   Searches for many, varied, and unusual possibilities; defers judgment

2   Separates idea generation from evaluation (defers judgment), but generates only a limited number of possibilities

1   Generates one option at a time, stopping to judge or evaluate each possibility, and generates only a limited number of possibilities

0   Thinks immediately of one option and accepts it with no generation of other possibilities; criticizes other ideas and rejects the need for more options

Similarly, a rubric for use of the evaluation matrix tool (using criteria to evaluate) for focusing options might be:

3   Formulates appropriate criteria, applies them systematically to options, and considers ways to overcome possible limitations, combine appealing possibilities, or produce new options

2   States appropriate criteria for analyzing options and applies them in a mechanical way to rank or rate the options, focusing only on finding the "best" idea

1   Lists several options and then judges them, stating reasons for accepting or rejecting them, without formulating criteria explicitly or applying criteria systematically

0   Declares any option "good" or "bad" (accepts or rejects) with no evidence of criteria, justification, or systematic analysis

Use Assessment Tools and Results Wisely and Appropriately

Finally, it is not wise to rely on a single instrument to assess a person's creativity or to use results as if they represent absolute, fixed classifications of creative ability. A single assessment tool cannot tell you everything about an individual's skill level, knowledge, or ability in a particular domain, let alone across many domains. Often test users overlook the fact that instruments that measure creative thinking through divergent thinking do not purport to be comprehensive assessments of the total construct of creativity. Some creativity assessment tools lack construct validity and have little or no evidence to support their effectiveness as predictors of future accomplishment (Zeng, Proctor, & Salvendy, 2011).

It is also important to be cautious in interpreting and using the results of rating scales, self-report inventories, checklists, and surveys. Each can be subject to influences that may impact results. For instance, in the case of a self-report instrument, the respondent may not have understood or paid attention to the directions. Idealizing or selective memory may have played a role in the response choice. Responses may have been chosen in an effort to please the person administering the instrument or some other person in a position of authority. Keep in mind that the spirit of most instruments is to help you become more aware of and responsive to individual needs and differences.

Wise and appropriate use of creativity assessment tools and data also involves avoiding stereotyping and rigid categorizations of people. Use all of the data you gather to understand the student's present characteristics, strengths, interests, and needs. In the best of circumstances, all of the data you gather can contribute to your understanding of the student's strengths and needs. Rather than making judgments about whether or not a student is creative or including or excluding individuals from a certain program, assessment data used wisely and appropriately provide insights into instructional needs (e.g., what to do or what *not* to do at a particular time). The data you obtain about students' characteristics and needs (their creative strengths) evident in their behavior or performance at the present time under particular circumstances or conditions (or within a particular talent area or domain) enable you to recognize and respond to their needs. You must always be prepared to reevaluate and update your decisions and plans about how best to respond.

In the next chapter, we'll guide you in moving from the basic concepts in Chapter 10 and the principles in this chapter to a detailed plan for implementation.

Taking the Chapter Forward

o Review the four basic principles presented in this chapter. Compare them with current practice in your school or district in one of two ways:

➤ How are these principles reflected (positively or negatively) in the policies and procedures for identifying students for any special programs (e.g., gifted or enrichment programs, special education services, athletic or music programs)? Which of the four basic principles in this chapter are best illustrated and supported? What policies and practices might benefit from changes?

➤ Consider the four principles in terms of what classroom teachers already do in planning and carrying out daily instruction in any curriculum area. What do they already do that best reflects and supports the four basic principles in this chapter? What might they do differently with these four principles in mind?

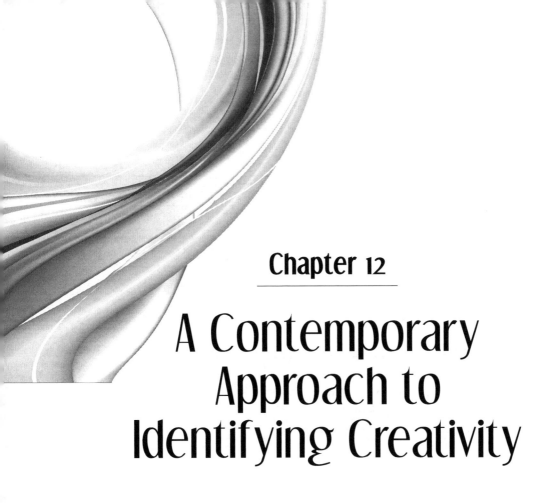

Chapter 12

A Contemporary Approach to Identifying Creativity

After reading this chapter, you will be able to design a sound, contemporary approach to identifying creativity. You'll have a plan that can readily be translated into practice in your own setting. As part of that plan, you'll be able to complete a Creative Strengths Profile, become actively involved as a creative talent spotter (and help others to play that role), and guide students in constructing, maintaining, and using a personal portfolio.

In Chapters 10 and 11, we argued that assessing creativity is a complex—but not impossible—challenge. It is complex because creativity is multidimensional and dynamic. Despite the fact that there is really no reason to expect that it would be reasonable for one test to yield a single score that would be a comprehensive indicator of a person's creativity, that remains a common question we have been asked again and again. Typically, the caller begins, "We need to identify students who are creative." It may be to evaluate the effectiveness or impact of a program or often because creativity has been identified as a school goal or an aspect of gifted and talented programming for which students must be identified and selected. The caller is often disappointed or frustrated when we reply that there is no single test that will yield what he or she is seeking. However, that does not mean that it is impossible to assess creativity (Treffinger, 2009). To help you address that challenge in a constructive way, this chapter deals with profiles and portfolios, two important kinds of tools for what is often known as alternative or authentic assessment (Hart, 1994; Herman, Aschbacher, & Winters, 1992; Treffinger, 1994).

The Creative Strengths Profile

Think about the Creative Strengths Profile as a tool to help you identify the ways any of your students demonstrate creative characteristics and strengths for a particular task or goal, in a certain setting, and under particular circumstances. It's not just a way to assemble or aggregate several scores in order to generate an overall index or categorical placement. More formally, preparing the Creative Strengths Profile refers to the development of a multidimensional framework to help understand, predict, and facilitate creative performance in a meaningful or valued domain (i.e., a worthwhile outcome).

The Creative Strengths Profile has seven important characteristics:

- *Flexible*: The profile may include a variety of data and forms of documentation; it does not have a single, fixed format.
- *Developmental and dynamic*: You may modify or change the profile at any time as new or additional data become available, not just at certain deadlines for an identification or selection decision.
- *Focused on strengths*: The profile emphasizes the search to identify what a student can do creatively in any area of talent, ability, or interest. It seeks evidence that affirms creative strengths.
- *Diagnostic*: The data in the profile help you plan for appropriate and challenging instructional activities or experiences.
- *Functional*: Profiles are active tools that students, teachers, and others can use to guide instruction and creative development; they are not "file drawer" documents.

○ *Varied data sources*: The profile can include many kinds of information (both qualitative and quantitative, formal and informal).

○ *Action oriented*: Profiles document actions to take and may include goals, objectives, person(s) responsible, evaluation, and timelines.

The Creative Strengths Profile can take a variety of formats, including physical documents in a folder, file, or container or documents in a digital format on CD or DVD, in a database, or in the cloud. It may be helpful to use a simple two-page paper summary of the profile to use in personal, peer group, teacher, or home conferencing and discussion.

Figure 6 provides an example of a Creative Strengths Profile summary. Note that the four columns under "Indicators of Creativity Characteristics" are the four categories we presented in Chapter 6, and the rows under "Data Sources" are the four groups of data from Chapter 11. The cells in this matrix might include data from a variety of different sources, depending on the tasks or goals for which the profile is being created.

Some specific data that might be incorporated into the Creative Strengths Profile draw from any of the four basic dimensions of creativity found in the COCO model, described in Chapters 5–9, and might include: characteristics (cognitive, metacognitive, personality and style, interests); context or dimensions of the situation (culture, climate, historical expectations and experiences, biographical data); operations and elements of the task (transferable process skills, research, inquiry skills, knowledge base); and outcomes (products and accomplishments, data from one's portfolio).

The "Additional Foundations" column on the right side of Figure 6 provides space to record information from a variety of other sources that extend and enhance your understanding of the student's creativity: motivation and task commitment, style preferences, climate or context, and knowledge and content expertise, which are all essential for creative productivity. The box at the bottom of the form provides space to synthesize the data from all sources, take stock of the overall level of performance, and anticipate actions that will promote creative growth and productivity.

Based on all of the data presently available, you might describe students' needs at four broad levels of performance (Treffinger et al., 2002). These are:

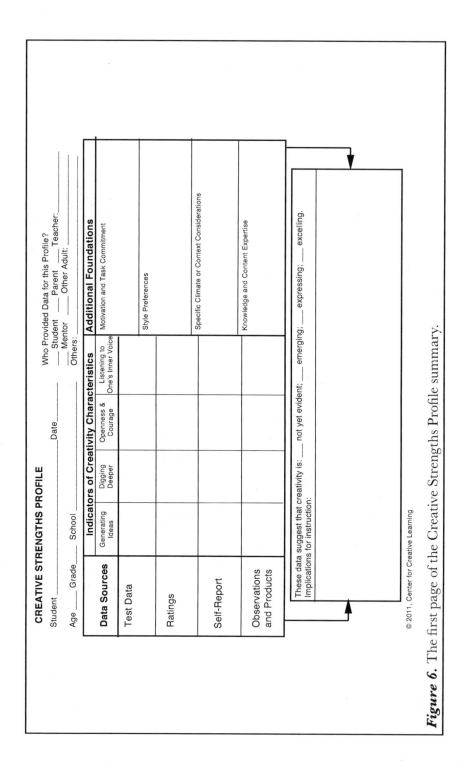

Figure 6. The first page of the Creative Strengths Profile summary.

- *Not yet evident*: This person's present level of performance may not reveal characteristics or behaviors that are consistent with the selected definition of creativity. Notice two important qualifications in this statement. First, the category is not called "uncreative" or "not creative." The category does not suggest that creativity is unattainable for the person, but only that creativity characteristics are not presently evident or observable. The category is about performance, not about ability, aptitude, or potential. Second, the category relates only to characteristics of creativity as defined for the assessment; under a different definition of creativity, which might involve other characteristics, the person's level of performance might differ.

- *Emerging*: There is limited evidence of creativity characteristics in the person's present performance. Creativity is beginning to emerge in ways that are consistent with the definition of creativity being assessed, although the creative behavior may be inconsistent, tentative, or limited in quality.

- *Expressing*: When data indicate signs of creativity characteristics in the student's present behavior with regularity and occasional signs of being high quality, you might characterize the student's present level of creativity as expressing. This category suggests that the characteristics of creativity can often be observed in the student's typical behavior and products.

- *Excelling*: When data indicate consistently the presence of creativity characteristics (as defined for the assessment) that are accompanied by creative accomplishments in one or more areas of performance or talent with outstanding depth, quality, and originality, you may categorize the student's present level of performance as excelling.

Let's look briefly at the three students we introduced in Chapter 1 in terms of these four categories. As Eric entered fifth grade, his interests and potential definitely had not been evident to his teachers. We can assume that they were evident to his family, but that information had not been communicated clearly to the school. Once his teacher had a more complete picture of Eric's potential, she was able to help that potential emerge and be recognized by others in the school. William's creativity in music was also emerging. His teacher helped him express his ideas by encouraging a public performance of an arrangement for band. However, in his other classes, we have a less clear picture about his level of creativity. The same is true of Sue. In science, she was able to produce excellent professional-level work that was recognized by experts in her field of interest. Again, we have a less clear picture of her other areas of interest. For her this was the end of a process of learning in which she explored several areas of interest. She displayed creative potential in several domains, but it was her passion for medical science that motivated her to produce consistently high-quality work. As she became more focused on this one area, other interests were set on the back burner.

It's important to keep in mind that these levels represent a continuum of performance, rather than separate, independent categories with rigid boundaries. They do not represent specific scores (such as a creativity index). As much as we all might yearn for precise, objective categories and exact numerical designations, the reality of the complexity of creativity, its attendant characteristics, and our assessment tools reminds us that such precision is seldom attainable at the highest levels of human behavior.

If you have multiple sources of data that all point to the same column, you can be reasonably confident that it correctly describes the person's present performance level. If you have some sources of data that suggest a certain present level of performance, but other data that suggest a different level, additional analysis may be warranted and additional data collection might also be helpful. In general, a plausible working hypothesis might well be to give greatest trust and weight in your analysis to the data from at least two data sources that support the highest level of present performance; that is, use the highest level of present performance that is supported by data from two or more data sources. There are two reasons for this recommendation: (a) if higher level performance is indicated in any column, that level of behavior existed, by definition, even if only through a single source; and (b) the instructional consequences of a false positive (i.e., proposing a higher present level of performance than actually might be warranted) generally seem far less worrisome in this area than the consequences of a false negative (i.e., proposing a lower present level than might actually be warranted). Withholding services that would be appropriate and challenging for a student seems to hold greater risk for disservice to the student than does providing opportunities for him or her. Because it is well established that creativity can be nurtured, providing opportunities that stretch the student will not be likely to be stressful or harmful; denying students access to services from which they might profit is a waste of potential. The rubric in Figure 7 may also guide you in determining a student's present level of performance on a certain creativity task or project.

The data from the first page of the Creative Strengths Profile provide the foundation for the actions on the second page of the profile, as illustrated in Figure 8. This form provides an opportunity to record decisions regarding actions that emerge from your review and analysis of the profile data. Teachers, parents, outside mentors or leaders, and students themselves can have collaborative input on this page. It is a working plan that may be changed or expanded on an ongoing basis as the result of additional data or refinements that emerge during the initial implementation. It is not intended to limit or control action, but to function as a plan of action that provides guidance, communication, direction, and feedback.

Why Engage in Profiling?

You might be able to walk into a classroom without knowing anything at all about the students and just begin to "teach" (whatever that might involve), but we certainly hope that's not the way you carry out your professional life. On the other hand, you may also know some people who seem to spend virtually every waking moment away from the classroom immersed in planning; they don't seem to have a life at all outside their work. Most likely, you strive for some happy medium between those extremes. If there's a continuum between winging it on the left and being overly compulsive on the right, is there a responsible, comfortable center point?

At first, profiling might seem to lean a bit to the right side of that continuum—seeming to be quite a bit of work. We wouldn't be truthful if we said that it's easy. What we do suggest is that once you start doing it and become comfortable with it, the process will not be as demanding as it might first appear, and it will contribute positively to making your work successful and rewarding—quite possibly exciting, too. Profiling involves active, informed participation by the students, so it's engaging for them, helps build independent, self-directed learning skills, and is not just more work for you. It provides richer, deeper understanding of your students'

	Not Yet Evident	Emerging	Expressing	Excelling
Tests	The student's scores on measures of creative thinking (verbal or figural) do not indicate proficiency in generating ideas with fluency, flexibility, originality, or elaboration at the present time (and in relation to the tasks and assessment context). Generally, this means standard scores that are below the mean of an appropriate comparison group (and taking error of estimate into account).	The student's scores on measures of creative thinking (verbal or figural) indicate average skills or proficiency in generating ideas with fluency, flexibility, originality, or elaboration, in relation to appropriate comparison groups. Generally, this means scores that are at or near the mean of an appropriate comparison group (and taking error of estimate into account).	The student's scores on measures of creative thinking (verbal or figural) indicate above-average skills or proficiency in fluency, flexibility, originality, or elaboration in relation to appropriate comparison groups. Generally, this refers to scores that are consistently above the mean for an appropriate comparison group (when such data are available and taking error of estimate into account).	The student's scores on measures of creative thinking (verbal or figural) indicate strongly above average skill or proficiency in fluency, flexibility, originality, or elaboration in relation to appropriate comparison groups. Generally, this refers to scores that are consistently well above average for an appropriate comparison group (when such data are available and taking error of measure into account).
Ratings	The student's ratings on specific creative thinking criteria or behaviors completed by a qualified rater do not reflect evidence of creative thinking proficiency at the present time, or in relation to the task or the specific talent area or domain being rated.	Ratings of the student's creative thinking skills or behaviors completed by a qualified rater and for a specific task, talent area, or domain being rated demonstrate some indications of creative thinking, but may be limited in breadth, depth, or quality as perceived by the rater. The student's ratings are at or near the average (in relation to local comparisons) and may be above average for a specific task or project.	Ratings of the student's creative thinking skills or behaviors completed by a qualified rater and for a specific task, talent area, or domain being rated demonstrate consistent indications of creative thinking in relation to that task or area. The student's ratings are average or better (in relation to local comparisons) and are above average in some of the indicators, in relation to varied tasks within the student's area(s) of strength.	Ratings of the student's creative thinking skills or behaviors completed by a qualified rater and for a specific task, talent area, or domain being rated demonstrate consistent indications of high levels of creative thinking in relation to that task or area. The student's ratings are above average to excellent (in relation to local comparisons), on several indicators, in relation to varied tasks within the student's area(s) of strength and over a sustained period of time (several months or longer).

Figure 7. Rubric for assessing present level of performance.

	Not Yet Evident	Emerging	Expressing	Excelling
Self-Reports	Self-description(s) indicate few or no characteristics associated with creativity. Does not demonstrate attitudes or interests that are indicative of creativity characteristics; does not demonstrate motivation or interest in pursuing creative activities or challenges.	Self-description(s) indicate some characteristics associated with creativity. Demonstrates attitudes or interests that are indicative of creativity characteristics, but may be tentative or uncertain about motives or involvement in creative activities or challenges.	Self-description(s) indicate several characteristics associated with creativity at an average to above-average level. Demonstrates positive attitudes or interests that are indicative of creativity characteristics and motivation to engage in creative activities or challenges.	Self-description(s) indicate awareness of many characteristics associated with creativity at a high level. Demonstrates very high level of interest, energy, enthusiasm, and motivation to engage in creative activities or challenges. May seem to be relentless or on one track in pursuing areas of creative interest.
Observations and Products	In the student's projects, products, or performances, we do not see indications of fluent, flexible, or original thought or of unprompted elaboration. Student may be reluctant or hesitant to engage in creative challenges or may withdraw from participation. Completes few or no original products, or products judged as below average on creative product scales or by judges (individual or by consensus panel).	The student's work includes some evidence of fluency, flexibility, originality, or elaboration in thinking when prompted by a teacher, supervisor, or peers in a team or group. Student participates in individual or team creative activities or challenges, but may be tentative or indicate lack of confidence in his or her contributions. Completes products evaluated consistently as average on creative product scales or by judges (individual or by consensus panel).	The student's products, projects, or performances consistently and spontaneously show evidence of fluency, flexibility, originality, or elaboration (in individual work or as part of a team or group). Student participates actively in individual or group creative activities or challenges and makes consistent creative contributions to the activity. Completes products consistently evaluated as above average on creative product scales or by judges (individual or by consensus panel).	The student's products, projects, or performances include evidence of spontaneous fluency, flexibility, originality, or elaboration recognized by others as high in quality and quantity (in individual work or with a team or group), with documentation of "real-world" accomplishments and products. Student initiates creative activities or challenge and is looked upon by peers and/or adults as an "idea leader" in activities. Completes products consistently evaluated as very high or excellent on creative product scales or by judges (individual or by consensus panel).

Figure 7. continued

143

PROFILE ACTION PLAN

Student _____   Date_____

Programming Actions	Who	Where	Timeline		Document/Evaluate
			Start	Review	
Goal:					
Activity 1:					
Activity 2:					
Goal:					
Activity 1:					
Activity 2:					
Goal:					
Activity 1:					
Activity 2:					
Goal:					
Activity 1:					
Activity 2:					
Goal:					
Activity 1:					
Activity 2:					

Figure 8. The second page of the Creative Strengths Profile Summary.

Table 8

Positive Contributions of the Creative Strengths Profile

> The Creative Strengths Profile should help you plan how best to:
> - know and teach through each student's strengths, interests, and talents;
> - create meaningful and effective instructional experiences;
> - help students understand, recognize, or identify their creative talents and "spot" emerging or developing strengths;
> - guide students in learning how to use their talents autonomously;
> - build bridges between past and future learning experiences;
> - involve students actively in learning; and
> - recognize and respond to gaps between the students' needs and their present instructional program or services.

strengths, talents, and interests (especially skills that involve real-world activities). It may stimulate many new ideas for engaging activities and experiences that will make your classroom more exciting and dynamic for everyone. Table 8 describes some of the positive contributions of profiling.

Creative Talent Spotting

Building profiles to recognize students' creative strengths and talents may begin with your deliberate efforts to be alert and watchful for creative strengths in your students. We have referred to this as "talent spotting" (Treffinger et al., 2008; Young, 1995). This phrase can be helpful, because it reminds people of the process that is often used to locate or discover talents in many real-world settings (e.g., music, dance, drama, athletics). By listing the attributes of an athletic scout, to use an example, we might find some helpful insights into the behaviors of an educator who is a talent spotter. The athletic scout:

- knows the sport;
- knows about the needs of the field;
- knows benchmarks of talent development;
- knows the difference between potential and performance;
- knows standards of excellence within the field;
- has an historical perspective and knowledge of the field;
- is able to recognize talent in raw form;
- is patient and persistent but knows when to move on to new prospects;

- relies on many sources of data—observations of performance, study of films, interviews with the prospect and others (e.g., coaches, players), player statistics, and press clippings;
- has sharp powers of observation;
- sees possibilities for playing other positions and roles on team;
- takes risks based on assessment of data and potential for talent development;
- spends a great deal of time in the field; and
- understands that there are many factors to consider in addition to physical skills (e.g., attitude, opportunity, training, coaching). (Treffinger et al., 2008, p. 71)

There are several similarities between the athletic scout and the classroom talent spotter. They both must have a thorough knowledge of, and experience with, the task, the people with whom they are working, and the methods and techniques they will need to use. They both deal with assessments that are complex, and to be certain, spotting students' creative talents, like finding the next athletic superstar, is hardly an exact science! Both athletic scouts and classroom talent spotters share some other common experiences. Both:

- possess and use general knowledge (e.g., effective teaching skills for the teacher) and specific expertise (e.g., knowing creativity characteristics to seek);
- hold high standards and have a good command of the expectations associated with excellence and accomplishment in the domain;
- know that talent can come from any place, any setting, and any walk of life, and so they are alert to signs of promise in every person;
- invest considerable time and energy in their search, keep good notes or records, and realize that the search is not a "one-time, one-shot" look, but may extend over an extended period of time; and
- gather many different kinds of data from a variety of sources.

There are also some differences, of course. As an educator, your job is not just to find the creative talent, but also to be able to work with the students to develop or nurture it. You are guiding your students in applying their creativity and preparing them to strive for future goals. The athletic scout may be searching for talent in one very specific area (e.g., baseball, basketball), but as an educator, creative talents among your students may arise in many different content areas or talent domains.

To be an effective classroom creative talent spotter, you must be able to deal with many different factors or variables. Although some people emphasize natural ability, we believe that the creative potentials that exist in all students and that can be influenced by work habits, motivation, and perseverance are often more important than raw natural power. That's why it is important for you always to be on the lookout for a creative spark in any of your students that you can build upon and also why deliberate efforts that you make to teach process skills and tools are so important.

Like Eric's fifth-grade teacher, by being alert and teaching those tools, you are setting conditions for creative productivity to develop and emerge. In some students, you may see the results early and often, while in others, it may take longer for everything to come together. Many of us have had the experience that, years later, students who were in our class met us again or even sought us out to say, "You may not know it, but what I did in your class opened great doors for me that have made all of the difference in my life!"

Student Portfolios

As noted, the second page of the Creative Strengths Profile is a planning guide that is useful primarily for designing and managing instruction. It's a teacher-oriented record-keeping document, although it may often be wise to review and discuss with parents, other educators, and, of course, students themselves.

Individuals who are engaged professionally or even as serious amateurs or hobbyists in creative work in many domains also maintain an ongoing, growing, and dynamic portfolio that documents their efforts and accomplishments. The contents of one's personal portfolio can inform an ongoing profile, of course, but their major purposes and contents are quite different. The goals and purposes of a portfolio may include demonstrating authentic achievements, helping students see their own progress (achievements, productivity, growth) over time, enabling teachers to assess complex outcomes and applications, and showing parents or outside audiences what the individual has worked on and accomplished (Hausman, 1992; Hebert, 1992). Some researchers argue that a portfolio can be an important tool for quality improvement in education (e.g., Belanoff & Dickson, 1991; Blackbourn, Hamby, Hanshaw, & Beck, 1997; Marx, 2001; Thomas et al., 2004–2005).

From an instructional planning perspective, a student's portfolio may contain resources that confirm (or contradict) other evidence, such as achievement test scores. It may provide long-term or cumulative indicators of creative growth and development. From the student's own point of view, a portfolio can help her to learn to chart her own course for future learning activities; affirm or verify her own progress, efforts, and outcomes; communicate with others about her creative work; and provide a tool for sharing and celebrating her creative work.

Portfolios represent ways to document and assess authentic real-world and higher level learning outcomes for which traditional tests are usually inadequate. They can be empowering experiences for students, helping them to expand their awareness of their own work, progress, and accomplishments and to set their own future goals. They are unique and personal ways for students to communicate a specific message to a certain audience at a certain time. Some people have the misconception that a portfolio is always a compilation of one's best work. Rather, the contents of one's portfolio may vary in relation to one's goals and the intended audience at any time. It can represent, for example, highlights of major accomplishments, evidence of activities and accomplishments across a variety of tasks or contexts, or documentation of how one's work in a certain area has grown or changed over time. Table 9 identifies several items that might be components of a student's portfolio.

Increasingly, technology has made it possible to create, maintain, and share portfolios in digital formats, although the portfolio might be a physical collection of materials and documents in a notebook, a folder, or even in a box. It may include actual objects or photographs, diagrams, or even text descriptions, along with letters, programs, certificates, or other items that we often describe as scrapbook documentation.

Note that Table 9 does not include test data or the results of rating scales or self-report inventories. Those data can be important elements of the student's Creative Strengths Profile, but the portfolio is concerned

Table 9

Components of a Student's Portfolio

Portfolios might include:
- products or work samples (completed or in progress; with dates);
- testimonials;
- evaluations, by oneself or others, of one's work or products;
- biographical resources, journal or diary entries or excerpts ("Me, in progress");
- documentation of participation in activities or specific events;
- recognitions, honors, prizes, or awards for one's work;
- external reviews or evaluations of one's work, growth, or accomplishments;
- visual documentation of work completed or in progress (models, prototypes, photographs, videos);
- podcasts;
- PowerPoint or other digital presentations;
- scrapbooks (media reports or clippings);
- material from websites or social media; and
- other items selected by the student for a specific purpose or need.

with providing evidence or documentation of products, accomplishments, or performance—evidence about the student's creative behavior and ability to use creatively what he or she knows and processes. Note also that work samples may be part of a portfolio, but that the portfolio is more than simply a compilation of student assignments or worksheets. (In some schools, we've seen what purport to be portfolios, but they might more accurately be titled "Famous Worksheets I Have Done.")

Another important distinction between the Creative Strengths Profile and the student portfolio involves ownership. Although the student's input and involvement in the development of the Creative Strengths Profile may be desirable and useful, it is primarily the teacher's document (because the teachers are generally responsible for classroom instruction). In some settings, the student may take greater responsibility for his or her own instruction, but in most daily classroom settings, that is the teacher's role and responsibility. By contrast, from its beginnings, the portfolio belongs to the student. Of course, that doesn't mean that teachers, parents, peers, or community members cannot provide support and assistance to a student in creating and maintaining a portfolio. Such assistance may be valuable and desirable—but it is provided to assist the student's goals, purposes, and action. Table 10 summarizes the main steps in assembling a portfolio.

Table 10

Assembling a Portfolio

1. Know why you're creating it. Identify your purpose(s) and audience(s).
2. Determine what will be best to include.
   - Best work?
   - Typical work?
   - Work showing change or growth?
   - A combination of these?
3. Consider various ways to assemble the data, to display or present it, and to convey your intended purpose(s) to your audience(s).
   - Physical collection (folder, box, scrapbook)
   - Digital tools
4. Provide "help" for the viewer or reviewer as appropriate for the context.
   - Table of contents
   - Labels or legends
   - Self-assessment
   - Self- or assessor forms or ratings

In the next section of this book, we turn our attention to methods, tools, and resources for nurturing or developing creativity, and at that point, we will turn our attention to the challenges of linking assessment (including both the Creative Strengths Profile and portfolios) with instruction.

Taking the Chapter Forward

o   Think about Sue, William, and Eric. If you were their classroom teacher, counselor, gifted and talented teacher, or coach, what additional information would you need to complete each student's Creative Strengths Profile? What assessments might you draw on? What next steps might you recommend in order to help them continue to grow? Consider ways that you might begin to develop Creative Strengths Profiles and portfolios with your students. How might you most effectively communicate to students the goals and benefits of these and engage them in planning, creating, monitoring, and using them? Do you have your own Creative Strengths Profile and personal or professional creativity portfolio? Consider the benefits of such an effort for yourself as well as for your students.

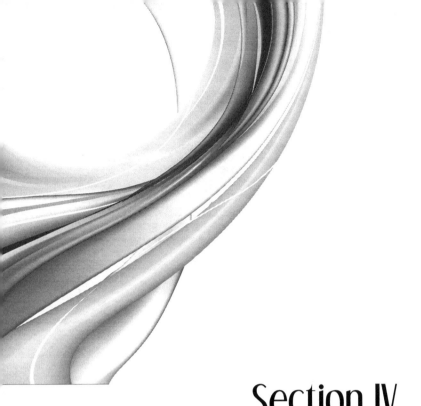

Section IV

How Do We Develop Creativity?

Chapter 13

Setting Conditions for Developing Creativity

Taken together, the chapters in this section reflect our belief that creativity need not—and should not—just be left to chance, but that it can be fostered through deliberate, intentional efforts. Parents, teachers, and individuals themselves can enhance or nurture creativity and creative behavior. This chapter lays the foundation for deliberate efforts to nurture creativity. Chapter 14 presents eight basic guidelines for creative and critical thinking. Chapters 15–18 each focus on one of the three levels in the model presented in Chapter 7 and with structured programs for deliberate creativity instruction. Chapter 19 links creativity instruction with other contemporary perspectives and themes on effective instruction and synthesizes the section's key ideas. You can use the resources and tools in this section (Chapters 13–19) effectively in any classroom, with students of any age, and in any subject matter or content area.

After reading this chapter, you will be able to describe six steps to take in laying a foundation for creative teaching and learning and ways to respond to the needs of learners who are at the four different levels of performance in relation to creativity.

Creative Teaching and Learning: Laying the Foundation

There is an old story (a myth, we hope!) about a very frustrated air traffic controller who gave landing instructions to two pilots, apparently without realizing that the instructions, if followed, would lead to the two planes heading directly at each other. The first pilot heard the second set of instructions, radioed the tower to note the head-on course, and asked if the controller had any advice. The controller's response was, "You all be careful now!" Developing creativity, just like landing planes safely, calls for more than hopeful good wishes, and just as content instruction requires careful preparation, efforts to nurture or develop creativity also require sustained planning, preparation, and effort to accomplish success-fully. Developing creativity involves more than just saying to your students, "I want you to be creative!" Laying the foundation for instruction that nurtures creativity involves several key actions.

- *Define and discuss the meaning of the terms* creativity *and* innovation *with your students.* Find out what they already understand about the concepts, and clarify misunderstandings they may have.
- *Pay attention to characteristics and talent spotting.* Be alert for evidence that your students are already thinking creatively and critically. Recognize and reinforce them for those efforts and, as we dis-cussed in Chapter 12, be an alert talent spotter for creativity and for opportunities to challenge students to demonstrate creativity. To see it, you have to be watching for it, but you also have to be certain to create opportunities for it to occur.
- *Work to establish and maintain a conducive climate.* Review the nine important factors in a climate that supports (and does not inhibit) creativity from Chapter 8, and work collaboratively with your students to create that climate in your classroom (and with your peers to create it throughout your school).
- *Teach and practice several basic guidelines for creative and critical thinking.* In Chapter 14, we will present and discuss eight specific guidelines to teach your students and to observe daily in your classroom.
- *Establish and maintain an ongoing classroom-wide commitment to creativity combined with quality.* A classroom that values, supports, and nur-

tures creativity is a place in which there is an ongoing emphasis and dialogue about the importance of quality work and the factors that contribute to creative products (as presented in Chapter 9), conversation about good thinking and ways to improve thinking continuously (or metacognitive processing), and time and encouragement for reflection each day.

○ *Begin work on the "foundation" skills and tools.* Review the foundations level of the model for teaching and learning productive thinking presented in Chapter 7 (Figure 4) and put it to work for you. This involves teaching basic tools for generating and focusing ideas, guiding students in learning and applying a variety of research and inquiry skills and tools, and making effective use of the powerful technology that is available to young people as well as to adults today.

Building the Structure: Gathering and Using Data

After the foundation is in place, the job of constructing a solid structure above it comes next. This structure includes the visible, tangible ways that teaching and learning for creativity and innovation will take place on a daily basis over an extended period of time. It may appear to be a large and difficult task, and in truth, it is; but, no one ever said that powerful, effective teaching is easy. In our own work, however, and in conversations with countless skillful and devoted teachers throughout the world, we have learned another important lesson: Difficult tasks are not necessarily onerous. So, although teaching that fosters creativity is difficult, it can also be highly rewarding and the source of some of the greatest professional satisfaction you will ever experience. Difficult? Yes. Worth it? Absolutely. So, once you've laid the foundation, what are the next steps?

Your early steps and activities may be targeted at informal groups or even at an entire class as you work with students to build important foundational skills. As you continue your efforts, however, it becomes more important to be able to vary or differentiate instruction based on students' interests, skills, strengths, and needs (at the very core of approaches such as RtI, as noted in Chapter 11). This involves developing and using

Creative Strengths Profiles (described in Chapter 12) as a foundation for planning and carrying out instruction. In Chapter 12, we described four levels of present performance that you will observe among your students (not yet evident, emerging, expressing, and excelling) and how to assess those as part of the Creative Strengths Profile. The important question is, "Once I know that, what do I do with the information?" Table 11 summarizes the four student levels of performance and their implications for one's general approach as a teacher or group leader, the tasks that may be particularly relevant (in relation to the model for teaching and learning productive thinking shared in Chapter 7), and specific considerations of characteristics and styles, tools, environment, and products or outcomes. We can also describe specific instructional differentiation needs for each of the four present levels of performance (Treffinger et al., 2002).

Not Yet Evident

If a student's present level of performance is in the "Not Yet Evident" column, it does not mean that he or she is not creative and never will become creative. Instead, this is your cue to design and carry out specific classroom strategies to help that student and others to discover, develop, and express their creative potentials. At this level, the programming actions may focus on the foundations discussed in this chapter, helping students to discover creative opportunities and to begin to examine their style preferences and potential creative strengths. Your role involves planning opportunities for students to grow in awareness of their personal characteristics, interests, and creative strengths. You will also provide direct instruction designed to help students discover, develop, and improve their competence in the four categories of characteristics discussed in Chapter 6 (generating ideas, digging deeper into ideas, openness and courage to explore ideas, and listening to one's inner voice). Extrinsic motivation (e.g., rewards, contests, teacher praise) focused on their efforts to learn about and develop their personal creative abilities may also be useful.

The primary starting point for the operations element of the COCO model (from Chapters 5 and 7) will involve teaching students a variety of tools for generating ideas and digging deeper into ideas (see Chapter 15). Students for whom creativity is not yet evident will also benefit from experiencing an open, safe environment in which they are comfortable learn-

Table 11

Responding to Present Level of Performance

	Not Yet Evident Leads to:	Emerging Leads to:	Expressing Leads to:	Excelling Leads to:
Teaching or leading approach	Directing	Coaching	Participating	Delegating
Characterization of approach	"Discovering or Reluctant": building the necessary foundation for creative learning	"Developing or Interested": developing and practicing tools and creativity skills	"Performing or Enthusiastic": applying tools and skills to realistic problems and challenges and to some manageable real-life challenges	"Soaring or Passionate": identifying and applying creativity tools and skills to a variety of real problems and challenges individually or with a group or team; demonstrating self-initiated and self-directed creativity
Tasks (Creative Learning Model in Chapter 7)	Foundations ————————→	Realistic ————————→		Real/Authentic
Tasks	Foundations: responses to exercises	Realistic: basic practice tasks, products	More complex realistic and some "safe" real problems	Full range of real problems and challenges
Characteristics and styles	Discovering style preferences and strengths	Building strengths	Applying strengths in one's own way	Optimizing style awareness and use; extending to reach new levels

Table 11, continued

	Not Yet Evident Leads to:	Emerging Leads to:	Expressing Leads to:	Excelling Leads to:
Tools	Provide awareness and introduction to thinking tools	Guided practice and building confidence, competence, commitment	Expanding one's toolbox, recognizing ways to apply tools	Personalizing or customizing tool selection and use for optimum effectiveness
Environment	Creating climate for discovery and inquiry	Environment supports and encourages safe practice	Environment that offers rich and varied opportunities for applications	Freedom to adjust, modify, and construct one's environment for productivity
Products and outcomes	Exploring products and methods of creative expression; learning about various product types used to document learning and to present creative solutions or ideas and important standards of quality (i.e., criteria) used to evaluate those products	Exposure to and development of various creative outlets of interest; providing opportunities for product development, product sharing, and product assessment; expanding product repertoire	Applying personal strengths in creative expression and product development to selected performance area; providing opportunities for product presentation and authentic assessment in realistic situations	Integration of personal expression (product performance) and productive tools to authentic problem-solving situations; authentic products produced for authentic purposes are presented to real audiences and assessed in that context

ing to generate and express ideas. The climate must be one that accepts and values new and different ideas, allows and promotes playfulness and humor, offers challenge and encourages involvement, builds trust, provides both idea time and idea support, and promotes freedom and risk taking (see Chapter 8). Finally, be certain to provide opportunities for students to explore and experience directly many, varied, and unusual methods and products for reporting and sharing their learning (e.g., written products, drama, videos, various kinds of digital products). Such varied experiences will help students begin to identify the area in which their creative passions may thrive.

Emerging

Students you might place in the "Emerging" column have most likely already demonstrated some key foundation skills and/or attitudes, but may need to refine, polish, and practice those skills. For these students, programming can focus on recognizing and nurturing their emerging characteristics, strengthening their competence, and helping them gain confidence in their own creative abilities.

The teacher's role might be considered coaching, because you are assisting and supporting efforts to identify and build creative strengths as you are also guiding the student's inquiry into more realistic endeavors. As the student's work moves into areas more closely tied to personal styles and interests, intrinsic motivation will begin to replace the need for extrinsic motivation. Students at this level will benefit from continued refinement of the creativity tools, as well as group problem-solving activities in which they can begin to apply the tools and processes they have learned to situations that are meaningful to them. In addition, metacognitive skills and processes are important for helping students learn how to monitor their own thinking. Reflecting on their instructional experiences during debriefing sessions will help them better understand and develop all creativity characteristics, but especially those in the categories of openness and courage to explore ideas and listening to one's inner voice.

A continuing nonjudgmental climate is essential for students to feel safe during guided practice and inquiry. Additional exposure to and extension of the ways and means of creative expression, specifically in tune with the students' interests and abilities, is appropriate here as well.

Expressing

Students whose present level of performance is located in the "Expressing" column have already demonstrated competence and are growing in confidence about their creative abilities. A strong foundation for creative productivity is in place, and they are ready to deal with realistic problems and situations. The focus for programming actions should be on helping students to apply their strengths and interests in their own way. At this level, they start to build commitment for a lifetime of creative accomplishments. Students whose creativity is expressing—and many who are also in the emerging category—often find great stimulation, enjoyment, and opportunities for creative growth, productivity, and celebration in structured programs and competitions (see Chapter 17).

The teacher's role is one of supporting emerging students' continued development by helping them initiate their own ideas and to identify realistic and meaningful situations where their creative skills and attitudes can be applied. Even though intrinsic motivation is in place, they will need reassurance as they work through the problems identified.

The environment should encourage initiative and action toward identifying real problems. Outcomes will be assessed through appropriate and creative performances. Although it still continues to be the ultimate responsibility of the teacher to maintain the climate that supports these students' efforts, the students themselves will also need to develop skills, attitudes, and procedures that will be supportive to themselves and others as well.

Excelling

Finally, students whose present level of performance is in the "Excelling" column have already demonstrated highly significant levels of creative thinking skill. Programming at this level will focus on extending their competence, confidence, and commitment to stimulate and enable them to reach new levels of creative productivity in real or authentic tasks.

The teacher's role is to delegate many of the process decisions and actions to the students, but also to be there to answer questions, cut red tape, support them as they struggle through inevitable bumps in the road, and then celebrate their successes. As the students move into areas of sustained personal interest or passion for learning, intrinsic motivation is in full force. Students who are excelling creatively in any area are often already engaged in activities outside the classroom or school. They may be participating in activities in the arts, drama, or in other community-based groups, for example, or they may be ready for teachers or parents to help them discover and become involved in such activities.

In working with students who are excelling creatively educators should continue to customize, personalize, and add to their repertoire of tools and strategies for working successfully on the real problems the students choose for their work. The students need a context that allows them the freedom to act on ideas and topics based on their personal interests. They are engaged in creating products to share with authentic audiences, and they are having real-life opportunities to express themselves creatively. Creative productivity is in action!

Taking the Chapter Forward

○ Consider the schools in which we found Eric, William, and Sue and their teachers. What specific steps were taken to identify and nurture creativity in all students? How effective were the teachers in providing programming designed to maximize each student's interests? Think about your school and/or classroom and the ways they operate on a day-to-day basis. How effectively are you setting conditions for the development of creativity? Which areas need improvement or greater attention? What are you doing most effectively? Educators, students, parents, and community members can all be active partners in setting conditions for recognizing, assessing, and developing creativity. A collaborative approach involves much more than just reaching into a grab bag of fun exercises and activities over and over again or treating creativity as play time for students; it will be exciting and rewarding for everyone involved.

Chapter 14

Basic Guidelines

A fter reading this chapter, you will understand and be able to identify and list the guidelines for generating and focusing ideas. You will also be able to create ways of introducing the guidelines into your classroom. This chapter will help you think of ways you can help your students understand and apply these important guidelines. Once you and they understand the generating and focusing guidelines and the tools, you will find new ways to use them on a daily basis. Your students will be better creative and critical thinkers in school and in life.

The Heartbeat of Effective Thinking and Balance

By now you understand that both generating options (creative thinking) and focusing (critical thinking) are necessary for a balanced approach to creativity, innovation, and effective problem solving. People often mistakenly think about creativity only in relation to generating ideas (or often as what you do when you're brainstorming). There are actually many tools for generating ideas, of which brainstorming is only one. In addi-

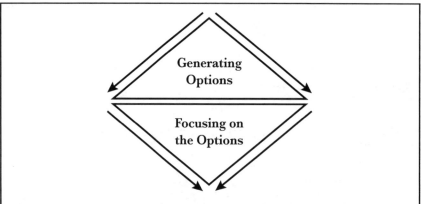

Figure 9. Using generating and focusing in harmony (Treffinger et al., 2006).

tion, effective creativity draws on both generating ideas and focusing your thinking working in harmony. We often demonstrate this mutual relationship with a diamond-shaped diagram that illustrates both processes as they work together (see Figure 9).

The top half of the diagram represents the generating phase, in which creative thinkers produce a pool of many, varied, unusual, interesting, and detailed responses (fluency, flexibility, originality, and elaboration in thinking). The bottom half of the diagram illustrates the focusing phase in the process; this involves sorting, sifting, prioritizing, categorizing, and choosing the options.

Anytime individuals or groups seek creative possibilities or implement any component or stage of Creative Problem Solving (CPS), they draw on both. This is the "dynamic balance . . . of two complementary kinds of thinking" (Isaksen et al., 2011, p. 36).

Treating these as complementary operations in which your thinking expands as you generate options and contracts as you focus (indicated by the arrows in Figure 9) occurs most effectively when you separate these operations, providing time and opportunity to use each independently. There are guidelines for both generating and focusing. These are rules— or at least rules of thumb—that can help your creativity and problem-solving efforts to be more effective. Just as any classroom or organization has rules to maintain order and control, these guidelines help individuals and groups manage their generating and focusing efforts in an effective and efficient way, too. This chapter presents both sets of guidelines. These guidelines draw extensively on the five-decade CPS tradition that began with Alex Osborn's (1963) work and is represented today in the contemporary CPS model (Isaksen et al., 2011; Treffinger et al., 2006).

Guidelines for Generating Options

In order to gather as many options and as many unusual or novel options as you can, it is important to set aside evaluation, critiques, criticism, or praise of any kind while you are engaged in generating. This is the principle we describe as remembering to *defer judgment*. It is the foundation for generating options. There are four interrelated guidelines for generating:

- defer judgment,
- strive for quantity,
- freewheel, and
- seek combinations.

Defer Judgment

It really doesn't matter the age group you work with, it is always important to avoid external or internal judgments. During a generating session, there will always be people who can't help but evaluate or criticize each option. Likewise, it is very hard for others not to praise options as they are generated with "great!" or "good job!" Especially as educators, we like to make sure everyone feels good about their ideas and know they will be considered. But consider what happens when you are part of an idea generating session. If you hear someone's ideas being criticized, are you as likely to throw your idea into the pool just to have it torn apart? And, if you hear praise being heaped on an idea, the reaction for you or for others might be, "Well, that's the one they were looking for. Guess we're done!" Tauber (1991) examined praise and suggested that it is an evaluation, albeit an apparently positive evaluation. It suggests that the person has met the mark. For a generating options session, it can imply that generating is all done, and the goal has been met. By allowing praise, the opportunity to generate new and very novel options has been shut down just as much as would criticism or a critique of an option. There are some who perceive praise as manipulation or control. The person giving the praise has the power to determine what is praiseworthy and thus can manipulate the situation, or in this case, the generating session.

Deferring judgment also means to avoid internal judgments, either positive or negative. We often question or second-guess our own ideas, and we need to turn those judgments off. There will be time to evaluate the options later during the focusing phase. So, during a session when you are working with your students to generate options, you can repeat what a person said (and write it down) to avoid saying anything that might be a criticism or praise. You can also simply say something like "okay," "another one," or "next." This will help keep the session moving and help *you* to defer judgment. With any age you will need to remind people to defer judgment. Use the term defer judgment so that everyone becomes used to it. (For younger children, you can always remind them what it means. For example, you might remind your younger students that "We listen to and write down all ideas!") You may need to emphasize the point by saying something like, "Remember that we don't say an idea is good and we don't say it is bad, either." Deferring judgment can help to create a healthy classroom environment. Applying this principle throughout the period of generating ideas and discovery will stretch everyone's thinking and create a thoughtful classroom where "thinking is systematically integrated" (Litterst & Eyo, 1993, p. 272). Deferring judgment is also important to keep the pathways of the generating session wide open. If praise or evaluation is allowed during a generating session, those who are generating the options will focus more on the promised reward or evaluation and will be less likely to explore alternative paths (Hennessey, 2010).

Strive for Quantity

Look for as many options as you can. In the classroom, help your groups look for options by encouraging them with things like, "Let's find three more ideas!" Regardless of age or grade, people will generally find more ideas—usually more than you ask for. Quantity of ideas usually breeds quality. The more you generate, the greater the possibility that some of the ideas will be very unique and promising. As you and your students generate options, make the statements as brief as possible. Ask for "headlines." If your students are very young, ask them to give their ideas a title. That way, you'll hopefully avoid the long essay! If you have students who have trouble finding a shorter version of their idea, you can summarize with a headline, stating it out loud as you record it. Make sure you check with the person to ensure that it is what he or she meant to say. Remember to just list the options; do not discuss them or allow anyone to critique or praise. As you list the options, number each one. It will make the focusing session easier to handle.

Freewheel

List and accept *all* options. Even if the ideas seem a little wild or way out there, write them down just the same as the other ideas. Always remember there is time to evaluate after you generate. Some of these wild ideas may just be the springboard that helps your students find new directions or possibilities that can become very real, but would not have been considered were it not for that wild and crazy option. Allow the sense of play, and give yourself permission to be playful with ideas. It is often easier to tame a wild idea than it is to make a dull idea exciting.

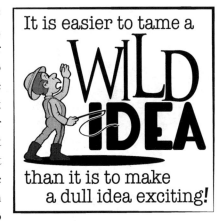

Freewheeling takes practice. As you generate options, it is often easy to slide into the kind of thinking that is easy, drifting along with habits of thought and basically ending up in a rut. Stretch your thinking and help your students stretch as well by extended effort. During the generating phase, you do not need to consider the usefulness of an option. This is a time to open the floodgates. Use all of your senses and help your students do the same. Stimulate their thinking with music or sound effects, different scents or odors, or visual effects. Sometimes just going for a walk can help jog your thinking out of its habit-bound rut into new paths. You can also stimulate new thinking by asking open-ended questions.

Seek Combinations

How often have you heard an idea mentioned by someone that makes you think of another idea? Your idea builds on someone else's idea.

Likewise, someone may build his or her idea upon something that you generated. These ideas that make new connections may be very different, even though they may be built on a previous option. These new connections are often called hitchhiking or piggybacking. Encourage your students to modify, alter, or build on other ideas as the generating session progresses. You never know which idea might be the one to lead to a new, very unique, and useful solution! You can also encourage this during a classroom discussion. For example, you might have your students generate a list of games, and then have them combine games to create something very new to them.

One example of a generating session is of a group of sixth graders who were developing a skit for a competition and they wanted to make their own costumes. The teacher did not have a sewing machine, and she did not want the students to use one. It was also important that the students do all the work themselves, so the options had to be something the students could actually do without help. The students generated many options about making their costumes. When they began examining their options they stated their concern as: "How to put materials together to make a costume." This opened up new paths for students to think of other ways to construct a costume and even helped them think of different materials to use. Here are just some of the options generated:

- staple the cloth together,
- tie it,
- glue with hot glue,
- fuse seams with iron-on material,
- use tiny safety pins,
- sew it by hand, and
- use our own clothes and pin on stuff to work as the costume.

We'll revisit this class later as the students focus on their options.

Ask your class to generate as many options as it can related to the word "rock." Have the students generate one option each time it is their turn. If someone doesn't have an option to contribute, let him or her pass and go on to the next student. Your role is to record each option as it is generated. Remember to simply repeat the option or say something along the lines of "next" or "okay." Go around the room at least twice. What did you notice?

Guidelines for Focusing Options

Once a group has generated a lot of ideas, perhaps even 20–25 possibilities, what happens next? Many of us have had the experience of either watching someone's ideas being shredded or having our own ideas pummeled. Adults and young people alike have difficulty in holding back on how they feel about ideas. You will hear things such as, "That was such a dumb idea!" Or, you may hear someone say, "That's an interesting idea, *but* . . ." or "That idea was so way out there; no way can we use it!" We need to avoid the criticism feeding frenzy that can happen without guidelines or rules. Just like generating options, there are four important guidelines for focusing:

O use affirmative judgment,

O be deliberate,

O consider novelty, and

O stay on course.

Use Affirmative Judgment

As you and your students look at all of the generated ideas, everyone should feel as though they have really accomplished something. Now is the time to begin sorting, sifting, and categorizing to find the ideas that will work the best. Look first for the positives or strengths of an idea. After that, consider concerns or limitations. But to avoid trashing, smashing, and killing ideas, state concerns by using a sentence stem such as "How to . . ." or "How might . . ." For example, let's visit the group of sixth graders who were developing a skit as part of a competition and wanted to make their own costumes. The teacher acted as facilitator and suggested they use ALoU: Advantages, Limitations (and how to overcome them), and Unique features. As the students listed the advantages they saw with the safety pin option, it occurred to one student, who was to be a "raggedy" character, that he could just pin rags all over his own clothes. In the end, nearly all of the options were used in some way and no one had to use the sewing machine.

One middle school teacher (Reynolds, 2009) has her students provide peer critiques during the time they are working on a large project. Reynolds found that although she had to work closely with her students to understand the concept of affirmative judgment, the students eventually became much more participatory in the classroom discussion following a student presentation.

Be Deliberate

As you and your students progress through a focusing phase for any open-ended task or problem, always be very specific as you analyze, refine, and develop the ideas and options. You will want to choose focusing tools to help you and your students make these decisions. Make sure that the goals or the plans are clearly in the open with nothing hidden. Sometimes there might be a hidden agenda that no one knows about except, of course, the person with that agenda. So, it is vitally important to make sure everyone is aware of and comfortable with the process and plan to avoid conflict and controversies as decisions are made. This shared goal or vision is important so everyone can clearly see where the group is headed. It can also make shared decisions much easier.

Ms. Pfeiffer's kindergarten classroom is a good example of shared decision-making. It was the beginning of the year and she wanted rules to be clearly laid out. In her opinion, however, it seemed to her that the students would pay more attention to the rules if they had a hand in generating them. Even though her students couldn't read all of the words, the list of generated options was helpful for her to have. She made the list very clear to her students so they knew what their choices were. Everyone was aware what the ultimate goal was: deciding on classroom rules. Ms. Pfeiffer used a unique way to focus on the list. She would read the option, and the students would raise their hands if they liked that rule. They eventually broke the rules down to inside rules and outside rules. Because the students helped to generate the rules and chose the ones that mattered most, they helped each other follow the rules when reminders were necessary. The students were able to come to this point because their teacher was very clear about why they were developing the rules and how they would benefit the class. There was a clear direction for the students to see. On the other hand, if the group being asked to generate the options has no idea how their options will be used, if at all, it creates an atmosphere of confusion and mistrust.

Consider Novelty

When you're seeking creative ideas or solutions for a problem, you're searching for options that are both useful and novel. For some it is not easy to love novel options. Some people may prefer options that improve things incrementally rather than make big changes. It might feel a bit prickly, like hugging a porcupine. (Remember the children's story, *How Do You Hug a Porcupine?* [Isop, 2011]?) Perhaps you have been part of a group that has generated a lot of options. Most of us have. But many times when it comes to choosing an option or two from the list, it is all too easy to toss out or ignore those that are very novel. Very often a group might end up choosing an option that is close to the expected or safe idea.

Two teachers who were team-teaching a mixed second- and third-grade classroom wanted their students to experience the CPS process. It took some courage for them to consider novelty. Each teacher took a group of students. One group generated options for a new stuffed animal, and the other generated ways to make computers appear more fun. Each teacher divided her large group into smaller groups in order to focus on the options they had generated. The small focusing groups shared their favorite options with the whole class. Later, one of the small groups decided to combine the stuffed animal idea with their computer option and embed a computer into the belly of a very large teddy bear. The teachers (taking a deep breath) let the students pursue their option and, with the help of a parent, found an old computer and an old teddy bear to work with. The students realized there were some drawbacks (the computer got a little warm!) with their teddy bear computer, but they made adjustments that worked for a little while. The teddy bear computer was used in a learning center until the computer fizzled.

Stay on Course

It is very difficult to get to a new destination without a map of some sort or even an address! Goals are like addresses in CPS. They help you to know where you want to go, and you generally have a picture in your mind of what this might look like. How you get there can vary depending on which route you take. In CPS, you may choose many different paths, and the tools you choose may determine the kind of path you take. If, for example, you are part of a curriculum planning team, you and your group may first want to consider where you are now with the curriculum and where you want it to end up in the future. Think carefully about where you want the curriculum to end up, what it "looks" like now, what you want it to look like in the future, and what benefits your students will gain from this new curriculum. You will need to take the time to evaluate the options carefully while remembering to consider novelty and not allow personal agendas to steer the process astray.

You, Your Classroom, and Your School

Applying these guidelines can take some practice, but the end results can be beneficial to everyone involved. Let's start with your classroom. Children can learn the guidelines. Just like adults, children have preferences for generating options and focusing. Some children may want to keep generating options while others may feel a strong urge to evaluate each option as it is generated. You can simply remind each student in a consistent way to defer judgment. By calmly and consistently reminding everyone to defer judgment, as well as modeling this guideline, the message will percolate throughout the classroom. Anytime there is an opportunity to generate options, help your students to stretch their thinking. Always ask for two or three more ideas. Encourage your students to piggyback and look for combinations. As you and your colleagues develop curriculum activities, you can apply the guidelines, too. For example, if you want your young students to learn to recognize letters, how might you do this?

Geist and Hohn (2009) gave the example of the students who were learning the letter "M." They were each given a sheet with a large "M" on it and instructed to glue macaroni onto the shape. The activity did not contain or stimulate creative thought on the part of the student and there was little thought to the outcome. A better approach for the teacher would have been to think about how the students might learn to recognize the letters. The teacher could also have asked, "In what ways might the students learn to recognize the letters?" Think about the process you use and that you ask your students to use, as well considering as the end product (e.g., recognizing the letter M). An example of a solution to this given by Geist and Hohn is to use student drawings that include an image with the name of their object. The students usually had help writing the letter or spelling the name of the object. But, the point is, the students were involved in their learning and helping to construct something that helped other students learn their letters.

Likewise with the focusing guidelines, you may need to remind some students to use affirmative judgment. Using sentence stems such as "How to . . ." or "How might . . ." will take practice. You can model the use of these stems as you hold class discussions about any number of topics or curricular areas. For example, if your class has just listened to a story about a character who is in a problem situation or who is about to make a decision, you can ask your students questions using one of the sentence stems, and they can then generate responses to help the character out of the problem. As your students examine the options that everyone has generated, remind them to consider the novel or unusual ideas, because you never know where it might lead. Remind them that very novel options can be made useful. All of the guidelines combined with the tools are a powerful set of skills you and your students will have for a lifetime.

You are the lead example for your classroom. Generating options can be done for any part of your curriculum. For example, you can have your students generate options about everything they know about a generic plant. Then you can help fill in the gaps for the things they did not generate. To focus, you and your students can categorize the parts of the plant.

You are also an example to your colleagues. If you have colleagues who also use the tools and guidelines, it will be simple to demonstrate the power of the CPS process and tools among the rest of your colleagues. If you are unsure of the acceptance of the process or tools, you can still lead by example. The next time you are in a meeting and someone suggests that brainstorming be used, you can offer some simple guidelines to make the generating session more effective. If it appears that nothing will happen with the generated options, you can suggest ways to work with the options and, at the same time, suggest guidelines for focusing. We have had some experience with this, and we know it is effective. People generally welcome ways to make their ideas useful and put them to work.

The next chapter deals with specific tools for generating and focusing options. Be certain to keep the guidelines for generating and focusing from this chapter in mind as you learn these tools and ways to apply them.

Taking the Chapter Forward

o After your students have learned the guidelines for generating and focusing, monitor their interactions with each other, especially when they are working in cooperative or collaborative groups. This will give you opportunities to guide them back onto the trail when they seem to be getting lost in old, unproductive patterns. Monitoring your own behavior will also be instructive, especially when you are dealing with problems beyond the classroom. After you have experimented for a while with taking these guidelines beyond your professional life, report your experiences to your students. Ask them to try the same, both in and out of school. Check in with them from time to time about their application of the guidelines when working in their groups or with family and friends in other settings. The discussions that follow will be valuable to both you and your students.

Chapter 15

Teaching the Foundational Tools
(Level I)

In Chapter 1, both Sue's and Eric's teachers gave them some direct instruction in the use of creative tools to improve the effectiveness of their efforts. After reading this chapter, you will be able to describe and use 10 foundational tools for generating and focusing ideas. You will also be able to describe those tools and their functions to others. This chapter will help you to design instructional activities aimed at teaching these tools to your students and enable them to gain competence and confidence in appropriately applying these tools in real problem-solving situations.

Thinking back to Chapter 7, you will remember the figure showing the model for teaching and learning productive thinking (Figure 4; Treffinger & Feldhusen, 1998; Treffinger et al., 2006). The diagram describes the model's three levels of creativity instruction, the first of which is the foundations level. At this level, students are introduced to the basic knowledge of the Creative Problem Solving process and tools, as well as associated terminology. Students need basic instruction as to how to use both the generating and focusing tools to expand and then focus their thinking. They also need to gain some basic understanding as to how these tools can be applied to research and inquiry, as well as their ability to expand their productivity and the effectiveness of their communications. The rest of this chapter looks at knowledge and skills at the foundations level, especially as it pertains to 10 basic tools for generating and focusing ideas.

Table 12 summarizes the goals of Level I and the roles of teachers, students, and parents.

The Pulse of the Process

There is a natural rhythm or pulse to the creative process. Some look at this as a cycle between creative and critical (or divergent and convergent) thinking. We use the terms generating and focusing ideas because they clearly describe the actual behaviors individuals and groups must engage in if they are to be creatively productive. As discussed in Chapter 14, we call the interaction of these two behaviors—generating ideas and focusing ideas—the heartbeat of creativity (Isaksen et al., 2011, Treffinger, Isaksen, et al., 2006). The process is driven forward by the recurring activities of generating and focusing and is supported by knowing and applying the guidelines in Chapter 14 as well.

When generating ideas, we need to open our minds to new possibilities, change our set perspective, be willing to follow new and unusual thoughts to wherever they may lead, and think differently about the challenge, the data surrounding it, the criteria that we will use to evaluate possible solutions, and the implementation of those solutions. Each stage of the creative problem-solving process—gaining clarity, generating ideas, or preparing for action—is approached more effectively if we are able to choose and use focusing and generating tools that are appropriate to the situation and to our problem-solving style (Isaksen et al., 2011).

Although there are hundreds of tools that can be effectively used to either generate or focus our thinking, we teach 10 foundational tools as part of our basic toolbox, five generating and five focusing tools (Treffinger, 2008; Treffinger & Nassab, 2011b; Treffinger, Nassab, et al., 2006). We start with these 10 basic tools because they are easy to understand and apply by individuals or groups and they are related to or incorporate fea-

Table 12

Goals and Roles for Level I (Foundations)

Goals: In relation to learning the foundational generating and focusing tools, the student:
- Understands and applies basic guidelines for both generating and focusing options.
- Knows, chooses, and uses basic tools appropriately and effectively for generating options.
- Knows, chooses, and uses basic tools appropriately and effectively for focusing options.
- Learns and uses vocabulary associated with tools.

Teacher's role: Through direct instruction, the teacher:
- Presents guidelines for generating and focusing options and guides practice in applying them.
- Presents tools for generating and focusing options (including the names of and purposes for the tools).
- Provides opportunities for students to apply the tools through varied activities (within the curriculum as well as drawing on everyday experiences).
- Challenges students to apply the tools to tasks that arise in the classroom setting.
- Asks questions that call for productive thinking, probes and draws out students' thinking, and engages students in posing their own questions.
- Helps students to learn how to select and use tools appropriately when they need to generate or focus options for any task.
- Models the use of the tools in her or his own thinking.
- Provides examples of how the tools are used in many situations in the real world.
- Provides time for planning, extended effort, reflection, and debriefing when using the tools and helps the students to do so effectively.
- Creates and maintains a classroom climate conducive to productive thinking and sets expectations that students will learn and use the tools.
- Uses assessment and evaluation methods that include challenges for productive thinking and use of tools.

Student's role: Working independently and in groups, the student:
- Learns, applies, and internalizes the guidelines for generating and focusing options.
- Learns tools for generating and focusing options (including the names of and purposes for the tools).
- Uses the tools through varied activities (within the curriculum, in dealing with everyday experiences both in and out of the classroom).
- Responds appropriately to questions calling for productive thinking.
- Initiates questions that involve higher level thinking.
- Recognizes when certain tools might be helpful and chooses appropriate tools to use.
- Demonstrates extended effort and reflection in planning and carrying out activities and engaging in debriefing activities with others.
- Demonstrates curiosity and interest in continuing to learn and use new tools.

Table 12, continued

> **Parent's Role:** In daily interactions with the student, the parent:
> - Observes and applies the guidelines for generating and focusing options in everyday situations involving individuals or the family together.
> - Provides opportunities for all family members to contribute ideas and to analyze, refine, develop, and select options.
> - Respects the student's participation and ideas (without being either closed-minded nor patronizing or condescending).
> - Knows and uses deliberate tools for creative thinking (generating options) and for critical thinking (focusing options) in his or her own life as well as in dealing with the student.
> - Uses games, family outings, play time, and many informal opportunities to reinforce creative and critical thinking.
> - Rewards and celebrates productive thinking on the part of all family members.
> - Discusses the student's school experiences in relation to productive thinking and creative activities or accomplishments, not just in relation to "right answer thinking" and test scores.
> - Finds out about the kinds of creative and critical thinking, problem-solving, and decision-making methods and tools that students will learn in school; compares these to the methods and tools the parent uses in his or her own work or career; and communicates about these with the student.

tures of many other useful tools. By concentrating on only 10 tools, we can provide uniformity of approach within an organization whether it be a school-based problem-solving team or a major corporation.

Five Generating Tools

Generating tools enable us to increase the fluency of our ideas, expand our thinking, look at the situation from many different perspectives, and open our thinking to novelty and originality. Use these tools when you need many new and different ideas, when you are seeking a variety of unusual possibilities or options, or when you need to explore ideas or solutions in more depth, adding details to existing suggestions or combining several promising possibilities. If you become bogged down or need to change perspective, you may need to change to another tool. Below we will briefly look at five generating tools (Treffinger, 2008; Treffinger & Nassab, 2011a; Treffinger, Nassab, et al., 2006).

In order to generate effectively, start with a clear, concise statement of the issue or question you want to address. Use a stem that is open and invites the generation of many possibilities such as, "In what ways might . . ." or "How to . . ." Avoid unproductive stems such as, "Can you . . ." or "How many ways can you . . ." (Treffinger, Nassab, et al., 2006). Often the responses to such closed-ended stems end up being "No" or "Three." It is also a good idea to review the key background data surrounding the task so that you and others with whom you are working have a good understanding of the main issue you are dealing with.

Brainstorming

The word *brainstorming* is often used inaccurately as a synonym for creative problem solving. It is only one of many tools. That said, there are many forms of brainstorming. All involve an effort to produce a large number of ideas basically by thinking out loud, in writing, or in a combination of the two and listing whatever thoughts related to the challenge that come to mind, as fast as they come to mind, without censure or judgment. Brainstorming is usually used when a large number of ideas are desired in order to break into new areas of thinking.

To use brainstorming, list as many ideas as possible that respond to the issue or question. Think of many varied possibilities. Make an effort to go beyond what you have heard or seen before. Stretch, combine one idea with another, and let your mind go off into different and unexpected directions. Our experience in the field shows that the first ideas are usually reflective of what has already been done or what is at the surface of your thinking. In order to begin to explore unusual, creative ideas, you need to go beyond the first ideas that come to mind, often stretching for 20–25 ideas (or perhaps even more).

A teacher decided to use the brainstorming tool to help her students expand their vocabulary with words related to water. She had them look through the newspaper for a week for anything having to do with water, including news stories, advertisements, or cartoons. They were to collect their items in a folder and bring them into class. Working in groups, students compiled a list of their items and then compared their lists to see which group had the most, which list had the most unusual item, and which list included an item that was an example of a very different view of water.

> At the conclusion of the lesson, the teacher lead a discussion as to how students felt about the different water items and the many ways we "perceive, understand, and react to items we encounter in the media every day" (Treffinger et al., 2003, p. 31).

In addition to the traditional approach to brainstorming, where participants sit in a group calling out as ideas come to mind, there are many versions and adaptations. One is Brainstorming with Post-it® Notes. In this brainstorming adaptation, participants still work in a group, but a facilitator is not required to capture ideas as they are shouted out, and the process is a bit less frantic. Participants think over the challenge and then write ideas one at a time on Post-it® Notes. After they've written down an idea, they read it aloud and then post it for all to see or read. Others might build on that idea or use it to help them generate another along the same line of thought. This process continues until the flow of new ideas becomes a trickle. If at that point a large collection of ideas has been produced, then it may be time to move the process forward; if not, then the group can be called on to stretch its thinking or to try another generating approach.

Brainwriting is the quiet, reflective approach to brainstorming. It can be carried out in person or online using a system such a Google Docs. In the in-person version, participants sit around the table, each with a sheet with 12 large blocks arranged in three columns and four rows. There is a blank sheet with 12 blocks in the middle of the table. After being given a clear understanding of the problem or challenge to be addressed, each participant, at his or her own pace, fills in the top three blocks with an idea or option. The first participant to complete the top row will place his or her sheet in the middle and take the blank sheet to work on. The next person to complete the top three blocks puts that sheet in the middle and retrieves the sheet that is there. That person then either adds three new ideas or options in the second row or builds on the ideas that are in the top row until the second row of three blocks is filled in. That sheet is then exchanged with another that is in the middle. This process continues until all 12 blocks on each sheet are complete.

Attribute Listing

Attribute listing is helpful when you want to break down a problem, question, or challenge into its essential parts or elements in order to generate change. It can also help you better understand the various elements of the issue in order to make changes or modifications that will incrementally, but positively, effect the whole. This is an organized, structured, analytical approach to generating ideas that often appeals to those less comfortable with the openness of brainstorming. It is useful when you are seeking improvement in a situation or of a product or procedure.

Begin using attribute listing by breaking the task or question into its main parts or components and then listing the major attributes. Next, consider the attributes one at a time. How might you change, modify, improve, or enhance each attribute? Could it take a different form? What would that look like? In what ways would it change the whole? Try to list several possible modifications for each of the attributes. Consider the result of combining some of the attributes or some of the modifications you have generated.

A football coach sat down with his team and listed the attributes of each position on the team, made another list of the attributes of each of his players, and finally, prepared a list of the attributes of the players on the team they would be playing on the coming weekend. They first discussed the team assignments. Was each team member using his position in a way that drew on his best attributes? What might they change as individuals and as a team to improve their performance? They next used the lists to begin a discussion of how they could devise and practice plays in the coming week that would build on their strongest attributes while exploiting the attributes of the opposing team.

Force-Fitting

Force-fitting helps us come up with new ideas by linking randomly selected objects to a question or problem in order to stimulate new ideas or relationships. Force-fitting enables us to look at the challenge from different perspectives and pushes our thinking in different directions. It can often be used to stimulate additional original ideas when the flow of ideas using other tools drops off to a trickle.

After stating the problem or task to be addressed, randomly choose an unrelated object or picture. The object can be anything. We often use a small box of toys. Each toy can stand alone or act as a model. For instance, a red toy car is made of plastic. It is pushed around by hand or runs down hill by gravity. It can also remind the problem solver of the real thing—a red Corvette, for instance. The question becomes, "What new ideas about the task are suggested by this red car?" When ideas based on the red toy car stop flowing, select another object or picture to stimulate your thinking. Continue this process, selecting one object after another. If one object does not lead to new connections to the task, go on to another one. Remember that your objective is many new and different possibilities or options.

Mr. Sanchez, an elementary teacher, was conducting a science lesson on conservation. He had collected a large number of random objects and pictures that included various toys (cars, a chess piece, a small ball, an X-Men action figure, and a Barbie doll), objects from around the home (a paintbrush, comb, couch pillow, fork, and paper clip holder), and dozens of random pictures cut out from magazines. After a short video on the need for conservation, he put the following challenge statement on his SMART Board: "In what new and unusual ways might we conserve our natural resources?" He then had the students pick one of his collected objects or pictures and asked them to consider how that object or picture, or anything about it, might suggest new or unusual ways to conserve natural resources. Following that prompt, students began to offer suggestions that were recorded under the challenge statement on the board. Mr. Sanchez encouraged the students to stretch their thinking and seek many wild and crazy options, letting them know that it was okay to have fun while doing the work of generating ideas. If students ran out of ideas when thinking about a specific object, he encouraged them to pick another one from the collection.

Morphological Matrix

The *morphological matrix* can help produce thousands of unusual combinations and ideas in a very short amount of time. It is at the same time both structured and expansive and is easy to use. The matrix is made up of a grid, usually four columns wide and 10 rows deep.

To use the morphological matrix, think of four or more parameters, characteristics, or major elements of the task or challenge. Think of elements that can take many forms. Use each of those characteristics as labels at the top of each column. Although you may have thought of many more than four, we have found that the matrix works best with three to five columns, and we usually focus on just four. For instance, in writing a short story, the elements might be: character, setting, goal, and obstacle.

Now generate 10 ideas for each of the elements. Generate ideas for one column at a time, with no regard for what has been generated in the other columns. Think of a variety of characters: real, historical, imagined, general, or specific. For instance, you might list politician (or be more specific, such as President Obama). In the second column, you might list outer space, Mars, or a trash can. Your matrix might look something like what you see in Figure 10.

The last step is to randomly draw one possibility from each column. You can do this by opening a phone book, pointing at any number and using the last four digits to form a unique combination of four options. Remember to remain flexible. One successful example was when students chose racehorse, south Florida, true love, and miss deadline from their matrix. The story they wrote was about a racehorse that retires so that he could travel to South Florida where his true love is living. He is followed, and his plans almost thwarted, by a former girl friend, another racehorse named Miss Deadline.

Keep in mind that the morphological matrix can be used in any domain, not just creative writing. If you can break a task down into three or four essential elements and can generate 10 options for each element, then this is an appropriate and powerful generating tool.

SCAMPER

The fifth of our foundational generating tools is known as *SCAMPER*. SCAMPER is a mnemonic device created by Eberle (1971), based on a

	Character	Place	Goal	Obstacle
1	Mickey Mouse	Mars	Solve mystery	The in-laws
2	President Obama	Classroom	Get rich	Outlaws
3	wicked witch	On a riverboat	Write novel	By-laws
4	Harry Potter	French Riviera	Find true love	Auto accident
5	James Bond	In an airplane	Win a contest	Broken leg
6	Barney	Beach	Skydive	Money
7	Tom Cruise	Mountain top	Become famous	Monsoon
8	Talking goldfish	Trashcan	Bake cookies	Bad hair day
9	Ballet dancer	In a greenhouse	Create a website	Long-lost uncle
10	Miley Cyrus	Paris	Escape	Fear

Figure 10. Example of a morphological matrix.

list of idea-expanding questions first proposed by Alex Osborn (1953). Osborn's questions were designed to stimulate the flow of new ideas by triggering new and unusual thinking and different ways of looking at a task or challenge. Each letter in SCAMPER stands for a key word that can remind us of these basic questions:

- S = Substitute: What or who might you take away, insert, or change?
- C = Combine: What elements or attributes of the task or challenge could be blended together?
- A = Adapt: What other ideas or actions does this suggest? What could be copied or used differently?
- M = Modify, Magnify, Minify: What elements might be done differently or changed slightly? What might be made bigger, stronger, faster, louder, or more colorful? How would elements react if toned down?
- P = Put to Other Uses: In what ways could elements of the task be used differently or the context in which elements are applied be changed?
- E = Eliminate: What elements, parts, or attributes surrounding or imbedded in the challenge are in the way or no longer needed? What might happen if they were done away with?

○ R = Reverse, Rearrange: What elements, parts, or attributes surrounding or imbedded in the challenge could be mixed up, moved around, or put in opposite order?

SCAMPER is useful when you or your group need to generate many unusual ideas by considering new and varied perspectives. It can help to speed up the pace of idea generation and provide opportunities for additional playful search and exploration of the task or challenge. After stating the challenge, pick a letter from the list and ask the questions above or others that might come to mind based on the key word. Apply the questions to your problem. If one trigger word does not lead to new ideas, go on to another. Although many people follow these words in sequence, you do not need to, nor do you have to use all of the words. Use what works, for as long as it works, and then move on.

A music teacher working with a group of high school composition students had them use the SCAMPER tool to explore new ways to expand on an original musical phrase. The students first developed an original phrase of four to eight measures. They then experimented with their phrase by substituting one or more notes; combining their phrase with another phrase of music from any source; adapting their phrase to a different meter; modifying it by making it longer or shorter or by changing key; change the tempo or mode so that the music might be put to other uses; eliminating a note or measure; and rearranging the notes, having them go upside down or backward or in an entirely different order. When students had explored many different ways to think about their phrase, they then selected those ideas that seemed to work best and completed an original composition.

Five Focusing Tools

After you have generated a list of 30, 40, or even hundreds of ideas or options, you are not finished. You need to narrow your possibilities to a few workable solutions and put those solutions into action. The focusing tools are designed to help make critical decisions, choose among ideas and promising possibilities, develop criteria, make comparisons, break a course of action into manageable steps, assign responsibility for those steps, and place them into a workable order. These tools can help you organize and prioritize your ideas and select the most promising option from a group of possibilities. Below are brief descriptions of five foundational focusing tools (Treffinger, 2008; Treffinger & Nassab, 2011b; Treffinger, Nassab, et al., 2006).

Hits and Hot Spots

The *Hits and Hot Spots* tool is used to reduce a large number of suggestions into a workable list of ideas and to arrange those ideas into promising clusters that invite further refinement. You start by arranging your suggestions in a way that each can be easily viewed and considered. Decide how many of these you will want to work with. If you are in a team, each member might be invited to mark three to five of the listed options. These will be hits: options that stand out; feel right; seem to sizzle; seem workable; are clear, exciting, or intriguing; or promise to move things in the right direction. If you allow five hits per group member, then each individual should mark (we often use markers or stick-on dots) five different suggestions. However, different group members can mark the same suggestion. Before proceeding, review all of the options. Remember that you are looking for novelty.

After the hits have been marked, look at them carefully. Are some of them similar? If so, gather them into like groups and form Hot Spot clusters. Look back at other ideas on the list and add other similar suggestions to the clusters. Review the suggestions in each cluster, noting what all of those ideas have in common. What creative direction do they represent? Give each of the clusters a title summarizing the essence of all of the ideas in each cluster. Restate those ideas in a single suggestion.

A high school guidance counselor was conducting a freshman seminar on choosing a career, prior to the students making their selections of elective courses for the following year. At the end of the previous session, students were asked to work at home and list their major interests, without worrying about whether those interests led to possible career paths. At the beginning of the seminar, the counselor assigned students to groups of five and asked them to share and combine their lists and to identify careers that were associated those interests. Group members were instructed to check three career areas on their group's list that really interested them, caught their attention, or seemed liked the right fit for them. The group then arranged these into Hot Spot clusters. Each cluster was given a title. Working with their groups, students wrote a simple statement summarizing each career opportunity. Individual students then selected one of these areas of opportunity to study in more depth and create a short presentation on that career area to the whole class.

ALoU

ALoU, which stands for Advantages, Limitations (and how to overcome them), and Unique features, provides an affirmative way to analyze and give a balanced and fair assessment of an option. It can help you to look at both the strengths and challenges of a proposal and consider whether those challenges can and should be addressed, while also considering its unique aspects and future potential. Using ALoU, you can explore a proposed solution more thoroughly or compare the potential of a few promising suggestions, focusing on the positives of each rather than the negatives.

To use the ALoU tool, first list all of the advantages of the option. What is appealing or positive about it? Next, list its limitations. However, state these limitations in the form of an open invitational problem statement. For instance, instead of listing, "We can't afford to do this," you would ask, "In what ways might we develop the resources that we will need to do this?" Notice, we said "resources," not "money." This allows us to open our thinking beyond just financial resources.

After considering all of the possible limitations, consider the option's unique features. What is truly unique about this idea? Where might it lead? What new opportunities might it open up? In what ways does it stand out against other options being considered? Finally, go back and look at your limitation statements. Note those that represent significant concerns or difficulties and explore ways that they might be overcome or be made less significant so that the option could be pursued.

An art teacher took her students to a nearby museum. The students' assignment was to pick one painting from the collection and critique it, based on points that they had been studying in class. Students were to list up to five advantages of the work. These would be areas of strength that made the work stand out. They next needed to note at least two limitations stated in a manner that invited a positive response (e.g., "In what ways might lighting have been more effectively used in this work?"). Students also noted the unique features of the work. What made it truly original? If the work influenced a paradigm shift in painting, they were to note the role that it played. When the students next met in their own classroom, they reported on their findings. Class discussion of each selected piece focused on the student's suggestions for overcoming the limitations noted about the work.

Evaluation Matrix

The *evaluation matrix* helps you to systematically evaluate a moderate to large (8–15) number of options against specific criteria. It provides an accurate, detailed examination of each option in relation to other promising options, ideas, or suggestions in the list and enables you to identify those options to develop further, implement immediately, study more, modify, or reject.

You can begin to form the evaluation matrix by either listing your criteria across the top of several columns or labeling each row with one of the options being considered. The criteria you choose should be relevant for all of the options. Although you need to generate criteria that are appropriate to your challenge, we find that the acronym CARTS (cost, acceptance, resources, time, space) is often a useful place to start. You also need to choose a rating system (e.g., 0 to 5, where 0 is *very poor*, and 5 is *excellent*).

Evaluate all of your options against one criterion at a time. Go down your list and rate all of the ideas against the criterion at the top of the first column. Then move on to the next criterion. Consider, for instance, if you select one option how much it will cost in comparison to the others or what kinds of resources each option will require and the availability of those resources. At the end of each row, add up the "scores" for each of your options. You are not simply looking for one winner but for options with the most potential for success. One suggestion might be rated with four 5s and one 0 under "time." Not having the time to implement the solution may make it unrealistic—and a candidate for rejection. You might end up with several options that if modified, combined, or used in sequence would lead to a very productive outcome. You might create decision columns on the right side of the matrix that will aid in analyzing your results.

At a Back to School night, two parents became aware of a teacher's efforts to teach the creativity tools to the students in his class. The parents got some reading material on the topic and decided to enlist their two children in the selection of a new family car using the evaluation matrix tool. They first decided on several criteria, including cost, miles per gallon, room, maintenance, and accessories. After researching the current market, they each made one or two recommendations that were placed in the matrix. Each vehicle was evaluated against each criterion on a 1 to 5 scale, with 1 being *very weak* and 5 being *very strong*. The car that was rated most highly on room, maintenance, and accessories was lowest on miles per gallon and average on cost. The family's selection, after considering each choice side by side, was less expensive and had the best advertised miles per gallon, while the other criteria had scores of 4 out of 5 (see Figure 11).

Paired Comparison Analysis

The *Paired Comparison Analysis* (PCA) helps you to make decisions about promising options (usually 4–6) by ranking them based on how strongly they are supported in relation to each of the other suggestions. It can also help to clarify your thoughts, feelings, and understanding of the options being considered and to build consensus within a group.

To use the PCA, write each of your options down, making sure they are parallel and distinct. Label each with a letter (e.g., A–F). Chose a rat-

Vehicles	Criteria					Total Score
	Low Cost	MPG	Room	Maintenance	Accessories	
Choice 1	5	5	4	4	4	22
Choice 2	3	1	5	5	5	19
Choice 3	3	3	2	3	3	14
Choice 4	2	4	2	3	3	14
Choice 5	4	2	3	2	2	13

Figure 11. Sample evaluation matrix for automobile choices.

ing scale that will indicate the strength of preference for one suggestion over another. You might try 1 for *weak*, 2 for *moderate*, and 3 for *strong*. Consider one option against each of the others by pairing the letters: A/B, A/C, A/D, and so on. Select the preferred option of the two and rate the strength of the preference. When all of the pairs have been rated, tabulate the scores.

Rank the options from the highest total to the lowest. In order to make sure they are ready to go, you might want to use the ALoU tool on your highest ranked options.

In order to practice using the PCA tool, you might tell your students that they have won a trip to one of six destinations, but they must all agree on the destination. List six destinations and have the students use the tool to reach a consensus on their final destination (see Figure 12).

Sequencing (S-M-L)

The *Sequencing (S-M-L)* tool helps to organize a potential course of action into discrete tasks, assigning timelines (short, medium, and long) and responsibility to each individual task. It provides a clear written timeline that identifies both the tasks to be carried out and the people responsible for each task. It enables us to get a project moving, keep it moving, and hold individuals accountable.

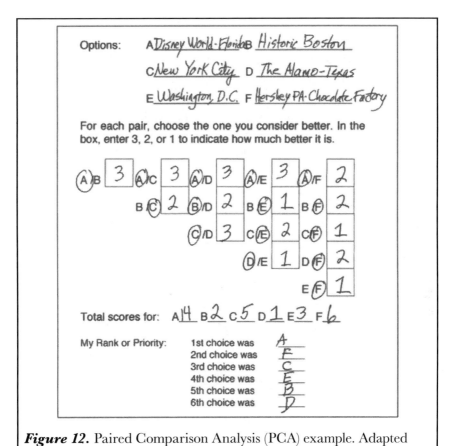

Figure 12. Paired Comparison Analysis (PCA) example. Adapted from Treffinger and Nassab (2011b).

A S-M-L chart has five columns. The first lists the tasks to be accomplished; the next three are labeled short, medium, and long; and the last is labeled who. You will need to define what is meant by short, medium, and long. Long is usually some deadline or due date for the project, medium is usually a time by which preliminary steps need to be accomplished, and short is an immediate benchmark date to ensure your plan gets off the ground. We often suggest that short be defined as the next 24 hours, because once started, projects are more likely to be completed. Our motivation to start a new project is highest in those 24 hours following the decision to implement a particular plan of action.

In the first column, list all of the tasks to be accomplished in no particular order. These tasks include how to make sure available resources and elements that will assist you in moving forward are brought into play. Consider how potential roadblocks might be turned into assets, neutralized, or avoided. Next, place a check mark next to each task indicating when it must be completed for the plan to succeed: short, medium, or long. Some tasks may need to be addressed in more than one time frame. After establishing the time frame for each task, name the individual or group who will be responsible for achieving each task. Make sure that you have the agreement of those individuals and that they have the ability to carry out the assignment before completing the SML chart. Then put your plan into action.

A seventh-grade social studies teacher assigned projects to groups of four students. Included in the assignment was the instruction to use the Sequencing (S-M-L) tool in their planning. The assignment was due in 5 weeks, which became the long date. Short would be the next 24 hours, with each group reporting on their short-term accomplishment the next day. Each group would decide on their own medium checkpoints. Group members listed all of the things that needed to be accomplished to produce a successful presentation. They then decided whether each activity had to be accomplished immediately, in the middle of the time period, or at the end. They decided that some activities needed to be worked on throughout the assignment period. Finally, the group assigned responsibilities for each activity and planned ways to monitor each other's progress.

Teaching the Tools

When teaching the tools, it is best to present them one at a time, making sure students understand how each tool is used and how it can be applied. Be aware, too, that individuals with different creative problem-solving styles may approach, value, and use each tool differently (Schoonover & Treffinger, 2003). Recalling Table 2 in Chapter 9, Explorers and Externals, for instance, may enjoy and look forward to a brainstorming approach that is wide open, with ideas being shouted out as soon as they come to mind. Internals and Developers, on the other hand, may work better using Brainwriting or Brainstorming with Post-it® Notes, two approaches that are more structured and allow for some reflection before sharing.

When first introducing a tool, provide opportunities for simple practice problems. When a degree of competence is built up, move on to providing opportunities for realistic applications and life-like situations with low risk. These opportunities should extend across content areas and represent varied experiences so that students can be confident in using the tools in a variety of situations. Creativity instruction is not a one-shot deal or an amusement that serves as filler in the classroom. It is most effective when adopted by a school or district as a long-term commitment. However, the lack of such a commitment does not mean that meaningful instruction cannot take place within an individual classroom. In either case, sound instruction builds on what has already been presented. Use the terminology and skills throughout the year and from one area of study to another.

Resist the urge to present too much new information at once. Introduce new content with familiar tools, and introduce new tools using familiar content. As you introduce any tool, be clear about what it is used for and how it is used. Help students think about how and where they might apply the tools in their everyday lives and in other content areas. This will help develop their metacognitive skills. Although you may introduce tools out of curriculum context, it will be valuable to move them promptly into applications in context. In this way, students build confidence in using the tool and have opportunities to apply it in meaningful ways. After students have used a tool, debrief them on their experience and on their thinking during the process. When evaluating students' performance, focus not only on content, but also on their growth in using the tools.

As with any instruction, begin by ascertaining each student's level of learning and readiness, considering, for example, the four levels described by Treffinger et al. (2002) and discussed in Chapter 13. For students whose present level of creative performance is not yet evident, emphasize building the foundations for creative learning: help them to become aware of productive thinking, the problem-solving process, and the tools in a learning environment that is safe and open for creativity to emerge. For those students whose confidence in their abilities is beginning to emerge, provide guided practice opportunities with the tools while helping them develop, use, and apply their metacognitive skills. Some students will display a firm grasp of the skills being taught and be able to apply their problem-solving strengths in personal ways. They will need help in recognizing appropriate ways to use the tools on their own, while expanding their skills beyond the 10 foundational tools. They will benefit from many rich and varied opportunities to apply what they have learned. Finally, there are those students who, due to pervious training or natural ability, will excel in the use and application of the tools. They will benefit greatly from being given the freedom to act on their own and to customize and personalize their use of the tools so that they can have optimum impact on real-life problems.

Potentially successful problem solvers, when working at the foundations level, also need to be familiar with a variety of other tools for research and inquiry as well as tools that might be called expression and productivity tools. Research and inquiry tools include research skills (including both traditional library and reference skills and contemporary web search tools) and a variety of age- and experience-appropriate data-gathering, data-analysis, and data-reporting skills (e.g., interview or survey methods, fundamental experimental design methods, statistical methods, methods for graphing, charting, or summarizing data). Expression and productivity tools include learning how to plan and deliver oral presentations; leading discussions; engaging in formal debate activities and techniques for persuasion and communication; and recognizing assumptions, generalizations, flawed arguments, and propaganda. This set of tools also includes using technology effectively (which we will consider in greater detail in Chapter 19), such as audio-visual equipment (e.g., projectors, media players, interactive whiteboards), presentation and graphics software and web-based resources, and other specialized scientific or technical equipment for any domain in which they are working. These tool skills also include important skills such as understanding the appropriate use of intellectual property (copyright and plagiarism issues) and developing wisdom about critical evaluation of material they locate (e.g., just because you read it on the Internet does not mean it is truthful, accurate, or even what or who it purports to be). These skills and tools are important for many reasons in addition to their relevance to creativity and innovation, but they are also important to keep in mind; there is a difference between being creatively open to ideas and experience and being gullible and potentially victimized.

Considering the Characteristics of the Learner

When helping students learn the problem-solving process and the use and application of the appropriate tools at the foundations level, we need to consider the individual's overall level of understanding and accomplishment in terms of personal productivity and the individual's style of problem solving.

Problem-solving style impacts not only how one chooses and uses a particular tool, but it also can act as a guide for delivering instruction most effectively (Treffinger, Selby, & Isaksen, 2008). As we pointed out in Chapter 6, by taking the various styles of our students into account, we can differentiate our lesson based on both level and style. During instruction, students with an Explorer preference may benefit from an explanation of the process and tools that encourages their use in a spontaneous or unexpected fashion. They will be encouraged by the recognition of their efforts to go in unusual directions and by being granted permission to deal with several challenges or several aspects of a single challenge at the same time. Developers will benefit from instruction that enables them to appreciate the structure provided by the CPS process and the tools themselves. They will be encouraged by the knowledge that they can be successful creative problem solvers and still proceed one step at a time in a planned organized manner.

Externals and Internals will also benefit from instruction that allows them to process information on their own terms. Externals will appreciate opportunities to gain understanding through engagement, exploration, and discussion. They will be motivated by working with others and by having permission to actively apply their newly learned knowledge and skills. Those with an Internal style need time to think about and reflect on new information before they engage most effectively. They also benefit from being able to pursue some projects on their own or with a trusted colleague and from being able to listen to the thoughts of others followed by ample preparation time.

Those with a strong Person-Oriented style of decision making look to tools that provide opportunities for collaboration. They appreciate the aspects of the problem-solving process that help bring a group toward consensus. Task-Oriented deciders appreciate the aspects of the process and tools that help uncover the underlying problem, build clarity, and help develop a sound foundation for future action.

During instruction, you may observe different individuals reacting to and building a preference for different stages of the process and for different tool choices. Explorers with a strong External preference may really enjoy and be energized by a traditional brainstorming session. Internals are more comfortable, and often more productive, using Brainwriting or Brainstorming with Post-it® Notes. Developers appreciate the structured nature of the morphological matrix, while Explorers appreciate a tool that can provide 10,000 new and unusual ideas in a short time. Person-Oriented deciders are encouraged by the fact that the ALoU begins with the listing of advantages, while Task-Oriented deciders see value in having an opportunity to not only formally list limitations, but also consider how those limitations might be overcome.

Taking the Chapter Forward

o Think about the 10 tools. How might you apply them to your own life? In what ways might you introduce their use to groups that you work with, both in your professional and private life? How might you teach the tools to your students? What types of practice problems might you provide? How might you ensure that the climate in your classroom is safe and open? What opportunities could you provide for your students to engage in realistic practice, applying the tools to build a better understanding of your course content? What opportunities might you suggest to your students to use the tools in real-life situations?

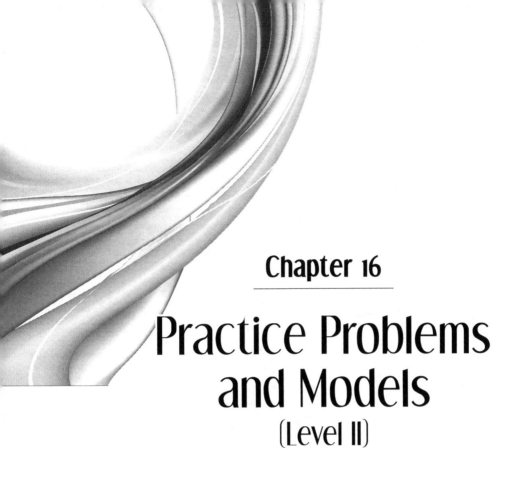

Chapter 16

Practice Problems and Models
(Level II)

After reading this chapter, you will have an understanding of how to extend the learning experience of students whose creative potential is emerging. You will be able to identify strategies to help students practice applying tools for generating and focusing ideas. You will also be able to guide students in learning and applying a deliberate creative problem-solving process.

Table 13 describes the goals for Level II and the roles of teachers, students, and parents in carrying out this level.

Who Needs Practice?

The simple answer to the question "Who needs practice?" is . . . everyone. Any good musician will tell you that practice makes up an important part of the day. Practice is also a vital element in effective instruction.

Table 13

Goals and Roles for Level II (Realistic Tasks)

Goals: The student:
- Becomes competent in the components and stages of CPS, the language or vocabulary of CPS, and the use of basic tools during CPS.
- Gains confidence in his or her ability to generate and focus options and to use CPS effectively through work on appropriate and realistic tasks.
- Develops commitment or conviction as an effective or productive problem solver.

Teacher's Role: When guiding and leading students in working on realistic problems and challenges, the teacher:
- Reviews and extends students' competence with tools for generating and focusing options.
- Reinforces thinking guidelines and positive attitudes.
- Guides students in learning and applying all CPS stages and components.
- Introduces roles of people in problem-solving sessions.
- Introduces task appraisal and process planning and guides students in developing metacognitive skills.
- Provides practice problems and leads students' work on those problems.
- Encourages students' confidence in, and commitment to, problem solving, identifying successes en route.
- Establishes and maintains a constructive climate for creative and critical thinking and problem solving.
- Sets up and uses performance tasks that enable students to practice problem-solving applications.
- Guides students in collaboration and teamwork.
- Provides space and resources for effective problem solving in small groups.
- Encourages students to stretch and be risk takers.
- Challenges students to look forward in their thinking and to enlist others in their efforts.
- Teaches students to be reflective and to debrief their problem-solving efforts, leads the debriefing, and guides groups constructively in learning and growing as problem solvers.

Student's Role. Working independently and in groups, the student:
- Knows the language and vocabulary associated with all problem-solving stages and components.
- Knows the purposes for each stage and component and chooses them appropriately in working on practice problems.
- Engages (with enthusiasm) in applying problem solving to tasks or challenges provided by the coach or teacher.
- Assumes the role of client or resource group member when working on practice problems and plays those roles appropriately.
- Collaborates with others in task appraisal and process planning when working on practice problems.

Table 13, continued

Student's Role, continued
- Demonstrates confidence in his or her ability to work successfully on a variety of problem-solving tasks.
- Demonstrates competence, individually and in small groups, in applying tools for generating or focusing options during any component or stage.
- Shows conviction by engaging in complex tasks and challenges and seeing efforts through to appropriate completion or closure.
- Engages in and contributes to debriefing of problem-solving sessions.
- Demonstrates active interest in continuing to learn and use new process tools.

Parent's Role: In daily interactions with the student, the parent:
- Strives deliberately to express problems as opportunities and challenges, not just as concerns or difficulties.
- Discusses opportunities for and examples of effective thinking and problem-solving in relation to storytelling (orally and from books), films, videos, or television programs.
- Takes examples from the media (e.g., newspapers, television) of current events that involve (or need) productive thinking and explores with the student or as a family how the situation might be addressed creatively.
- Supports the student's participation in creative activities and programs (in much the same way as we support athletic participation).

It reinforces students' learning and helps to establish a given skill set as part of their repertoire. As you introduce new creativity and problem-solving tools and skills to students, practice will help them to refine, polish, and apply those skills appropriately during the stage that Treffinger et al. (2002) described as emerging. The goal of instruction at this level is to help students use their emerging characteristics to strengthen the three Cs: competence, confidence, and commitment. Table 14 summarizes some indicators of these factors.

Practice early on allows students to gain and build their strengths and their understanding about the application of the creative process and tools and to receive and benefit from meaningful feedback. As with musicians and other professionals in many domains, creative problem solvers need to continue to practice their skills long after they reach proficiency and are able to easily apply those skills comfortably and consistently across a broad range of tasks and situations.

The activities and challenges presented to the student are designed to be low risk, but meaningful. The greatest risk to the student may be an emotional let down if his or her efforts are not successful, but with

Table 14

The Three Cs to Accomplish in Level II

Competence (knowledge and proficiency with methods, tools, and applications)
- Able to generate ideas and focus their thinking
- Knows and follows guidelines for thinking
- Knows the vocabulary of process and uses it appropriately
- Knows thinking tools, selects and applies them appropriately
- Demonstrates fluency, flexibility, originality, and elaboration
- Able to self-assess, monitor, adapt during problem solving
- Follows through on new ideas and solutions to problems
- Recognizes situations in which process tools are relevant

Confidence (belief in one's ability to use or apply process successfully)
- Shows initiative
- Demonstrates leadership
- Ready to work on challenges others may consider risky or too difficult
- Eager to share ideas and solutions with others
- Ready to describe and discuss strategies and uses of tools
- Not intimidated by obstacles or barriers; ready to overcome them
- Organizes or mobilizes others; sets the pace
- Expresses belief in the probability of success ("We can do this!")
- Undaunted by challenges, blocks, or difficulties

Commitment (initiating, eager, excited, passionate)
- Passionate and excited about opportunities for creativity and problem solving
- Becomes immersed in a task even when it is difficult
- Shows pride in work; optimistic; motivated
- Eager to share ideas and solutions with others
- Persistent and goes beyond the minimum that is required
- Constant source of energy for others; enjoys collaboration and competition to accept and reach high standards

guidance such setbacks can lead to new opportunities. At first, provide well-structured practice opportunities. Then, as the student's abilities develop, practice challenges can become more complex, open-ended, and challenging. You might begin with simple practice exercises or activities. These can be light-hearted, whimsical, or playful open-ended questions with little need for background research or preparation that can be completed in as little as 10–20 minutes and that emphasize applying a basic generating or focusing tool. Additional practice might involve an event task; a brief, contrived scenario; or a practice problem that a class or small groups can work on in 45–60 minutes. Several collections of tasks of this kind are available, including *Pickles, Problems, and Dilemmas* (Draze, 2005a);

Primarily Problem Solving (Draze, 2005b); *CPS for Kids* (Eberle & Stanish, 1996); *Be a Problem Solver* (Stanish & Eberle, 1997); and *Practice Problems for Creative Problem Solving* (Treffinger, 2000). Figure 13 presents a sample of a one-page practice problem (Treffinger, 2000).

As students' competence with the problem-solving process and tools grows, you can involve them in extended problems and challenges, with more complex material or cases involving background study and research and extended working time. Extended problem-solving challenges, for example, include those suggested by Problem-Based Learning advocates (e.g., Gallagher, 2009) or teacher-directed small-group projects (e.g., Buck Institute, 2011).

Working through problems that pose an increasing level of difficulty continually pushes students out of their comfort zone and into their Zone of Proximal Development (Vygotsky, 1978; Woolfolk, 2010). It helps students become creativity conscious (i.e., aware of their creative tendencies; Davis, 1987), giving them the confidence to make deliberate efforts to apply their creative thinking skills when confronted with new and challenging situations.

At Level II (where students' skills are emerging), the teacher's role becomes that of coach, helping students identify and develop their strengths and engaging them in strategies that will strengthen areas of weakness. Working individually and in groups, students refine their use of the creativity tools and begin to apply the tools and processes to situations that are more meaningful to them. The teacher guides his or her students toward taking on more realistic challenges and therefore more risk in a nonjudgmental climate that provides a safe foundation for growth (Treffinger et al., 2002).

The Practice of Practice

Because practice reinforces learning, we need to begin a regimen of practice (in the sense of doing or performing often effectively and confidently, rather than merely in the sense of mechanical repetition of a memorized algorithm or prescribed steps) after initially learning new information, skills, or tools. Over time, practice within a domain builds competence in that domain, leading toward the development of expertise. Meaningful, sustained practice will allow your students to learn how and

GONE FISHING

Messy Situation

For several days, as usual, your father has been talking about wanting you to go fishing with him this weekend. He says the fish will be biting and just waiting for you both to catch them. You and your dad don't get to spend too much time together, and you really appreciate his thought, but ... your dad is a great fisherman. He is always able to catch the most and biggest fish on any fishing trip with you or with his friends. You know that he has asked you because he loves to fish and because he wants to spend time with you. He is busy most of the week with his job, so you don't get to see a lot of each other.

He started taking you along on his weekend fishing trips a few years ago and has invested quite a bit of money into equipment for the two of you. You have all the best in tackle and equipment, but you are not good at fishing. Your dad's skill and interest in the sport has increased. Your skill has remained at the beginner stage, and your interest has been reduced to absolute boredom. Each time you go fishing, you never catch any fish and you are totally bored. The time and opportunity to be with your dad and talk together is important to you, but you wish there were another way.

Lately, you have become so bored on these fishing excursions that you haven't even been able to enjoy the time. Your dad is always landing the big ones while you just sit there. You might enjoy the trips if you caught fish, but you don't know for sure because you never catch any. This weekend, there is an activity at your school that you could use for an excuse. It is not something that you really care a lot about, but it wouldn't be as boring as fishing. The last three times your dad has asked you about fishing, however, you have made up an excuse. You fear that he may be suspicious, and you don't want to hurt his feelings. But, you don't think you can stand another whole weekend of boredom.

The weatherman just predicted a beautiful weekend ahead, and your dad is making preparations for the trip. What are you going to do about this Mess?

Figure 13. Example of a practice problem. From *Practice Problems for Creative Problem Solving* (3rd ed., p. 28), by D. J. Treffinger, 2000, Waco, TX: Prufrock Press. Copyright 2000 by Donald J. Treffinger. Reprinted with permission.

where to choose and apply tools with confidence, how to choose and combine them in a variety of situations, and how to recognize where and when it is appropriate to use the problem-solving process and tools. Practicing a variety of tools and applying problem-solving skills in a variety of settings as part of ongoing learning activities helps to ensure that, as domain expertise grows, students will not fall victim to the risk of losing the flexibility of thought and varied perspectives that are needed for creative productivity (Runco, 2003a). We suggest that you vary the tools practiced and the ways you apply each tool and not limit practice to a constant, fixed time or class. In this way, students will avoid the incorrect impression that a tool can only be used in a specific situation or in a certain combination. Distribute opportunities across the curriculum and in situations relating to daily life. This will help promote broad access to, and use of, the skills and contribute to their availability to the students as their expertise grows, promoting flexibility across many and varied open-ended challenges. Teachers and parents can work together to encourage such practice and to explore different ways of applying the tools and problem-solving process skills until students becomes experts in their use.

Practice With Tools

As you teach and practice several generating and focusing tools and the elements of a problem-solving model, you will probably work on them one at a time, but only until the students are confident in their use and application. Musicians learn and practice one set of scales at a time. As they become proficient in recognizing chords and harmonies and applying that knowledge, they are able to combine their knowledge and skills to work on more difficult compositions. As your students become proficient in the use and application of tools for creativity and problem solving, encourage them to practice applying them in appropriate combinations as they work on increasingly complex challenges.

In presenting and then practicing tools, remember to give attention to both generating and focusing tools. You may introduce one generating tool and then share one focusing tool to apply for a specific practice activity. As practice continues, encourage the students to use different combinations of tools so that they do not lock themselves into assuming that a specific generating tool is always linked to a specific focusing tool.

To begin, you might review the examples in Chapter 15, presenting the various examples of how the tools were successfully applied in different settings. It can also be interesting to consider various products or innovations that may have resulted from the use of any of the tools, whether unintentionally or deliberately by their creators. For instance, Reese's Pieces combine three types of ingredients: chocolate, peanut butter, and hard candy. Was the force-fitting generating tool used to develop this product? Might it have been used?

Torrance Incubation Model

The Torrance Incubation Model (TIM; Torrance, 1979; Torrance & Safter, 1990) is an instructional planning and delivery model that focuses specifically on teaching creativity skills and concepts. It involves three broad stages: Heightening Anticipation, Deepening Expectations, and Extending the Learning. Each stage includes several cognitive, metacognitive, motivational, and affective strategies to consider when planning creativity-related instruction. Several examples and illustrations of the model, its strategies and skill set, and applications for lesson design were provided by Murdock and Keller-Mathers (2002a, 2002b) and Keller-Mathers and Murdock (2002). The TIM was intended to be a dynamic and flexible tool for organizing and delivering creativity skills and providing for practice, incubation, and application of those skills in any content area—not to define or prescribe a specific set of creativity skills or tools.

Learning and Practicing Problem Solving

An explicit, deliberate approach to problem solving serves a number of purposes that extend beyond what people might do using only individual generating or focusing tools. For example, knowing and applying a problem-solving model or process can help you to be aware of, and to extend, your natural problem-solving strengths. It can help you to ensure that you are asking the right questions and identifying the real opportunity or challenge; to expand the number, variety, or quality of options you might consider; to change perspective; and to extend your efforts beyond your beginning comfort zone. A structured process can also help you focus on relevant data and options, navigate your way through a maze of resistors and distractions, and guide you as you define and implement a workable solution or plan of action. All of this takes place within the framework of an explicit, organized process within which you make informed decisions about how to proceed. In an interview for *Educational Leadership,* consultant Ken Robinson highlighted this, noting that:

> a creative process may begin with a flash of a new idea or with a hunch. It may just start as noodling around with a problem, getting some fresh ideas along the way. It is a process, not a single event. (Azzam, 2009, p. 22)

There are several approaches to the process and models to describe creativity and problem solving. Several early models described a broad series of stages. Wallas (1926), for example, described four steps: preparation, incubation, illumination, and verification. Torrance's pioneering work on creative thinking (synthesized, for example, by Millar, 1995, and Torrance, 1995) also proposed four steps: sensing a problem, forming ideas, testing the hypothesis, and communicating the results. Many approaches through the years have described problem solving in relation to a series of steps or stages (e.g., Polya, 1957; Simon & Newell, 1970; Simpson, 1922). Basic tools, such as the generating and focusing tools presented in Chapter 15, often provide the basic building blocks for those stages. After gaining confidence with those basic tools, students will benefit from instruction in a problem-solving process, learning how the basic tools fit as part of that process and how the steps or stages of the process might best be applied.

Edward de Bono's CoRT Thinking and Six Thinking Hats

Edward de Bono (1981) developed an extensive set of tools in his CoRT thinking program. These included five groups of 10 tools each, concerned respectively with breadth of thinking, organization, interaction, creativity, and information and feeling. A sixth set of tools, focused on action, proposed a structured model for drawing on all of the tools to solve problems, involving "target, expand, and contract" in stages described as purpose, input, solutions, choice, and operation.

Subsequently, de Bono (1985) suggested that problem solvers often try to do too much at once. He advised that they divide their thinking into six clear components, with the problem solver's role changing as he or she engages in that component. He used colored hats to symbolize each component of the process: white for the gathering of facts and information; yellow for exploring the positive aspects of a situation or option, where the problem solver probes for value and benefit; black for probing for possible difficulties or dangers, looking for where things could go wrong; red for those points in the process where feelings, hunches, and intuition are explored—where fears, hates, likes, and dislikes are placed on the table; green for an open focus on creativity, the point where possibilities, alternatives, new ideas, new concepts, and new and varied perceptions are considered; and finally, blue for the metacognitive aspects of the process, where the problem solver manages the thinking process and determines which functions should be in play at any time.

Six Sigma

The Six Sigma approach was originally developed at Motorola as an approach to quality control in business. The model is widely discussed as a metric (a statistical concept or expression), a mindset that focuses on the customer and creative process improvement, and a method of strategic improvement (Brue, 2002; Goffnett, 2004). The approach involves components that parallel problem-solving processes in seeking breakthrough thinking and carefully specified improvements, following five steps with the acronym DMAIC (define, measure, analyze, improve, control). The methodology asks the problem solver to first define goals that are consistent with customer demands and to measure the current practice while collecting relevant data. The data are then analyzed to determine cause-and-effect relationships and to determine if consideration has been given to all pertinent factors. Based on the data, problems solvers explore ways to improve practice and to focus more effectively on the target. They set up pilot runs prior to moving into production and then engage in ongoing monitoring of production to allow for continuous improvement. Kowaltowski, Bianchi, and de Paiva (2010) included Six Sigma in a review of methods that stimulate creativity in architectural design education. Ruff (n.d.) reported on applications of Six Sigma in educational contexts, some involving business or management problems (e.g., purchasing processes, improving air quality in a school) and others involving educational and curriculum-related challenges (e.g., preassessment of student knowledge, clarifying faculty teaching assignment procedures).

Synectics

The Synectics approach was developed by William J. J. Gordon (1961) and George Prince (1970). Both Gordon and Prince were associated with the Arthur D. Little Co., a well-known management consulting firm. They were interested in the processes and strategies used by managers and other businesspeople to solve problems and develop new ideas. Their study and personal experiences led them to conclude that metaphor and analogy played an important role in many new creative breakthrough ideas. As a result, they began to devise strategies for individuals and groups to enhance their creative productivity. Although Gordon and Prince later followed separate pathways in their work, both remained actively involved in training and consultation with their own unique ways of developing and using Synectics. Prince and his group focused primarily on business applications, while Gordon and his associates maintained an active interest in education (Gordon & Poze, 1979, 1980).

Two fundamental operations provide the operational starting point for the Synectics approach: making the familiar strange and making the strange familiar. Synectics holds that creative ideas frequently arise from these principles. People make new connections when they can look at something that is familiar and see it in a new way, discovering new possibilities that are often overlooked by others. The importance of a fresh perspective, or finding the new and strange in the familiar around us, is reflected, for example, in the common advice, "We'll have to look at this in a new light."

The opposite process—making the strange familiar—can also be a catalyst for creativity. When people can look closely at something that is very unfamiliar, unusual, or strange and relate it to another part of their experience that is commonplace and familiar, it can be easier for them to deal with the new idea or experience. The strange idea can be dealt with or applied in a new and creative way. Using metaphor and analogy can be a very helpful way to translate those two basic principles into practical strategies or methods. When something is familiar and we want to stretch our thinking or get a new perspective, it can help to compare it to something completely different. On the other hand, when confronted with a new and strange challenge, it can be easier to deal with if it can be compared to an analogous problem or situation that we already know how to handle.

Creative Problem Solving

The Creative Problem Solving (CPS) framework most directly associated with our work today builds on the approach first formulated by Osborn (1953) and extended by Parnes (1967) and Parnes, Noller, and Biondi (1977). Their models eventually led to the formation of a linear CPS model (Isaksen & Treffinger, 1985) with six steps: Mess-Finding, Data-Finding, Problem-Finding, Idea-Finding, Solution-Finding, and Acceptance-Finding.

Work on refining the CPS framework has continued. Isaksen et al. (2011) recognized that in the real world, the process of thinking and solving problems creatively is not always linear, starting with a problem and working step-by-step toward a solution. Although a linear, step/stage approach is often used, many people have found that they enter a process at different points and at different times, depending on the task and their actual needs. If they have a good understanding of the problem or challenge, they might enter the process by generating ideas for a solution. As a result, contemporary research and development has led to a more fluid, natural, and dynamic approach to the process, monitored by a metacognitive component; this framework is called Creative Problem Solving, Version 6.1™ (Isaksen et al., 2011; Treffinger et al., 2006). Figure 14 presents the graphic representation of this model.

In contemporary CPS, Isaksen et al. (2011) proposed that problem solvers may work in any (or all) of the components and stages of the model. Each stage in CPS includes both a generating phase (drawing on the basic generating tools) and a focusing phase (applying the focusing tools). The CPS components and stages include:

- *Understanding the challenge* or gaining clarity about the problem or situation, with three stages: Constructing Opportunities, Exploring Data, and Framing Problems.
- *Generating ideas,* in which problem solvers produce a variety of options for a well-defined problem statement.

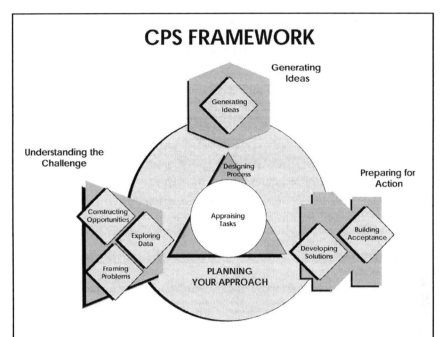

Figure 14. Creative Problem Solving Version 6.1™ framework. From *Creative Problem Solving: An Introduction* (4th ed., p. 18), by D. J. Treffinger, S. G. Isaksen, and K. B. Dorval, 2006, Waco, TX: Prufrock Press. Copyright 2006 by Center for Creative Learning, Inc., and Creative Problem Solving Group, Inc. Reprinted with permission.

- *Preparing for action*, in which problem solvers use the Developing Solutions stage and/or the Building Acceptance stage to move from promising solutions to a detailed plan of action for implementation.
- *Planning your approach*, a metacognitive component, guides problem solvers in Appraising Tasks and Designing Process to prepare for and manage effective and efficient process applications.

Creating Opportunities for Effective Practice

Regardless of the model selected for use in an educational program, the challenge for teachers is to offer students opportunities to learn and practice that model—and the foundational tools within the model—in ever-increasing levels of difficulty and risk. For example, a science teacher set up small groups with the assignment of developing a science project that would be presented at the science fair in the spring. She suggested that students use the CPS framework and a variety of generating and focusing tools to choose a topic, research and plan their project, and carry out their plan in time for the fair. She provided them a list of possible questions their projects might address, but offered them the option of choosing another question with her approval.

The members of one group decided that they needed to know more about the topics suggested by the teacher before they chose. They divided the list among them, and each student conducted online research on several of the topics, including current questions that the scientists still had about each. After sharing their findings, they reduced the list to four topics that had intriguing questions that the group thought that they could explore. Using the Paired Comparison Analysis (PCA) tool, they settled on their topic and question. They then arrived at their problem statement: "In what ways might we devise a study that will address this question?"

Realizing that they needed to know as much about the topic as possible before devising their study, they went back to gathering the data concerning their question, with an eye on studies that had already been done on the topic. An analysis of their findings helped them narrow the data and confirm their problem statement. It also laid the foundation for generating ideas about how to devise their study. In addition to brainstorming, they considered the attributes of the question, looked at previous studies and applied the force-fitting tool (including some random objects they introduced to help them vary their perspective). They also used analogies, such as, "How is this question like a spaceship?" The group used several focusing tools to narrow down their options to a few promising approaches that would help them gather data on their research question. The students then moved on to developing a plan, identifying possible resources and hurdles that they would have to overcome. As the plan developed, they identified specific action steps, assigned individual responsibilities for each, and used the Sequencing (S-M-L) tool to determine the order in which they had to be accomplished.

As with teaching and practicing the basic tools, a creative problem-solving process can be taught and practiced across the curriculum, in afterschool activities, and at home. For instance, looking at the evaluation matrix example presented in Chapter 15, the family might have realized that the perfect car for their needs was too expensive. They might then have decided to look for ways to obtain the resources needed to buy the car (forming a problem statement such as, "In what ways might we, as a family, work toward affording our perfect car?"). Using a generating tool like brainstorming, they might have listed 30 or 40 options and then used a tool like Hits and Hot Spots to narrow that list down to a manageable 5 or 10. As they continued to look at their list of options, they might have narrowed them down even more by again using the evaluation matrix, resulting in two or three promising options that needed to be strengthened and refined. To develop the solution, the family members might have looked at the attributes of both the problem and the solution to make sure that the wording and intent were clear and on course. They might have used the ALoU tool to address possible limitations and prepared a plan of action identifying actions that family members would commit to in the short, medium, and long term, ending with the purchase of the car.

Debriefing and Feedback

Systematic practice in Level II also helps students develop metacognitive skills as they learn to monitor their own thinking and to reflect on feedback through the experience known as debriefing. Debriefing involves reviewing any session involving applications of tools or problem-solving methods to examine the process that occurred, the choices that were made, and the results or effectiveness of the efforts. The major purposes of debriefing and feedback are to build competence, confidence, and commitment or to find ways to improve or enhance future performance—not just to identify what was "good or bad" or "right or wrong" in the work. It is often helpful, for example, to use a four-part format for debriefing, as illustrated in Table 15. (In working with adults, based generally on

Table 15

A Four-Part Debriefing Structure

Identifying Positives	Seeking Clarification
Begin by listing the aspects of the activity or session that were positive or successful. Ask questions such as: • What did we do that really worked well? • What were the best parts of this session or activity? • What happened exactly as planned or anticipated?	Next, identify areas of uncertainty or aspects of the activity that were unclear. Ask questions such as: • What wasn't clear to you about anything that happened? • What were you unsure or confused about, or what was puzzling or perplexing? • What do you wish you understood better or knew more regarding what we did (or did not do)?
Seeking Improvements	**Seeking Novel Connections**
Consider anything that might not have been effective or successful by posing constructive questions, such as: • How might we have improved or done this better or more effectively? • What do you wish we had handled differently and in what ways? • What might we have overlooked or forgotten? • What do you wish we had done more (or less)?	Be alert for any discoveries or unexpected outcomes and their implications. Ask questions such as: • What did we discover from this activity that we didn't know or hadn't tried before? Did any new possibilities come to mind? • What surprised us or happened that we didn't expect? What did we learn from that? • Are there any new ideas that we might want to try out in the future?

work by de Bono, these four categories are alternatively labeled Areas of Praise, Areas of Clarification, Areas of Improvement, and Areas of Amplification.)

A positive debriefing session allows students to reflect on their instructional experience and to think about their decisions while in process. Supportive and honest feedback helps students to become comfortable listening to their inner voice, be open to considering novel approaches to a challenge, and have the courage to pursue courses of action that promise to bring about an appropriate conclusion. With guidance, students are able to recognize relevant and appropriate ways to use the problem-solving tools and process independently and to expand their personal toolbox (Treffinger et al., 2002).

Taking the Chapter Forward

○ This chapter addressed Level II of the model for teaching and learning productive thinking discussed in Chapter 7, concerning systematic practice with creativity tools and problem-solving skills. Level II challenges students with realistic tasks involving a growing degree of openness and risk, extending the students' competence, confidence, and commitment as they gain experience. Many publications and web-based resources (e.g., Schoonover, Treffinger, & Selby, 2012) offer ideas for realistic practice problems. Explore these sources and try several of these suggestions with your own students. Many structured programs and competitions are also open to individuals and teams locally, nationally, and internationally. Several of these also offer publications that provide practice problems you can adapt to your setting; these programs are the focus of Chapter 17.

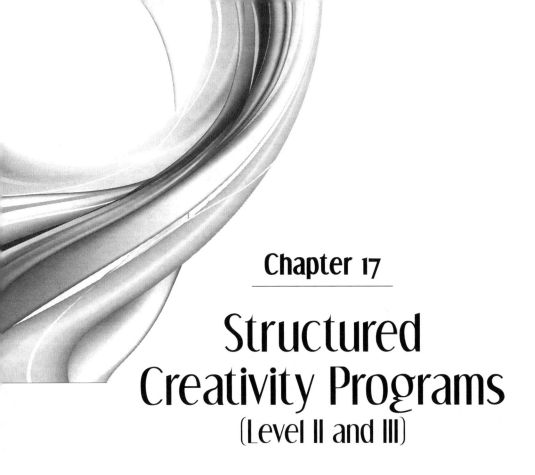

Chapter 17

Structured Creativity Programs
(Level II and III)

When students engage in creative problem solving as part of a structured program or competition, they must put their acquired skills to the test in ways that are intrinsically motivating and that offer meaningful in-depth feedback and new learning. After reading this chapter, you will have a better understanding of how structured programs that are part of the regular school offerings can promote learning and practice of the creative problem-solving process and tools. You will also have an awareness of some of the many programs and competitions available to students that are provided by not-for-profit and for-profit organizations. Participation in these programs may take place in the classroom or after school in a club setting. Students who belong to certain homeschool groups may also enjoy these programs. Various community organizations like the Boys and Girls Club or the YMCA may also offer structured creativity programs and/or competitions.

Structured Creativity Programs

Many structured programs are available both within and beyond the school setting that offer realistic opportunities for students to put their problem-solving skills to work while trying to attain a specific objective. They might be offered as part of a course, often for gifted and talented enrichment, or as extracurricular offerings. For the most part, participation is left up to the student and is open to anyone interested. Meador, Fishkin, and Hoover (1999) reviewed research evidence relating to a number of models and programs for fostering creativity and concluded that evidence supported beneficial effects of training on initial development of skills, while noting that additional support and training may be necessary to promote transfer of learning to real-life problem solving. This underscores the importance of extending creativity instruction through all three levels of the model presented in Chapter 7, viewing tools instruction, practice problems, and programs for real problem solving as essential elements of a comprehensive and ongoing instructional approach, rather than treating instruction in tools alone, practice problems alone, or participation in programs alone as sufficient. As an important component of a comprehensive instructional approach, then, structured creativity programs can also provide excellent opportunities for engaging students in finding and solving real problems, building on and extending their expertise in creativity and problem solving. Structured creativity programs are additions to in-class assignments and help put course content into a meaningful context. Ozturk and Debelak (2008) noted that "in academic competitions, it is possible to make the depth and breadth of content limitless" (p. 47).

Structured School-Sponsored Programs

There are many opportunities to structure school programs in ways that promote the use and practice of the creative problem-solving process and tools. The efficacy of a school newspaper or yearbook editorial board might be greatly increased if the members were well versed in the CPS process and tools and they were part of the standard operating procedures of the group. The process and tools can enhance the efforts of any teacher preparing students for a science fair. For 25 years, a music and drama teacher in a northeastern school district directed a program in which students wrote and produced an original musical play. Sixth- and seventh-grade students would begin work in late May, work through the summer and fall to produce a story and musical score, go into auditions and begin rehearsing in January, and present their production to the community in late March.

During the early years of the project, there was little attention to process and no attention to problem-solving tools beyond brainstorming. However, with ongoing study and training on the part of the instructor, both tools and the problem-solving process were gradually introduced, improving the efficiency of the work sessions and the outcomes of the program. Eventually, the various elements of process could be observed in almost every aspect of the project: script and score development, set and costume design, choreography, and sales. Students used several generating and focusing tools. During preparation, feedback among the students and the professional staff members involved flowed freely. Problems were addressed jointly. Changes and improvements in the production were made up to the closing performance. The productions also required students to draw widely on their content knowledge as writers, composers, designers, and even engineers. Typically, by opening night, more than 25% of the school's population had played some part in bringing the production to the stage.

National and International Programs

Most structured programs and competitions are sponsored by organizations outside of the school. All of them have a fee schedule for team and individual participation. Many programs also have printed and electronic training and instructional material available for purchase. We will look closely at four of these programs and then more briefly at a sample of the much longer lists of opportunities for students to practice applying their creative problem-solving skills.

Future Problem Solving Program International (FPSPI). E. Paul Torrance, a pioneer in creativity research, founded the Future Problem Solving Program (International was added later), also known simply as FPS. For more than four decades, the program has presented challenges to students designed to stimulate their interest in creativity and problem solving while providing opportunities for talent development across several domains (Treffinger, Nassab, & Selby, 2009). Under the direction of their teacher or coach, students in grades 4–12 use a six-step problem-solving process to explore and propose plans of action to complex social challenges. FPS offers opportunities for students to learn their skills in a noncompetitive component or to compete at the local, affiliate, and international levels. The program's stated goals for participants are to enable them to:

- develop and use creative thinking skills,
- learn about complex issues that will shape the future,
- develop an active interest in the future,
- develop and use written and verbal communication skills,
- learn and utilize problem-solving strategies,
- develop and use teamwork skills,
- develop and use research skills, and
- develop and use critical and analytical thinking skills.

The program offers four principal components designed to address these goals. Each calls for the participants to develop and exercise skills in creativity, problem solving, teamwork, and collaboration, emphasizing a concern for the future. Often teams are classroom based, where the teacher becomes the coach and uses the challenges and other program material as an approach to Problem-Based Learning. For competition purposes, there are three divisions for grades 4–6 (Junior), 7–9 (Middle), and 10–12 (Senior). Top-scoring local teams on the qualifying problem are invited to participate in Affiliate Bowls held each spring. Wining teams at the regional level are invited to compete at the annual International Conference. The program's principal components are:

- *Global Issues Problem Solving (GIPS).* This component is available to individuals or to teams of four students, who are provided opportunities to apply their research, analytical, and writing skills. Participants complete two practice problems and one qualifying problem, which are scored by trained evaluators. Evaluations are returned with feedback that includes suggestions for improvement. Specific topics are selected each year for the two practice problems, the qualifying problem, the Affiliate Bowl, and for the International Conference. For example, the 2010–2011 topics were healthy living, air transport, genetic testing, water quality, and emergency planning. The topics for 2011–2012 included all in a day's work, coral reefs, human rights, trade barriers, and pharmaceuticals. For 2012–2013, the topics are culture of celebrity, robotic age, megacities, and ocean soup.

o *Scenario Writing.* In this component, each year students choose from the same topics as the GIPS component to compose a futuristic short story. In order to meet this challenge, students research the topic and current trends to project a solution 20 years in the future.

o *Community Problem Solving (CmPS).* This component is also offered for teams or individual participants. CmPS teams may exceed four members based on the challenges that they adopt and local realities. Community problem solvers apply their academic and problem-solving skills to real problems in their school or community, tackling a challenge defined on the FPSPI website as "a problem that exists within the school, local community, region, state or nation." CmPS provides students with action-oriented opportunities to link creative problem solving directly to community service and to follow their efforts from their initial ideas into action and results.

o *Action-Based Problem Solving.* This yearlong component is noncompetitive. It is designed specifically for use in the classroom. Students learn the skills of creative problem solving in an approach that is nonthreatening and hands-on. Teams of four to six students work on one topic each semester. Unlike the other components, the three divisions for Action-Based Problem Solving are grades K–3 (Primary), 3–6 (Junior), and 6–9 (Middle).

The FPSPI program models activities that offer opportunities for students to develop their talents and problem-solving skills, with each component adding educational value in its own unique way. Students engage in real-world issues, applying their strengths, interests, and passions. Training is available for adult leaders in the program, and a variety of well-developed training and instructional materials are available. The program's effectiveness and impact has been supported in several published studies (Buckmaster, 1994; Cramond, Martin, & Shaw, 1990; Crenwelge, 1992;

Olenchak, 1994; Tallent-Runnels, 1993; Treffinger, Selby, & Crumel, in press). For more information about the Future Problem Solving Program International, visit http://www.fpspi.org. Recent presentations by program alumna to both adults and student FPSPI participants (one at the FPSPI International Conference in 2010 and the other at the Florida State Bowl in 2011) also provided significant insights into the personal impact and value of participation in the program. Both presenters gave us permission to share their presentations.

My very first FPS International Competition was here in Wisconsin for my scenario and with my booklet team. I stood on the main stage and read my scenario about toxic waste with my mother watching in the audience. And she's here again, so students, hear it now, proud parents of FPS are always proud parents of FPS. But that scenario in eighth grade was really the beginning of my writing career in many ways, and the skills from the booklet competition have helped me take that career to the next level.

I came to FPS Internationals for the next 4 years doing both the booklet competition and writing scenarios. Now how many of you are on a booklet team? So, if you were anything like my team, we had the quirky thinker who often cracked jokes to keep things light, the scientific mind who sometimes drove us mad with her science fiction ideas, the writer who always ended up racing to finish that best solution, and the mediator who would keep us from killing each other. Ah, yes, this seems to sound like a lot of your teams. Well, honestly, the skills I learned in that room have helped me be successful in Hollywood.

I was a writer for a new television show, which meant that I spent all day, every day in a room with eight other talented writers. We learned each other's strengths and weaknesses, and truly had to work as a team to meet our deadlines. Now, I'm not going to say we didn't disagree sometimes, but at the end of the day, you only have each other to make it happen. It was us against the world. Well, one day, the producer came into the room and said that Tori Spelling had to postpone her appearance on the show, and the episode we were about to shoot had to be scrapped. And after about 3 minutes of stunned terror, we all began to brainstorm. As FPSers, we use both the logical side of our brain and the creative side, which is a rare and great talent. It's how many of you will excel in college while driving your roommate mad—to this day my freshman roommate hates that I write so fast, thanks in part to FPS. So there we were, trying to come up with a new script and as I helped brainstorm new plotlines, or new solutions so to speak, I was also able to see the inherent problems we might run into if we only had a day to prep the shoot. And when I met up with my friends for dinner that night, mentally exhausted, I said that a lot of my coworkers had looked at me funny for jumping all the way from Problem A to Solution Z while they were still at the beginning. My friends said, "You do that all the time, Allison." I laughed, "Well, I am a Future Problem Solver." So much so that apparently they've stopped planning ahead when I'm around. Anyone else have that problem?

In life, we don't always get to be part of a team, for good or bad. In 10th grade, my team headed off to pursue other interests, so I began to compete as an individual in the booklet competition. There is nothing better in this world than learning young that you can be given a huge project and deadline and make it happen all on your own. It's something a lot of your peers now and in the future will admire about you: your confidence in both writing and critical thinking. If you're here today, then you all have those skills. My most recent project has been writing on *Mean Girls 2*, the sequel to the Lindsey Lohan original *Mean Girls*. Now admittedly, some of the antics in that film I learned during my off time at FPS, say at the dances, but we won't go into that now. In the competition, I learned how on my own to dissect a story, find the inherent problems, and set out to solve them, which is exactly what I did with *Mean Girls 2*. I was hired to come in and rewrite an existing script. They gave me an idea of what they were looking for, so I read the script and immediately was able to list certain problems: character arcs, lack of meanness in the mean girls (which you know, is sort of important), and a few fun moments that could be amped up. But it's not just about identifying the story problems as a writer, it's about being able to fix them.

Scenarios made me realize I loved to write, to create new worlds and characters. It was important that someone outside of my circle of family and teachers said to me, "You're a good writer, you have talent." Because it's not always easy in life to follow your dreams, but if you truly know what you're good at and what you love, you can be successful.

Working on *Mean Girls 2* has been so much fun, especially since they start shooting the movie in July. So now they give me new problems to tackle like locations, timing, and budget. My producer said he loved how I thought about the budget before I wrote a scene because a lot of creative types let their imagination run wild without thinking about how to implement their vision. That's what you all do: You think of the best way to solve a problem, a way that someday in the future can truly be a reality.

As we face all these serious problems in the world, like your topic of green living that's so very topical with the recent oil spill, I can only hope that some of you will go on to use these skills to not only fix our problems, but think and avoid them before they happen. Whether it be in the arts or sciences, whether your problems are as large as world issues or as artistic as theater, every contribution you make is an important one. FPS will help you excel not only in the rest of your education but in your career and your relationships. Congratulations to all of you on the excellent work you've done and will do in the future.

—Allison Schroeder, WGA writer

The Future Problem Solving Program taught me to be a creative thinker. When in my undergraduate career at the University of Florida, I wanted a pair of very expensive blue jeans. When I asked my parents to buy them for me, they said the three words college kids dread most: "Get a job."

I had to think of a way to make some money, which is when my FPS instincts kicked in. I brainstormed ideas until I found the perfect one—I would clean houses after class and eventually I'd be able to buy all of the blue jeans I wanted.

Now, almost 3 years later, my small idea has turned into a large-scale business operation. My company, Student Maid™, has provided more than 900 jobs and 75 internships since its existence. We have completely changed the reputation of the cleaning industry by only hiring students who meet a minimum 3.5 GPA requirement. With a little creativity, I took a business model that had lost its pizazz and turned it completely upside down.

I know parents and teachers will always tell you that the stuff you are learning now you will use later in life—and trust me I didn't believe them either—but it is true. I used every step of the FPS process in my journey as a young entrepreneur, and I am confident that the reason I am successful is because of the program. I had to brainstorm business ideas, generate criteria to choose the best one, and then write the action plan that would allow it all to happen. I learned how to be a part of a team, which has ultimately made me a better boss and business owner.

I truly believe that my FPS skill set is my competitive advantage and is what sets me apart from the rest. It can be yours, too! This program reinforces that with creativity and out of the box thinking, anything can be accomplished.

—Kristen Hadeed, founder of Student Maid™

Destination Imagination (DI). The DI program was founded in the summer of 1999 at an international meeting of almost 200 volunteers dedicated to creating a global program that would provide students with a positive, exciting, and supportive experience in creativity, problem solving, and teamwork. The program now serves students in more than 30 countries. At its core, it is an educational program in which students develop and present solutions to open-ended challenges in a tournament setting. The program describes its mission as encouraging:

> teams of learners to have fun, take risks, focus, and frame challenges while incorporating STEM (science, technology, engineering, and mathematics), the arts, and service learning. Our participants learn patience, flexibility, persistence, ethics, respect for others and their ideas, and the collaborative problem solving process. (Destination Imagination, 2012b, para. 2)

Destination ImagiNation's challenges are open-ended and motivate students to work creatively in a team of up to seven members to solve both a Team Challenge and an Instant Challenge. The challenges are multidisciplinary in nature. It usually takes from several weeks to several months for a team to choose a challenge, work on solving it in their own creative way, and develop their solution for tournament presentation. According to DI (2012a),

> There are seven new Challenges to choose from each year. Each of the Challenges is developed by a team of educators and industry experts who target a particular area of the curriculum and its related standards of content and performance. The areas of focus include: Technical, Scientific, Fine Arts, Improvisational, Structural and Service Learning. There is also a non-competitive Early Learning Challenge that allows participants to develop social and problem solving skills. (para. 4)

A preview of the current year's challenges can be found online at http://www.destinationimagination.org/challenge-program/challenge-previews.

Supportive national program evaluation results have been reported for DI (e.g., Callahan, Hertberg-Davis, & Missett, 2011; Treffinger, Selby, & Schoonover, 2004). While practicing to solve their DI challenges, students develop skills that they carry over into real life as they work their way through the 21st century. One alumna of the program, for example, is Dr. Kristen Jerger, a patent holder for many high-tech tools that provide surgeons increased control and precision. Her patents include one for the design of the Cavitron Ultrasonic Surgical Aspirator (CUSA), which is used in neurosurgery and liver procedures. For several examples of stories of individuals for whom DI has made a difference, visit http://www. destinationimagination.org/who-we-are/success-stories.

Odyssey of the Mind (OM). A founder of OM, Dr. Sam Micklus, was a professor of Industrial Design at New Jersey's Rowan University (formerly Glassboro State College). Challenges that he gave to his undergraduate students to create interesting devices like a mechanical pie thrower were evaluated not so much on the success of the solutions as on the ingenuity and risk taking that was involved in their solutions. In time, this approach brought about the development of a competition for students, kindergarten through college, emphasizing creative problem solving in a supportive, low-risk environment. Today, OM is an international educational program that, as reported by its literature, involves thousands of teams from approximately 25 countries.

Although the CPS framework and tools are not explicitly part of the program, they are implicit in the challenges students face, and we have known a number of coaches who have applied them with their OM teams. Students tap into their creativity and are encouraged to explore imaginative options and paths to a solution through the creative thinking process. Team members practice divergent thinking by tackling open-ended problems covering a wide range of content and interests while developing team-building skills. These challenges are in two main problem categories, long-term and spontaneous. Long-term problems are worked on over a period of one or more months. They are described on the organization's website as being "fun activities" that require time to create a satisfactory solution. Students can compete in five categories of long-term problems: mechanical/vehicle, technical performance, classics, structure and performance.

Spontaneous problems are designed to be "brain builders." Solutions can be created and implemented in about 10–30 minutes. These problems may build on verbal or mechanical skills or a combination of both. Teachers find that these problems and other OM offerings can provide the foundation for a well-rounded education.

Participation in OM teams is divided into four divisions based on grade level and age. Allowances are made for differences in grade level experienced by international teams. Schools, community groups, and homeschool groups are invited to enter one team per problem for each division. The divisions are: Division I (grades K–5 or under 12 years of age), Division II (grades 6–8 or under 15 years of age), Division III (grades 9–12 or where the oldest team member does not qualify for Divisions I or II and is attending regular school—not a college or university), and Division IV (collegiate teams).

Materials are available to teachers and coaches that are designed to help students develop their thinking skills and/or prepare for the team competition. They include creative competitions books, learning activities, online games, and curriculum activities designed jointly by Odyssey of the Mind and NASA. The learning activities provide parents and teachers with hints to imbed the activities into content areas like science in ways that will make school instruction more exciting. Meador et al. (1999) summarized studies that indicated support for the effectiveness of OM on several affective and cognitive variables for certain students. For more information about Odyssey of the Mind, visit http://www.odysseyofthemind.com.

Camp Invention. Unlike the three programs already discussed, Camp Invention is noncompetitive and almost totally school based. Designed to support and enhance the science education programs already provided by local school districts for elementary students in grades 1–6, the innovative and timely curriculum and instructional materials are delivered to participating educators in an all-inclusive package. The package includes detailed step-by-step instructions and staff training materials. Generally, the cost of operating a Camp Invention program is covered by parent-paid tuition.

Camp Invention is a program of Invent Now®, Inc., formally known as the National Inventors Hall of Fame, a nonprofit organization dedicated to promoting creativity, advancing innovation and entrepreneurship, and bringing recognition to inventors and invention. Invent Now®

curriculum writers are charged with producing innovative instructional activities and materials that align with state and national standards. The problem-based approach to instruction fosters teamwork, creative problem solving, and other important life skills identified as imperative for success in the 21st century.

The Camp Invention program typically takes place over the course of a single week, with young students rotating daily through four different modules. Each module "encourages working in diverse teams, engaging in investigations, experiments, and engineering challenges that combine science, technology, engineering, and math (STEM) in fun, hands-on activities" (Camp Invention, n.d., para. 1). A sample from a long list of module titles include:

- W!LD: Wondrous Innovations and Living Designs™,
- The Curious Cypher Club™,
- Bounce! An Atomic Journey™,
- Problem Solving on Planet ZAK®,
- Saving Sludge City™,
- Hatched™, and
- I Can Invent: Edison's Workshop™.

In most of the modules, students receive direct instruction in generating and focusing their ideas, as well as the guidelines for generating ideas. Students are encouraged to apply their skills to solve the problems that form the basis of each lesson. For instance, in the I Can Invent: Edison's Workshop™ module, students learn both the joys and challenges that real inventors face when engaged in the process of inventing something totally new. Working in teams, participants create multistep inventions built with parts of broken appliances and recycled materials. This invention requires that students apply both creative and critical thinking, not only to the design of their machine but to other problems and challenges that arise during the week.

In an evaluation study (Saxon, Treffinger, Young, & Wittig, 2003), the overall satisfaction of those involved in the program (teachers, students, and the parents of participating students) was very positive and supportive. Words used by campers included fun, challenging, exciting, and interesting. The hands-on nature of the curriculum and the enthusiasm for the program displayed by their children greatly impressed those parents responding to the study. For more information about Camp Invention and other Invent Now® programs, visit http://www.invent.org/camp/ teachersbringcamp.aspx.

Other structured programs. In 2008, Ozturk and Debelak reported on 32 academic competitions, including three of those reviewed above. Yahoo.com has a directory of K–12 academic competitions at http:// dir.yahoo.com/Education/academic_competitions/k_12/ that you might find useful to explore. Although not all of these provide explicit materials that support creative problem-solving instruction or the application of the process or tools of creative problem solving, many provide opportunities for educators to facilitate the use of the creative process and tools while preparing for the challenges each program presents. Below is a brief sample of these programs.

- *Doors to Diplomacy*: The U.S. Department of State sponsors this international e-learning challenge in order to teach communication and collaboration skills and to raise awareness of the importance of diplomacy. It is managed by the Global SchoolNet Foundation. Teams of two to four students ages 12–19 are guided by one or two adult coaches to produce web projects that will teach others the importance of international affairs and diplomacy. Students compete in three areas: Collaborative Web Project, Project Narrative, and a Peer Review Process. For more information, visit http://www.globalschoolnet.org/gsndoors.

- *ExploraVision*: Toshiba and the National Science Teachers Association started this science competition in 1992 for students in grades K–12. Working with their teacher in class or with a coach, teams of two to four students choose a relevant technology to explore in depth, and then they project what that technology will be like in 20 years. Competition winners are awarded cash prizes in the form of savings bonds. For more information, visit http://www.exploravision.org.

- *Future City Competition*: This is a national program designed for students in grades 6–8, who are challenged to imagine, design, and build a city of the future. Teachers may also use the program's challenges and materials in their classroom without competing. Students work with both an educator and engineer mentor and test their designs using SimCity™ software. The program helps students build 21st-century skills, including the application of math and science to real-world issues, communications skills, research skills, and the ability to work with a team. For more information, visit http://futurecity.org.

○ *Math Olympiads for Elementary and Middle Schools*: Founded in 1977, the program has teams from all 50 states and 30 countries in grades 4–8 participate. The program's goals include stimulating a love for mathematics, teaching major strategies for problem solving, and fostering mathematical creativity and ingenuity. For more information, visit http://www.moems.org.

○ *Science Olympiad*: This program has operated for 28 years, serving students in grades K–12. Younger students engage in exciting programs in the school setting. Competition divisions are provided for students in grades 6–9 and 9–12. The program operates in all 50 states with about 6,200 teams competing. Participating students are exposed to practicing scientists and mentors. For more information, visit http://soinc.org.

○ *The Discovery Education 3M Young Scientist Challenge*: This competition for students in grades 5–8 attracts hundreds of applications a year. Finalists compete for a cash prize awarded after a series of challenges. The student's scientific knowledge and ability to creatively communicate the scientific process used are considered in awarding the prize. The program offers lesson plans, webinars, interactive video resources, and other materials. For more information, visit http://www.youngscientistchallenge.com.

○ *The Promising Young Writers Program*: The National Council of Teachers of English established this program in 1985. It is school-based for students in the eighth grade and is designed to develop writing skills and to recognize writing talent. Each year, teachers are invited to incorporate a theme and set of writing prompts into their curriculum. Students explore the theme in their reading and writing and submit entries to a school committee that nominates submissions to the program. For more information, visit http://www.ncte.org/awards/student/pyw.

○ *Young Playwrights, Inc. National Playwriting Competition*: This competition is sponsored by an organization founded by Stephen Sondheim with the goal of developing playwrights up through 18 years of age. Theater professionals read and evaluate each submission. Selected writers are invited to attend a Young Playwrights Conference in New York. For more information, visit http://www.youngplaywrights.org/National_Comp..html.

Taking the Chapter Forward

o Space does not permit us to include a complete list of structured opportunities available for students to practice their problem-solving skills in interesting and exciting applications. We have had direct experience with several of these programs. Based on that experience and feedback from literally thousands of students, parents, and teachers, we know that a well-supported, well-run, and well-coached program has the potential to instill confidence, competence, and commitment in students both in terms of expanding their content knowledge and in developing important skills for life.

o Now that you have read this chapter, go online and investigate the programs that interest you. Think how you might incorporate one or more of these programs into your own instruction. Are there program opportunities already offered to students in your school, district, or community that you can tap into? If not, we suggest that you talk to others in your area that might be willing to help in offering one or more of these programs to your students. You may find, in the long run, that the intrinsic benefits to you equal or exceed those realized by your students.

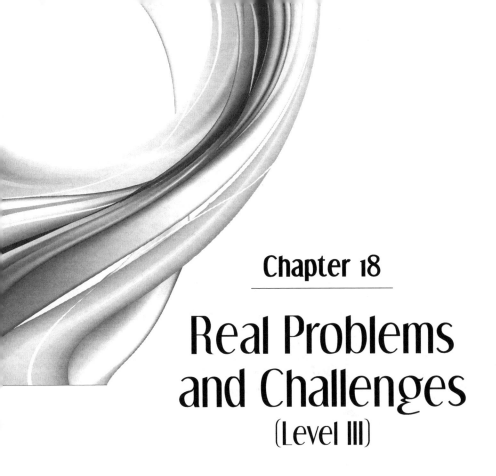

Chapter 18

Real Problems and Challenges
(Level III)

The third level of the model for teaching and learning productive thinking discussed in Chapter 7 is dealing with real problems and challenges. This is an exciting and challenging experience for both educators and students. After reading this chapter, you will be able to define real problems and challenges, define the goals for working on them with students, and explain why these are important aspects of educating for creativity. You will be able to describe several types of real problems for educational settings and to identify a number of resources to help students learn to locate, define, and solve real problems and challenges.

Table 16 describes the goals for Level III and the roles of teachers, students, and parents in carrying out this level.

Table 16

Goals and Roles for Level III (Real Problems and Challenges)

Goals: The student:
- Identifies and assumes ownership for and involvement in real problems and challenges.
- Demonstrates a constructive outlook toward real problems and challenges.
- Demonstrates expertise and imagination in dealing with a variety of complex tasks, opportunities, or challenges.

Teacher's Role: As a manager and facilitator for real problems, the teacher:
- Creates a setting in which real problem solving is valued.
- Stimulates searching for real challenges within and beyond curriculum areas.
- Assists students in identifying real problems and opportunities and in locating and preparing clients.
- Clarifies problem ownership and responsibility for taking action.
- Facilitates process use in problem-solving sessions.
- Serves as a guide to resources (or source of resources).
- Provides encouragement and support.
- Helps cut through red tape and the biases of others.
- Provides appropriate time and materials for students to work on real problems.
- Helps locate audiences and outlets.
- Facilitates effective follow through with and by clients and students; helps students see their efforts through to appropriate closure or completion.
- Guides accountability (record keeping, documentation).
- Introduces new process tools when needed.
- Facilitates debriefing of problem-solving sessions.
- Creates and sustains expectations of quality and effort.
- Models problem solving and reflection in personal behavior and in dealing with day-to-day situations.
- Recognizes and celebrates accomplishments and successes.
- Remains detached from the content of problems and avoids teaching about content or process during problem-solving sessions.

Student's Role. Working independently and in groups, the student:
- Searches actively for and identifies real problems and challenges for applying problem solving.
- Seeks opportunities to serve as a client or resource group member in problem-solving sessions.
- Accepts ownership for personal tasks or challenges and follows through with appropriate actions.
- Discusses or explains to others his or her successful CPS applications using appropriate vocabulary.
- Uses time for independent or group problem-solving sessions productively.
- Maintains records of activities and outcomes for problem-solving sessions or projects.
- Creates and shares products based on problem-solving activities using appropriate and varied products, outlets, and audiences.

Table 16, continued

Student's Role, continued
- Creates, maintains, and shares personal portfolios documenting problem-solving skills and accomplishments.
- Expresses curiosity and interest in learning and using new process tools.
- Celebrates successful outcomes of CPS projects.
- Takes problem-solving tools outside school, applying processes at home or in other group settings.
- Initiates use of CPS for new tasks and begins efforts to be a facilitator for other groups.

Parent's Role. In daily interactions with the student, the parent:
- Provides time for the family to pose problems and challenges and to work together on solving them creatively using appropriate methods and tools and involving all family members.
- Encourages the student to think on his or her own and apply good problem-solving methods and tools when faced with problems with siblings or peers in school or in the neighborhood.
- Supports the school's efforts to involve students in a variety of real-life problem-solving activities and programs.

Defining Real Problems and Their Importance

Learning and practicing a variety of tools for generating and focusing ideas (Level I of the model; see Chapter 15) and working on realistic or practice problems (Level II; see Chapter 16) help students develop the competence, confidence, and commitment they need to be successful in dealing with real-life opportunities and challenges. If students were to have experiences only at Levels I and II, they would miss the most important and strongest reason for creative learning and creative problem solving: acquiring powerful tools and skills that work when people really need them! Level III provides students with experiences that demonstrate and affirm the importance and value of being a creative and critical thinker and an effective problem solver.

In Chapter 1, William's band teacher was slowly encouraging him to accept more risk in his band arrangements. His next step was to work on a piece for public performance. Eric's first presentation was in the relative safety of his classroom. As he and his friend Jimmy took their show on the road, the experience and ownership of it became more real. With success, they were able to continue seeking these challenges as they moved on to middle school. Sue was offered and accepted several opportunities to deal with very real science problems. These opportunities helped her learn, grow, and become even more productive in her field. In each case, the teachers charged with guiding these students held firm to the goal of having them enter adult life with the skills needed to be independent problem solvers.

The renowned educational theorist and philosopher John Dewey (1933, 1938) argued for the importance of relating education to real-life experience, with students learning to find, think through, and solve real-life problems. He saw these tasks as being essential to the whole process of education. When people face a new, uncertain, or changing situation—one in which they are challenged to think of, and act upon, novel ideas and solutions—they need to be able to draw on much more than memory and recall. They are challenged to engage in thinking that matters in life and can make a difference.

We often distinguish between "realistic" and "real" problems and challenges. Table 17 summarizes the key factors that distinguish these from each other.

In understanding real problems, it is important to be clear about who actually has interest and ownership: who wants to solve the problem and who has actual responsibility for taking action or implementing new ideas and solutions. Without that clarity, the problem might appear to be real—to someone—but the students may not actually be able to translate their creative efforts and problem solving into action. We often refer to the person or group with responsibility for action as the "client" for the task and to the members of a group who support the client by generating ideas and helping the client to focus or make choices and decisions as the "resource group" (because they serve as a resource for thinking for the client).

Sometimes students will identify individual or group challenges of their own, for which they will actually be able to carry out their own solutions; in this situation, they might be both the client and the resource group (the problem solvers) at the same time. At other times, a problem that is real may come to the students from someone else: a teacher or administrator, a parent, or a person or organization from the community. The key questions for identifying a real problem are:

Table 17

Contrasting Realistic and Real Problems

Realistic Problems Deal With Tasks or Situations That Are:	Real Problems Deal With Tasks or Situations That Are:
• *Plausible.* Students recognize they could actually occur. • *Interesting.* Students are curious about them or have read, seen, or heard about them; they recognize them as pertinent to others. • *Engaging.* Students perceive them as worth their time and effort. • *Detached.* Not actually part of the students' current personal experience. • *Action unlikely.* Not a situation about which students will actually carry out the plan or solution.	• *Pertinent.* Actually present in the students' experience. • *Intensely involving.* Students feel personal concern about them; they have an impact or personal effect on the students' lives and experiences. • *Demanding.* Students perceive them as being important and necessary for investing time and effort. • *Immersed.* Part of the students' current personal experience (living it). • *Action essential (possible and intended!).* A situation the students will actually do something about or take action on.

- Do you (or does a group that matters to you) really need new ideas for dealing with the situation?
- Are you ready and willing to invest the time and effort that will be required to work on this challenge?
- Will you alone (or with the person or group with whom you are working) have the authority to carry out new solutions and ideas?

Working on real problems is not an exercise or simulation; it's real life, and it counts for more than a grade on an assignment or project. When we had an opportunity to talk with some sixth graders about real problems that they'd like to be able to solve, they provided many and varied responses. Table 18 summarizes their responses.

Finding Real Problems and Challenges

What kinds of tasks or challenges constitute real problems, and how can students or educators locate them? Real problems can be opportunities or challenges of personal interest or concern to an individual student

Table 18

Real Problems Identified by Sixth Graders

• Managing my allowance	• Making chores easier
• Getting along with others	• Feeding the cat; not missing the
• Getting our cat to stop clawing	school bus
• Managing time–lots of after school	• Getting homework done
activities each week	• Balancing chores; time for home-
• Waking up in the morning	work; fun time
• Getting parents to understand what	• Explaining what happens each day
we mean (fads, styles, girl/boy)	at school
• Communication	• New times (stay up later as we get
• Getting parents to buy something	older)
we want	• Listening to my music
• Watching my little brother or sister	• Getting something new when old
who won't mind	one was ok
• Convince mom I'm not cold	• Dog follows me to school
• Friends ask if I like someone and I	• Bundling up your little brother/
don't want to answer	sister, then they have to go to
• One kid messes up, but we all get	bathroom
punished	• School secretary tells mom every-
• Younger child without homework	thing that happens in school
teases me	• Pressure to take after your parents
• Drug, alcohol pressures	(business)
• Mom and dad work long hours; I	• Not enough private time
need someone to whom to tell my	• Picking my own clothes
problems	• Teenage sister brings boyfriend
• I must do homework after school;	home; I get kicked out
brother does his homework later	• Teachers compare you to older
• Parents want you to do better than	brother/sister
they did in school	• Parents nagging me about time
• Big brother or sister is bossy when	playing video games
parents aren't home	• Getting hassled about time on
• Trying not to forget to take things to	computer/Internet
school	

or a small group, projects related to the needs or interests of a class or school, or problems brought to a group by other clients (an outside person or group who wants and needs assistance with an important, open-ended opportunity or challenge).

Treffinger and Shepardson (2012), in the second edition of the *Real Problem Solving Program*, presented guidelines for locating and contacting prospective clients to work with students and for carrying out real problem-solving projects, from planning and design through implementing and evaluating action plans. Real problems can take many forms or varieties. These programs also offer students opportunities to compete with other individuals and teams and to compare their projects, solutions, and products with other students on a local, state or province, national, or even international level. Students engaged in these ways can also benefit from rich experiences, involving travel and networking with other students who share similar interests or passions for creativity, problem solving, and engaging in important community service initiatives.

Project-Based Learning or Enrichment Projects

According to the Buck Institute (2011), Project Based Learning (PBL) is a learning experience in which students "go through an extended process of inquiry in response to a complex question, problem, or challenge" (para. 1). Rigorous and in-depth PBL involves an open-ended driving question or challenge, heightens the need for knowledge of essential content and skills, requires inquiry to learn or create something new, allows for some student choice, and incorporates feedback and revision. PBL involves communication, collaboration, and higher level thinking, including critical thinking and problem solving. It results in an outcome (product or presentation) that is open to public scrutiny and critique.

Many projects that Renzulli and his associates describe as Type III Enrichment (Burns, 1990; Renzulli, 1977a, 1982) also involve attributes of real problem-solving activities. Renzulli (1982) proposed that real problems must have a personal frame of reference (affective as well as cognitive components) and do not have an existing or unique solution already established. He distinguished real problems from puzzles, training exercises, simulation activities, or units of study based on social issues. Renzulli (1982) proposed that the purpose of working on real problems is to bring about change or make a new contribution to a domain.

Components of Structured Creativity Programs

Structured creativity programs can also provide excellent opportunities for finding and solving real problems. In the Future Problem Solving Program International, for example, the projects that students conduct in the Community Problem Solving (CmPS) component (see http://www.fpspi.org/Components.html) have students identify and solve real problems in their school, community, or even on a wider scope, whether working individually or on a team.

Independent Study Projects

Johnsen and Johnson's (2007) *Independent Study Program* provided extensive materials that teachers (or students working on their own) can use as they engage in independent study projects that include real problems. This kit included resources for selecting a topic; asking questions; choosing and using a study method; collecting information; developing a product; presenting information; and evaluating the independent study. Johnsen and Goree (2005) also provided resources to guide students in selecting, planning, carrying out, and evaluating independent study projects.

Classroom- or School-Based Real Problems

Individual students, teams or small groups, and classroom groups who learn generating and focusing tools and a structured problem-solving process, such as the components and stages of the CPS Version 6.1™ framework (Isaksen et al., 2011; Treffinger, Isaksen, et al., 2006), can also engage in real problem solving on a wide variety of opportunities and challenges. They can work on problems of their own design or challenges that arise in their school or community, even if they are not involved in a structured or competitive program for that purpose.

The *Creative Problem Solving Kit* (Treffinger et al., 2006) provided a comprehensive set of activities and resources that individuals or groups of students can use on their own or with guidance and instruction from a coach, leader, or teacher to learn and apply generating and focusing tools and the CPS framework. It also includes a problem solver's *Action*book that can be used to record and document the results or outcomes of any real problem-solving project. Students can use the kit to work on a variety of different real problems. Table 19 describes four broad categories of real problems, based on whether the problem is initiated by students or by an external client and whether an individual or a group will be working on the problem.

Often people ask, "If an outside client (individual or group) presents a problem to students, can it be a real problem to them? Isn't it just "real" for the client?" Regardless of their specific nature or content, problems

Table 19

Real Problems: Opportunities and Challenges

1. Student Client: Individual

An individual student identifies an opportunity or challenge of personal interest or concern and works on it alone or by convening a resource group to engage in CPS.

2. Student Client: Group

A group of students identifies a task relevant to their own school setting, learning, or interest area, on which they are motivated to work collaboratively.

3. External Client: Student-Initiated

A group of students identifies an external task (opportunity, challenge, or area of concern), which they address by using CPS, and then seek to engage the external agent as a CPS sponsor.

4. External Client: Initiated

An outside client (an individual, an agency, or group represented by an individual) brings a real opportunity, challenge, or concern to a group of students and enlists their involvement and support as a CPS group. The external agent may serve as a client or as a sponsor for the group's efforts.

presented by clients can indeed be real for many students. Many students, and many teenagers in particular, demonstrate a high degree of concern for important issues in their school and community. In addition, they are often keenly interested in areas they perceive as involving strong values or emotional positions. They have a strong sense of fairness or justice in their dealings with the adult world. Especially as they enter their adolescent years, students are progressing from roles in which they are dependent upon the judgments and decisions of others (parents or teachers) into new roles in which they must demonstrate independence and responsibility. They need constructive and self-affirming opportunities to learn and apply the skills that will make the independence they desire possible, worthwhile, and enjoyable for the future. They are quite often interested in, and highly motivated to work on, challenges in which other people (especially adults!) will listen to them and take their ideas and contributions seriously. After seeing that the school board had actually carried out the solution to a local problem developed by a student group, for example, one high school senior said, "That's the first time in 12 years that I remember any adults here listening to something kids said!"

Client-initiated real problems are particularly powerful when it is clear that the client really does want and need new ideas and will be in a position to translate new ideas and solutions into action. The need, the challenge, and the potential for action to take place contribute to the students' involvement and motivation. The solutions will not simply culminate in a class presentation, an essay, a poster, or a project, but in people really doing something about the problem. Finally, students who are concerned with exploring career possibilities and future personal choices will benefit from opportunities to be involved in situations and processes that model future possibilities. Thus, problems presented by others can be real opportunities and challenges that are worthwhile and motivating for students.

Changing Roles for the Teacher (Again!)

Just as the teacher's role changed from providing skill instruction in Level I to guiding and leading practice in thinking and problem solving skills in Level II, there will be another shift when you become engaged in Level III opportunities with students. This shift will be from leadership that guides the students into the role of facilitator. The students' goals are shifting from learning new skills and practicing them to applying the skills they have learned to real concerns and challenges. The important outcomes at this stage are to identify and solve problems, not to learn a process or skill. Accordingly, your role is now to serve as a facilitator, working with clients and students together to help create and maintain a setting in which effective thinking and problem solving results.

The facilitator must be prepared to work with the client and the resource group to establish an environment and guide the group in its thinking (generating ideas and focusing their thinking).

Overcoming Concerns About Independent, Real Problem Solving

Some parents or fellow educators may express concerns regarding the importance and value of work on independent projects and real problem solving. Table 20 presents 16 concerns and possible ways to respond to them.

Table 20

Concerns and Possible Responses

Concerns	Possible Responses
• Independent projects may not be worthwhile elements of the classroom or school program.	• Invite people to observe and participate in project activities. • Distribute specific schedules and plans in advance. • Share products with other teachers and parents. • Prepare news releases to inform others about students' progress at various stages of projects.
• Students will not be covering the curriculum or learning essential basic skills, or important topics may be missed or skipped over.	• Provide specific lists of both process and content skills students will learn and use. • Demonstrate importance of process and teamwork skills for careers and the workplace. • Gather student performance data to monitor their progress.
• Students will choose topics that are too broad or too narrow.	• Teach and apply questions to frame the questions students pose. • Guide students in knowing and applying productive thinking processes. • Develop criteria before starting projects. • Use specific planning forms and contracts to guide students and to individualize.
• Necessary resources are too difficult to read or unavailable for students studying a particular topic.	• Tape record difficult reading material. • Use interviews, guest speakers, and online resources to gain access to information not easily attained in print form. • Use parents and community resource people.
• Students will fail to do deep inquiry, gathering very little or superficial information about a topic or question.	• Use contracting and conferences to explore challenging possibilities. • Link evaluation to higher level outcomes. • Before starting projects, work with the entire group to generate, discuss, and determine quality standards and expectations.
• Students will not know or will be unable to use research skills, data-gathering or organizing skills, or productive thinking.	• Provide prior and concurrent instruction and practice in research skills and in productive thinking strategies (for individuals and groups).

Table 20, continued

Concerns	Possible Responses
Too many students may be unable to move away from being dependent on the teacher.	• Define smaller progress goals to help the students monitor successful progress. • Provide explicit times for conferences with the teacher. • Build explicit peer support structures and responsibilities. • Introduce gradual self-direction through variations in teaching styles.
Students may be reluctant to show or present their results.	• Include opportunities for pairs or teams to share. • Provide a variety of reporting options. • Use student learning style preferences to guide choices for reporting or presenting.
Students may repeatedly seek to change the topic they have selected or the product they will make.	• Establish timelines for project stages at the beginning. • Use contract planning forms. • Require (and establish procedures for) justification with peer and teacher review for any proposed changes.
Unsure about how projects will be evaluated or graded.	• Use contract or point system grading. • From the beginning, involve students in establishing criteria for quality work. • Use a variety of evaluation forms and feedback or debriefing activities.
Some project work may appear to be the work of eager parents as much as (or even more than) the work of the students themselves.	• Communicate goals, processes, expectations, and criteria to students and parents at the beginning (e.g., meeting, newsletter). • Use contracts on which students (and parents) sign off to attest to the originality of the student's work.
Too many students may be unable to complete projects (and some may not be able to finish anything they start).	• Head this off early by using contract forms and establishing criteria and due dates for specific stages of the project. • Identify smaller subgoals or tasks to be completed en route to full project report.

Table 20, continued

Concerns	Possible Responses
• Small-group projects may result in one or two students doing all of the work for the entire group.	• Use group contracts that specify the duties of each group member. • Have a periodic review by the teacher with each group to monitor participation and progress. • Use work record sheets or logs in which each group member records time and activities contributed to the project. • Include evaluation checklists in which all group members evaluate each other (focus on specific criteria).
• Students may rely too much on looking up facts and have difficulty moving away from the knowledge level.	• Work on creative/critical thinking strategies before and during project activities. • Use small-group brainstorming sessions to help stretch each person's ideas about questions to pose, resources to use, and how to organize and present results. • Use deliberate strategies (e.g., webbing) to encourage students to look beyond the knowledge level. • Don't evaluate only with tests of recognition and recall. Develop and use performance criteria and rubrics.
• Parents or others may fear that independent projects mean students will become isolated or fail to learn social or group skills.	• Clarify ways to blend individual activities with other formats (e.g., pairs, teams, small-group and whole-class activities).
• Students may become so immersed in one project area that they may not want to do or work on anything else (fear of over-specialization or not being well-rounded).	• Communicate explicitly how other content areas will also be addressed. • Share and discuss the importance of a passion for learning in the development of high-level talents. • Show how students' special interests can be springboards for learning other skills.

Taking the Chapter Forward

As we have illustrated in Chapters 15 and 16, all students can learn and apply successfully the Level I tools for creative thinking (generating) and critical thinking (focusing). They can also learn a problem-solving process or model and apply it across many curriculum areas and in working on a variety of engaging practice problems, Problem-Based Learning units, or project-based learning activities. To support learning and instruction in these areas, you can do the following:

○ Locate and use web-based resources. The Center for Creative Learning (http://www.creativelearning.com), for example, offers resources relating to the CPS framework. The Prufrock Press website (http://www.prufrock.com) also offers a variety of resources and links to other useful sites. Any of several other structured process models for creative and critical thinking and problem solving, as described in Chapters 16 and 17, can also be applied for similar purposes and goals. One of the major goals of any creativity and problem-solving program in a school setting is to help educators access and use specific methods and procedures to move toward the goal of better thinking for all students.

○ As a teacher and/or a parent, teach the specific skills and tools for creative and critical thinking and problem solving, and then seek *real* problems and challenges for young people to work on.

○ As students work on real problems and challenges, they will grow in confidence and skill. But remember that not every student will be engaged in any real problem to the same extent or in the same way. Provide options that enable students to use the process for individual or small-group problems that are of personal interest. Some students may work best as part of a team or group, while others prefer to pursue extensive projects on their own.

○ Be alert for real problem-solving opportunities and challenges in a variety of settings. Engaging challenges might involve one classroom, an entire school, the home setting, or the community. Consider becoming involved in structured programs that provide ways to apply a CPS process while doing community service (see Chapter 17).

Chapter 19

Creativity and Education Today

After reading this chapter, you will be able to describe and explain at least four ways that creativity and innovation are important to contemporary educational issues and priorities. You will be able to identify practical implications of creativity for students and adults regarding mentoring, at-risk students, curriculum standards, and technology as examples of significant opportunities and challenges for schools and schooling today.

A Plethora of Opportunities and Challenges

There has been a love/hate relationship between education and creativity for many decades. The pendulum seems to swing in a regular cycle between embracing creativity and dismissing it as a frill that there is no time or need to address. Nonetheless, every generation seems to encounter a fresh set of opportunities, challenges, and concerns that seem unparalleled by those confronted by any previous generation. As you move from being a student to becoming a parent or grandparent, or if you work as a professional in education for long enough, you will experience the relentless swing of that pendulum, and you will probably find that with each swing, everyone feels that no one before them has ever encountered challenges of the same magnitude or complexity. (You are also very likely to discover that, in one form or another, many of the same issues and concerns come back to vex each new generation. In the 1950s and 1960s, for example, many were concerned that programmed learning and "teaching machines" were threatening to displace human teachers and turn education into a robotic, assembly-line experience. We have heard similar concerns in the past decade about the incorporation of computers into classrooms, and new concerns are arising about the impact of the Internet and the virtual classroom.) Today, then, as in generations past, there is a plethora of opportunities and challenges facing education.

Many writers have chronicled a variety of problems and challenges relating to building a constructive role for creativity in the classroom (e.g., Beghetto, 2010) and have enumerated many challenges facing education in the first decade of a new century. Boyerand and Hamil (2008) reviewed several key issues, including rising teacher attrition rates and limited parent involvement. Boling and Evans (2008) highlighted a widespread lack of literacy skills and reading failures. Jalongo and Heider (2006) reported that 46% of new teachers in the U.S. left teaching after 5 years or less, and Kopkowski (2008) also described the problem of new teachers entering and leaving the profession. Sitler (2007) wrote about the disheartening and disillusioning experiences of many new teachers, and Anhorn (2008) identified many reasons for rising attrition rates, including inadequate resources, difficult work assignments, and role conflict. As we completed work on this manuscript (in early 2012), there was no shortage of challenges for education. These included:

- policy and governmental mandates and programs (e.g., No Child Left Behind, Common Core State Standards, Race to the Top, Investing in Innovation, high-stakes testing, debates over vouchers, privatization, and charter schools);
- the challenges of technology (e.g., social media, uses and abuses of smartphones, iPods, tablets, podcasts, webinars, real-time video conferencing, Web 2.0 in the school and classroom);

- social issues placing children at risk (e.g., economic issues, with 4 in 10 students in the U.S. today on free or reduced lunch programs; high mobility of families and attendant transitions in attendance; equity and efforts to close the achievement gap);
- administrative and management issues (e.g., suspension and expulsion as disciplinary tools, dress and appearance codes, uniforms, single-gender schools, transportation, year-round schooling, merit pay, limits on teacher tenure, teacher evaluation and accountability, systematic approaches to school improvement); and
- personal issues (e.g., bullying, cheating and plagiarism, school violence, teen pregnancy, responses to gender identity and LBGT concerns).

A Call to Creative Action

Please be assured that our purpose in identifying a lengthy list of challenges and concerns was not to heighten your frustration, nor to communicate a sense of discouragement, despair, or defeat. On the contrary, we believe that these concerns provide a strong testimonial for the importance of, and the need for, creativity and innovation skills for adults in education as well as for the students they serve. Each of the challenges and concerns discussed above presents an opportunity for creativity and problem solving to be applied by educational professionals, parents, community leaders, and students collaborating to make a difference.

Four examples of opportunities for creative action illustrate applications of creativity to educational challenges: mentoring, at-risk students, content or curriculum standards, and technology. In each of these areas, there are implications for creativity for both adults and students.

Mentoring

A number of definitions of mentoring appear in the literature. Roberts and Inman (2001) defined mentoring as "a one-on-one relationship between a young person and someone who is an expert in a field or has passion and knowledge in a particular area" (p. 8). They described a number of mutual benefits of a mentoring relationship for both the mentor and the mentee (the person being mentored). Torrance (1984) also proposed a powerful definition: "A mentor is a creatively productive person who teaches, counsels, and inspires a student with similar interests. The relationship is characterized by mutual caring, depth, and response" (p. 2). The creative opportunities and benefits of such relationships apply for both the mentor and the mentee.

These definitions are appealing because they establish high expectations about the nature of mentoring as a relationship in which the actions, benefits, and learning extend beyond transmitting information for one person to another; this distinguishes true mentoring relationships from coaching or tutorial activities. Some of the key attributes of a mentoring relationship were identified by Treffinger (2003b). A mentoring relationship:

- is a relationship, not just an event or an activity;
- emphasizes mutual involvement in creative work, in which the mentor and the student both contribute in important ways (i.e., it is not simply a one-way relationship);
- is self-actualizing, as it stimulates growth and fulfillment for both parties;
- builds heightened awareness of one's own ability (and responsibility);
- often involves creative and critical thinking, problem solving, and inquiry—not routine tasks;
- includes substantive intellectual and emotional engagement in both process and product;
- involves work that is authentic—representative of the activity of practitioners in the real world—not merely exercises or contrived practice exercises and addresses topics, themes, problems, or issues that really matter to the mentor, the student, or others in the domain; and
- often involves projects or initiatives that lead to tangible results, outcomes, or products, as well as to personal and professional growth for all involved (Treffinger 2003b, p. 2).

Mentoring can have a powerful, positive effect on performance in many contexts, including for children and youth in creative development (Torrance, 1984) and in talent development programming (Haeger &

Feldhusen, 1989; McCluskey & Mays, 2003; Purcell, Renzulli, McCoach, & Spottiswoode, 2001), for at-risk young people from minority groups (Royce, 1998), for preservice teacher education programs (Baker, 2008), and for career growth among adult professionals (Noller, 1997; Noller & Frey, 1983, 1994). The benefits of mentoring have also included supporting vulnerable youth by sharpening their decision-making skills (Ferguson & Snipes, 1994), improving school attendance (Lee, Luppino, & Plionis, 1990), and reducing drug usage (LoSciuto, Rajala, Townsend, & Taylor, 1996), as well as supporting youth in programs such as Big Brothers/Big Sisters (Grossman & Tierney, 1998). In a meta-analysis of more than 50 studies assessing the impact of mentoring programs, DuBois, Holloway, Valentine, and Cooper (2002) identified many benefits of mentoring, especially for marginalized youth. Nash (2001) described the importance of mentoring for parents and provided information about two structured mentoring programs for youth.

Bennetts (2004) interviewed people in the arts, including dance, theatre, music, poetry, writing, painting, and sculpture, regarding their experiences with mentors and creative activities. These professionals reported that mentors acted as critics (providing expert practitioner feedback), as sources of support and affirmation of creative achievements, and as sounding boards for new concepts or project ideas. In these ways, mentors contributed to self-image, self-esteem, self-confidence, and self-worth throughout each artist's life. Early mentors in childhood recognized and validated the creativity of the child, respected the "self" of the child in its uniqueness, enabled the child's self-esteem to develop, acted in a trustworthy manner that commanded respect, and provided opportunities for creative achievement. During adolescence, mentors "supported creativity by providing opportunities for collaborative or personal achievement, helped with transition from youth to young adulthood in school and college, and provided resources and inspiration to feed the creative spark (Bennetts, 2004, pp. 380–381). In adulthood, the artists reported that mentors took their creative work seriously, provided respected critical reviews and feedback, listened supportively to new ideas, and understood their cycle of creative activity.

Nash and Treffinger (1993) described the application of CPS stages and tools as an important step in planning and carrying out successful mentoring initiatives. Frey and Noller (1992), Nash and Treffinger (1993), and Noller (1997) also described the important role of creative thinking and creative problem solving in mentoring relationships; these process tools are important at many levels of age, ability, and experience. Through the application of powerful process methods and tools, children and youth can actually attain mentoring relationships at the high level of expectations proposed in our definition across a broad spectrum of age, ability, and experience. Other critical elements contributing to successful mentoring programs and experiences include fostering strong two-way communication and relationships between mentors and mentees; offering support and direction for the mentors before, during, and after their service; and assessing outcomes objectively.

Noller and Frey (1995) described several factors that motivate mentors, mentees, and action. They emphasized the importance of affective and interpersonal factors in the mentoring relationship and highlighted the need for mutual investment, vision, and creativity. Noller and Frey (1995) proposed that effective action results when there is a focus on teamwork, innovation, discovering and developing talent, removing barriers, and the ability to make deliberate efforts to support and redirect the relationship when necessary. Noller (1997) defined 12 strategies for effective mentoring: a positive attitude, valuing, an open-mind, interrelations, creative problem solving, effective communication, a sense of discovery, focusing on strengths and uniqueness, confidence, awareness, risk taking, and flexibility.

Noller (1997) proposed that effective practices for successful mentoring included encouraging people to have a positive attitude in pursuing goals; to examine their ideals, beliefs, and values; to be assertive questioners and attentive listeners; to be independent thinkers; to assume responsibility for their own actions; and to take risks as an active participant rather than as a spectator.

Mentoring initiatives offer an engaging and cost-effective method to reach out to youth and to provide hands-on training and professional development for both preservice and in-service teachers. Mentoring is a powerful way for teachers of the future to gain real field experience, while at the same time serving as role models and building creative relationships with children and youth. For experienced educators, it offers ways to build bridges between the classroom and the real world outside the school.

At-Risk Students

The formidable challenges in guiding and supporting at-risk students and enabling them to become successful personally and academically also involve creative opportunities. Adults who accept these challenges are called upon to be creative and critical thinkers and problem solvers in many ways. However, we have also learned that creative engagement for at-risk students can give them a new and powerful sense of self-worth and constructive accomplishments that can turn their lives in powerful directions.

In a regional consortium of several school districts, several administrators were concerned about the number of at-risk students who had either dropped out of school or were about to do so. These students were capable of being successful learners, but they often found the school setting socially, emotionally, or intellectually unpleasant and not motivating. The greater their dissatisfaction grew, the more frequently they became involved in behavioral problems and conflicts with teachers and with other students, which in turn heightened their dissatisfaction and often led to poor academic performance. Others often viewed these students in the schools as nuisances, troublemakers, misfits, or other undesirable terms. Many of the students had become so negative and lacking in self-esteem that they did not view themselves as having any worthwhile strengths or talents. They were floating aimlessly, had serious substance abuse problems, and/or were in trouble with the law.

The concerned adults realized that the future life and career prospects were very poor for young people who became school dropouts. Students who failed to complete their education would seriously harm their future career prospects, and many dropouts were at risk of becoming involved in gangs or criminal activities. The adults also knew that many of these young people had talents and potential that might go unrecognized and undeveloped to the youths' disadvantage, as well as to the ultimate disadvantage of society.

This task, like so many complex social problems and issues, was initially surrounded by frustration, negative experiences and attitudes, and anxieties for many different stakeholders. The students were unhappy, as were the school personnel, the parents, and other community members and agencies. The administrators also knew that they would face several challenges: overcoming resistance from some teachers and students, arranging activities outside the typical school setting, and establishing a positive climate for learning, for example. The administrators had studied the content by reading about at-risk students and by talking with a number of students, teachers, parents, and community leaders. The concept of "reclaiming lost prizes" (as it was expressed by one of the group members) began to emerge as a key issue. The students had lost the sense of their own personal "prizes" (their own strengths and talents), and if they could not be reclaimed, valuable prizes would be lost to society, too.

To respond to the challenge, the administrators applied CPS and developed a multiyear initiative (McCluskey, Baker, Bergsgaard, & McCluskey, 2001; McCluskey, Baker, & McCluskey, 2005; McCluskey, Baker, O'Hagan, & Treffinger, 1995, 1998; McCluskey & Treffinger, 1998; Place, McCluskey, McCluskey, & Treffinger, 2000) to connect with these at-risk students and identify and develop their talents.

The project has been successful in helping many young people from the participating communities complete their secondary education (using a variety of alternative pathways), to develop effective life management skills, to find employment or move into postsecondary study opportunities, and to discover and apply their personal talents. Over the life of the 3-year project, 88 students participated. During the first month of the program, a facilitator engaged the students in an off-site classroom. Course content included workshops on conflict resolution, learning styles, nonverbal communication, self-concept, and career awareness, as well as intensive training in CPS. Using CPS tools, the students learned how to move from their "current reality" to a "desired future" (Treffinger et al., 2006). The participants formulated individual growth plans to help them identify and work toward goals. They gained experience in confronting real-world issues, generating new ideas and options, and taking action. Each student who completed this in-class phase earned one high school credit. The second month of the program included a work experience placement, which exposed students to an employment setting (where they had a chance to deal with real-life issues with the help of mentors in the business community). As much as possible, an attempt was made to match student interests to their job placement. Participants who successfully finished this phase of the program earned a second credit.

In both portions of the training, the students were actively involved in the process of recognizing and taking ownership of their own talents.

Many businesspeople were, in fact, happy to provide training grounds and support. Several became mentors to the students and stayed connected to them long after the project ended.

Members of the group found great benefit in their use of CPS. Many once unhappy, relationship-resistant dropouts responded to the Lost Prizes opportunity and turned their lives around dramatically. Fifty-seven of the 88 at-risk youth who participated (65%) returned to high school and performed well, successfully undertook university or community college programs, or obtained full-time employment. The program has subsequently been expanded and extended to a number of other diverse cultural settings (Baker, McCluskey, Bergsgaard, & Treffinger, 2005).

Curriculum Standards

Over the past decade, there has been steadily growing attention to identifying the essential content standards that should be at the heart of curriculum and instruction. Many states have developed and adopted curriculum or content standards. The Common Core State Standards Initiative (http://www.corestandards.org) sponsored the development of standards in mathematics and language arts that are proposed for nationwide use (and have been adopted by a majority of states). Several Canadian provinces have also pursued curriculum reform, and efforts to raise standards for student performance in core content areas have also taken place in a number of other countries worldwide (in many of which the curriculum is already established on a national basis). Proponents of new or expanded standards initiatives hold that such efforts provide information to guide educators, parents, and community leaders in understanding the learning outcomes that are important for all students. According to the Common Core State Standards Initiative (2012b):

> The Common Core State Standards provide a consistent, clear understanding of what students are expected to learn, so teachers and parents know what they need to do to help them. The standards are designed to be robust and relevant to the real world, reflecting the knowledge and skills that our young people need for success in college and careers. With American students fully prepared

for the future, our communities will be best positioned to compete successfully in the global economy. (para 1)

In addition:

> The standards have been informed by the best available evidence and the highest state standards across the country and globe and designed by a diverse group of teachers, experts, parents, and school administrators, so they reflect both our aspirations for our children and the realities of the classroom. These standards are designed to ensure that students graduating from high school are prepared to go to college or enter the workforce and that parents, teachers, and students have a clear understanding of what is expected of them. The standards are benchmarked to international standards to guarantee that our students are competitive in the emerging global marketplace. (Common Core State Standards Initiative, 2012a, para. 6)

The standards movement has not been without its critics (e.g., Kohn, 2010), however, and a number of concerns have been raised: narrowing of the breadth and scope of curriculum, driving teaching ever more toward a "teach to the test" mindset that stifles higher level thinking and inquiry, reducing local or state flexibility and choices regarding appropriate content, overemphasizing minimum competencies at the expense of excellence, confusing rigor with difficulty, and overemphasizing knowledge, recall, and the amassing of large sets of useless information that students fail to be able to apply. Some critics, therefore, view standards and creativity as oppositional constructs for teachers and students.

We have reviewed the content standards from states throughout the United States and from educational agencies in a number of other countries, including the Common Core State Standards. After we completed our own review, examined the work of several other writers and developers, and reviewed other discussions of standards in the literature, we concluded that standards and creativity are not actually incompatible—when approached effectively (and separated from any assumptions that the standard's content must be assessed by standardized, objective tests, an assumption that is not necessary to make). Of course, it is necessary to think creatively and critically and to solve problems that have some kind of content. It is possible to think creatively and solve problems involving rigorous, challenging content (and certainly more important to do) than it might be to think about trivial content. Hence, we decided that it would be possible for any teacher or curriculum developer to construct learning activities in which content standards and tools for creative thinking, critical thinking, and problem solving could be integrated harmoniously. To translate that belief into practice, we designed a variety of classroom activities in which we incorporated specific tools for generating and focusing ideas along with specific curriculum standards. We have now completed more than 80 such activities, spanning language arts, science, social studies, and mathematics content standards. These activities can be useful for classroom teachers, but more importantly, they can serve as models of ways that teachers or other curriculum writers can link thinking tools with a broad range of rigorous and challenging curriculum topics. They illustrate that, when educators apply creativity in approaching educational challenges, innovative resources and practices are possible to attain. You can obtain more information about this project and download several free samples of these activities by visiting http://www.creativelearning.com and selecting "Standards Instructional Activities" from the "Quick Links" menu on the home page.

Technology

It seems that everyone today, regardless of age, is immersed in technology. Computers, iPods, iPhones or other smart phones, and iPads and other tablets are all pervasive in our society and globally. As a result, technology is a powerful force that acts on learning and teaching (both informal and formal) today. This creates a new set of creative opportunities and challenges for educators, parents, leaders of community groups, and students. Adults face the challenge of change and the need to adapt to new technology (and new ways of thinking and relating that accompany it) in their personal life as well as in their interactions, in school or out, with youngsters. In addition, today's technology provides new ways for students to express and apply their creative and critical thinking skills. There are many ways to enhance your students' creativity through technology, and it involves much more than simply giving every student an iPad.

The impact of technology is not only evident in the rapid expansion of personal computers in homes and schools over the past two decades, nor even in the explosive changes in the hardware we access and use. Even greater change and challenge arise from the phenomenon that has come to be known as Web 2.0 (or a second generation of the web). Web 1.0 involved traditional websites: publishing pages, putting information on the web for others to read or copy, or having access yourself to almost unlimited amounts of information from your computer. By contrast, Web 2.0 involves participation, interaction, contributing, and relationships. It is dynamic, on the go, and widely accessible through many handheld devices; it is rapid-paced, mobile, and flexible. It is an image of a web with no hard boundary, a platform for assembling and harnessing collective intelligence through blogging, wikis, social networking, social bookmarking, media-sharing services, and social presence systems, collaborative editing tools, syndication, and notification technologies (Franklin & van Harmelen, 2007). Technology in the schools is now about creativity, collaboration, and connection.

Web 2.0 has the potential to elicit the wisdom of the crowd and also to generate the madness of the mob through virtually unrestricted freedom to contribute. Because users control their own data with Web 2.0 tools, the systems should, in theory, improve as more people use them. A broad array of Web 2.0 tools gives students widely varied learning and sharing experiences. Ausband and Schultheis (2010) argued that these tools would facilitate communication between the students and the construction of knowledge by the students.

It is important to remember, however, that simply using technology does not make teaching with it any more or less creative. Technology is simply another set of tools like white boards, chalkboards, or pencils. The essential element is what you *do* with these tools to enhance your students' creative and critical thinking skills and their Creative Problem Solving abilities. Just because a child uses a colorful marker or crayon to draw a picture does not make his or her product creative. There is a great difference between a paint-by-number painting and an original painting.

Computer technology can facilitate creativity, connections, and collaborations from teacher to teacher, teacher to student, and student to student—and from school to home and vice versa. Fish (2009) described, for example, a case in which students from the Urban School of San Francisco interviewed Holocaust survivors and Japanese internment camp victims and others whose stories would otherwise die with them. The audio interviews were transcribed and were uploaded along with digital photos to the Telling Their Stories (http://tellingstories.org) site. These students took on the role of historians, organized the information along with photos, and uploaded them to the website.

Online tools such as Google Docs are used to create collaborative documents, blogs, and slide shows and to organize data. Google Docs and Google+ are ways for individuals and organizations to share information. Through Google+, teachers can create a classroom "hangout" time for students to talk with the teacher if they are not in the classroom, or teachers can work with other teachers to generate options for curriculum activities. If some of the students are working on a CPS project for a program such as Future Problem Solving International, they could create a hangout, too. Google+ has chat and video chat similar to Skype and iChat, which are other important communication tools. Google+ can also be used to post photos and artwork. Web 2.0 resources encompass literally dozens of interesting and fascinating sets of tools, many of which are free, especially for educators. Of course, they vary widely in scope, purposes, and quality, but these tools could be valuable resources to use in conjunction with a variety of creativity and Creative Problem Solving applications (e.g., when applying generating or focusing tools). Wikispaces includes an interesting site for educators called "Web 2.0: Cool Tools for Schools (http://cooltoolsforschools.wikispaces.com). Schoonover et al. (2012) compiled and compared many Web 2.0 resources and presented a discussion of their potential role (along with blogging, social networking, and gaming) in creative teaching and learning.

Taking the Chapter Forward

o In this book, you have learned about characteristics, operations, context, and outcomes that contribute to creativity and ways to apply them with students. In addition, however, there are abundant opportunities in education today for adults to apply creativity and CPS. In this chapter, we highlighted four examples of such opportunities: mentoring, working with at-risk students, addressing curriculum standards, and utilizing technology. Be on the lookout for ways you can use your knowledge of creativity to address significant issues that your community, school, or school district may face, in addition to bringing creativity into your instructional efforts. In what ways might you also guide your students to seek many and varied opportunities to use their creativity on a daily basis?

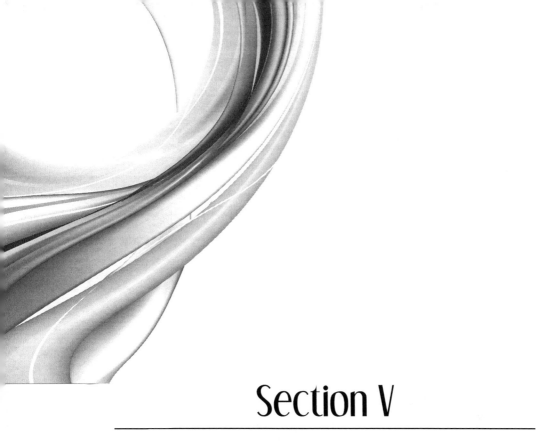

Section V

Looking Ahead

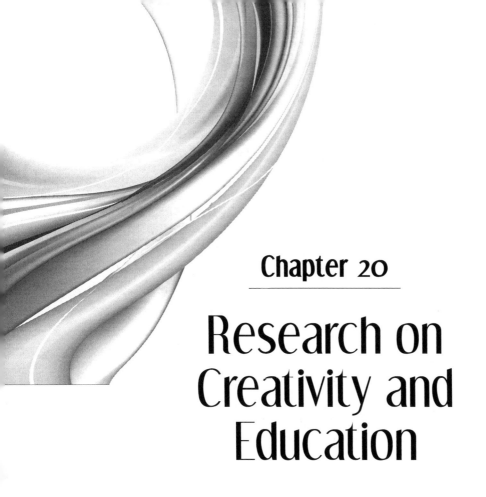

Chapter 20

Research on Creativity and Education

After reading this chapter, you will be able to describe four important purposes of research on creativity. You will also be able to identify nine general approaches to research and give examples of ways each approach might be used in studying creativity. Finally, you will be able to identify at least six areas in which current research on creativity now focuses or in which future research is needed.

Research Purposes and Approaches

If you review any of a number of research methods books or do an Internet search on the topic "purposes of research," you will find many lists with a varying number of overlapping responses. Perhaps at the broadest level will be statements, such as "research is the search for knowledge or any systematic effort to establish facts or principles, establish relationships or causes, or test hypotheses that will support, dispute, or reject theories." Commonly stated purposes for research include describing, explaining, predicting, or controlling phenomena or relationships. Some lists add exploratory purposes (searching in new directions to uncover or discover new insights or issues). One website, Experiment-Resources.com (2012) offered a broad definition of research as "any gathering of data, information and facts for the advancement of knowledge" (para. 1). Creswell (2012) defined research as "a process of steps used to collect and analyze information to increase our understanding of a topic or issue" (p. 3).

Research is often categorized broadly as

- pure or basic;
- action or applied;
- involving qualitative, quantitative, or mixed methods (in describing measurement);
- either library or web research (more often described in scientific settings as "review" than strictly as research); or
- "original" research (involving data collection and carefully specified methods of data analysis and interpretation).

Isaksen, Stein, Hills, and Gryskiewicz (1984) proposed a provocative and more extensive model for formulating or classifying research on creativity with three dimensions: the *unit of analysis* (individuals, dyads, small groups, organizations, or societal/cultural groups), *principal contexts for research* (conceptual/theoretical, stimulation/training, instrumentation/assessment, applications/product development, or identification/selection), and *process aspects* (data retrieval, problem formulation, ideation/generation, decision making/evaluation, and implementing). Isaac and Michael (1997) described nine basic approaches to scientific research, which we have adapted and illustrated specifically in relation to research on creativity in Table 21.

Table 21

Nine Basic Approaches to Creativity Research

Type of Research	Description	Creativity Example
Historical	Reconstructing the past objectively and accurately, often in relation to the tenability of an hypothesis.	What are the origins of the myth that "there is a fine line separating creative genius from insanity"? How did this myth develop? When and how was it debunked?
Descriptive	Describing systematically a situation or area of interest factually and accurately.	Thorough description of the nature of divergent thinking, including its components, instruments used to measure it, and the rationale for its relationship to creativity.
Developmental	Investigating patterns and sequences of growth and/or change as a function of age, time, or human development variables.	Do creative characteristics change with age or gender? Are efforts to enhance creativity at various age levels differentially effective?
Case/Field	Conducting an intensive study of the background, current status, and environmental interactions of a given individual or group.	In-depth study of the ways that architects express and apply creativity in their personal and professional life.
Correlational	Investigating the extent to which variations in one factor correspond with variations in one or more other factors, using correlation coefficients to describe the relationship.	What is the relationship between measures of various creative thinking components (e.g., fluency) and other variables (e.g., problem-solving style)?
Causal-Comparative or Ex Post Facto	Exploring possible cause-and-effect relationships by observing some existing consequences and searching back through the data for plausible causal factors.	Observing that personal criticism inhibits the creativity of children and searching through data from parents and teachers to examine interaction patterns that encouraged or discouraged creativity.
True Experimental	Investigating possible cause-and-effect relationships by exposing experimental group(s) to treatment condition(s) and comparing results to control group(s) not receiving the treatment (random assignment being essential).	Experimental (training in CPS) versus control (no CPS training) comparisons, with subjects randomly assigned to conditions; assessing creative thinking and problem-solving skills and attitudes as outcomes.
Quasi-Experimental	Approximation of true experiment, in which not all relevant variables may be controlled or manipulated (but in which experimenters take these limitations into account).	Conducting a training program in creative thinking in a setting in which intact groups must be assigned to treatments or in which one has little or no control over subjects' other activities or experiences.
Action	Developing new skills or new approaches with emphasis on direct application within an applied setting (e.g., classroom or organization).	Creating a new program to help parents stimulate creativity among infants and preschool children.

Note. Research categories and descriptions adapted from Isaac and Michael (1997).

Issues and Themes for Needed Research on Creativity

Treffinger (1986) reviewed current research on creativity and identified future research needs in relation to the nature and definition of creativity, identification of creativity, and nurturing creativity. Noting the absence of a single, unifying theory and definition, he called for efforts to be more systematic in understanding, describing, and categorizing our theories and definitions. Similarly, he noted, there was no universally accepted instrument for assessing creativity. In order to overcome the fallacy of a single score (or "creativity quotient"), he proposed the need for research and development that would guide the appropriate use of multiple instruments in a profiling approach. In relation to nurture, Treffinger (1986) argued that creativity had been established as a viable and worthwhile educational goal, but that many questions remained to be addressed to make its nurture or development practical in educational situations. He advocated greater attention to instructional challenges, noting that efforts to make creativity a vital factor in education must extend beyond viewing creativity instruction as a grab bag of enjoyable exercises and isolated activities, and instead build on approaches supported by evidence of effectiveness, impact, and transfer to other learning outcomes. He also identified the emerging influence of technology and computers as a significant factor in nurturing creativity.

Nearly three decades later, many of the same broad issues, themes, opportunities, and needs still exist, and several additional areas of concern about creativity in education have emerged. Treffinger (2004) noted that progress had been made in several areas (and particularly in relation to justifying creativity as a valid educational goal), but that many of the core issues and research needs identified previously still remained open challenges for inquiry. Rank, Pace, and Frese (2004) identified three broad themes for needed research on creativity: differential predictors of phases of creativity and innovation, integrating concepts of initiative and voice behavior with other variables in studying creativity, and enhancing an understanding of the effects on creativity of cross-cultural differences in values, motivational orientations, and leadership preferences.

As we consider the present and look to the future, the diverse issues, challenges, and opportunities for research on creativity in education include the following.

- *Conceptual issues.* There is an ongoing need for clarity and explicit presentation of conceptions and definitions that are used in studying creativity (Batey & Furnham, 2006; Beghetto, 2008; Gilson & Madjar, 2011; Plucker, Beghetto, & Dow, 2004). This includes the need for creativity researchers to state their definitions clearly and relate their assessments specifically to the stated definition. It also involves an ongoing need for classification of models and variables used in research, assessment of multiple components, the importance of considering demographic and cultural differences, and the need for longitudinal studies of predictors of creative achievement. The field would also benefit from continuing research that would sharpen our understanding of creativity as a multidimensional construct and promote efforts to inform teachers, administrators, and parents of the nature and importance of creativity.

- *Studies of the "ecology of intervention."* In a complex ecosystem, many components are interrelated and interdependent. The challenges for research on creativity in education are similar. We must be aware of, and concerned with, the total context of the school or classroom (e.g., environment, core educational and community values, professional development, home and community support) as a setting in which creativity and innovation thrive or wither. Education for creativity and innovation can never be reduced to taking out one's creativity book and doing a few pages. There will always be an interaction among many factors addressed in this book. Thus, we need research on how these factors weigh individually and in combination and contribute to meet the goals of creative productivity and innovative accomplishments. With this in mind, research is needed that will provide both comprehensive tools and data regarding the ecology of effective practice in schools today to provide for creativity and innovation. This calls for much more than a catalog of activities in areas that might be considered "creative" and will involve the input from many stakeholders in the educational endeavor.

o *Relationships between creativity and other skills.* In a complex system such as education, and when we are concerned with a complex set of outcomes such as creativity and innovation, our emphasis cannot be only on whether the efforts lead to gains on standardized achievement tests. Focusing exclusively on those criteria overemphasizes the importance of such tests as the ultimate criteria of school success when clearly they are not. In addition, given the richness and complexity of creativity (whether Big C, little c, or mini c), the outcomes are necessarily more diverse and complex than anyone might document and evaluate using standardized test criteria alone. However, even though educators' concerns should not rest exclusively on data from standardized tests, a plausible case might be made that it would be beneficial to know more about the effects or impact of instruction for creativity and innovation may actually have on performance of students on those measures. Inquiry might also be worthwhile on the relationships between creativity and innovation and other essential skill sets, especially those often characterized as life skills, 21st-century skills, or workplace skills (e.g., teamwork, collaboration, leadership, or interpersonal skills).

o *Multiple measures.* Research would also be beneficial in guiding educators in the effective and appropriate use of multiple measures when assessing creativity. The process of constructing and using Creative Strengths Profiles would be enhanced, for example, by research evidence concerning the contributions of various instruments, singly and in combination, to the prediction of actual creative accomplishments in various subject areas or disciplines. The profiling process would be enhanced by greater knowledge of the extent to which tests, checklists, and rating scales provide unique, overlapping, or redundant information and by investigations of effective combinations of various assessment tools in relation to age, gender, and subject area or content discipline. Given ongoing debates (e.g., Baer, 1994a, 1994b, 2011a, 2011b, 2011c; Cramond, 1994; Kim, 2006, 2011a, 2011b) about the extent to which creativity includes generalized factors, domain-specific factors, or a combination of both, research is clearly needed on the instructional implications of various general and domain-specific creativity assessment strategies and assessment tools and combinations of those tools.

o *Cross-cultural studies.* In the ever-more global context of teaching and learning, research is needed on the differential effects of school climate, instructional approach, class size, and related variables on creative learning within and across cultures. This includes, for example, studies that address the extent to which creative thinking tools and process stages are readily "transportable" from an educational setting in North American to other cultures, the ways in which environmental or climate factors may differ across cultures, or the extent to which multicultural exposure and experiences can facilitate creativity (e.g., Maddux et al., 2009). "Little m" multicultural experiences (e.g., exposure to ideas, websites, foreign friends, foreign music) or "Big M" experiences (e.g., living in another culture for an extended period) may both have influences on creativity (Leung & Chiu, 2008; Leung, Maddux, Galinsky, & Chiu, 2008; Rich, 2009).

o *Developmental, neurological, and biological factors and influences on creativity.* There is still no one who has done for the field of creativity what Piaget and Bruner contributed to our understanding of other aspects of intellectual development. Nonetheless, a number of researchers have contributed to a greater understanding of developmental processes that are important in creativity (Russ & Fiorelli, 2010), including cognitive and affective processes and studies of play. There are also numerous emerging studies of biological and neurological factors that relate to creativity (e.g., Bekhtereva, Danko, Starchenko, Pakhomov, & Medvedev, 2001; Kaufman, Kornilov, Bristol, Tan, & Grigorenko, 2010; Klijn & Tomic, 2010; Mölle et al., 1996; Reuter et al., 2005). Longitudinal studies would also be valuable in enhancing our understanding of creativity development across the lifespan (from early childhood through adulthood).

o *Effects of instruction and differentiation.* An abundance of research needs and opportunities exist regarding teaching, learning, and instruction for creativity and innovation. It is no longer relevant or meaningful to pose the simple question: "Can we enhance students' creativity and problem-solving skills?" The answer to that question is "Yes." The contemporary and more important question is: "In nurturing creativity and problem-solving skills, what works best, for whom, and under what conditions?" (Isaksen, Murdock, Firestien, & Treffinger, 1993a, 1993b; Treffinger, 2004). This challenge invites research on themes such as:

> - differentiation by key creativity characteristics of learners (which raises issues that are similar to the challenges of differentiating instruction for many other instructional goals and important skills).

> - impact of the teacher's style, the students' styles, and their interactions on instructional effectiveness.

> - impact and effects of instructional programs and strategies on individual, team, and group creative accomplishments (across all levels of the model for teaching and learning productive thinking). Research in this area might also profitably contrast programs or approaches delivered in different ways (e.g., within curriculum, extracurricular but in school, outside school) and comparisons under varying conditions of teacher/leader role.

> - inquiry that moves beyond the question: "Should creativity development involve direct instruction instead of being content-embedded?" The more important questions today challenge researchers to think about how and when direct and content-embedded instruction are best suited for various learners, tasks, or circumstances (returning to the question: "What works best, for whom, and under what conditions?"). Although creativity may now be more readily accepted as a valid educational goal, for example, Beghetto and Kaufman (2009) proposed that academic learning and creativity should be pursued simultaneously, but are now often arbitrarily separated in ways that are potentially mutually detrimental. They proposed the need for a new metaphor—intellectual estuary—to underscore the idea that both academic and creative streams in education can be integrated.

Taking the Chapter Forward

o Reflect once more on Eric, William, Sue, their friends, and their teachers. Think also of Lucy, Michael, Cheryl, their writing team, and their teacher. How might their educational experiences have been improved in ways that would have more effectively helped these students grow? Would some of the approaches taken by their teachers have benefited student creative productivity among many students? What more would you like to have known about these students and their problem-solving styles? What assessments would have most effectively provided that information? How might the answers to these questions inform your own instruction? What more do you need to know about educating for creativity that we were not able to include in this book? These are just some of the question that we hope you will consider as you go forward in your work.

o Throughout this book we have attempted to illustrate that research and practice can be intertwined. Practitioners today have benefited from research, and their questions can be starting points for future inquiry. By the same token, researchers can influence, and be influenced by, awareness of the challenges of effective practice. Both concerns face an abundance of opportunities and challenges. Whether your role is primarily rooted in practice or scholarly inquiry, creativity and innovation continue to be sources of exciting new challenges. We hope you will pursue your work with energy and passion, and with a commitment to sustaining a relationship of openness and support for both sets of activities. As a practitioner, your work will be enhanced by knowledge of research and by efforts to plan and conduct action research in your own setting. As a researcher, your inquiry will gain power and relevance through your efforts to understand and address the interests, concerns, and needs of educational practice.

Wrapping Up: A Framework for Action

We hope (and believe) that, beyond the function of sharing information and ideas, this book can be a resource that influences the *beliefs* educators hold and therefore can have an impact on what they do; it can be a catalyst for creative teaching and learning in action. We close, therefore, with a review of key ideas and concepts throughout the book that identify what informed, engaged educators believe, know, and do. The chapter-by-chapter list featured in Table 22 is a brief synopsis that may guide you in your own personal review, reflection, and planning.

Table 22

Chapter Synopsis

Chapter	Educators Who Foster Creativity and Innovation		
	Believe That:	**Know:**	**Do:**
2	Creative learning is important for all students; everyone has some creative ability.	The importance of setting aside myths or misunderstandings, keeping an open mind to spot creativity when it happens, and ways to engage colleagues and students in idea generation and focusing.	Dispel myths they may hear about creativity; design activities to help recognize unique potential in all students and to find ways to teach and apply productive thinking tools and processes in the daily curriculum.
3	Everyone sees and views creativity differently; creativity can happen without innovation but innovation cannot happen without creativity.	Several widely accepted definitions of creativity and innovation, the theory and research that supports each, and their real-world implications.	Formulate a personal definition of creativity and innovation based on study and experience and apply that definition to instruction.
4	Creativity and innovation are essential elements of a program of lifelong learning aimed at meeting the challenges of constant change.	An understanding of the processes and tools of productive thinking contributes to one's sense of self-efficacy, productivity, and self-worth in the face of constant change.	Find deliberate ways to teach the processes and tools that are basic to creative productivity in the daily curriculum, engaging students in applying processes and tools independently and through collaborative projects.
5	It is important to understand the essential factors that contribute to creativity and to understand how students experience those factors.	Because students approach each of the four COCO factors differently, there will be rich variability in their thinking and problem-solving choices and behavior.	Discuss with students the relationship among the four COCO factors and help students identify each factor's contribution to their creativity.
6	Characteristics and problem-solving style preference impact how any student will acquire information, learn and apply problem-solving tools, and engage in problem solving.	Unique personal characteristics and style preferences among students; their impact on the ways they approach learning, understand problems, search for solutions, and prepare for action; and ways to differentiate instruction in order to accommodate students' characteristics and style preferences.	Instruct students about creative characteristics to enable them to recognize and appreciate each other's unique abilities, and design activities that accommodate each student's needs in appropriate and challenging ways.
7	Students can learn and apply the mental operations that support creativity and innovation and, with guidance, they can function with competence, confidence, and commitment.	How to guide students in choosing, applying, and managing specific tools for creative productivity and how to encourage students to develop and apply metacognitive thinking skills when generating and focusing ideas, solving complex problems, or managing change.	Design and conduct activities, employing both direct and content-embedded instruction, that provide a strong foundational understanding of creative problem-solving tools and their applications, encouraging students to reflect on their experiences (e.g., through journaling or online blogging).

Table 22, continued

	Educators Who Foster Creativity and Innovation		
Chapter	Believe That:	Know:	Do:
8	A healthy classroom climate is important for productive thinking.	How to create and maintain a classroom climate conducive to productive thinking, including nine specific factors that contribute to a positive climate for creativity and innovation.	Establish and maintain a climate with trust and openness, conducive to student challenge and involvement and with time and support for curiosity, playfulness, constructive debate, freedom, and risk taking.
9	It is important to be explicit about expectations and criteria for creativity in assignments or projects.	Three major sets of criteria in order to assess creativity: Novelty, Resolution, and Elaboration and Synthesis (Style), and ways to engage students in assessing their own work and that of others.	Employ a variety of assessments, including student self-assessments, peer assessments, and assessment by teachers or mentors, to work toward deeper understanding of outcomes.
10	It is possible and important to assess creative characteristics, styles, and creative productivity in ways that are sound and consistent with measurement and assessment principles.	The meaning of important concepts and principles of measurement and assessment and their relevance to assessing creativity.	Conduct the necessary research and inquiry about possible assessment resources to use as a basis for selecting tools wisely and appropriately.
11	It is important and possible to identify creativity among students in a classroom setting.	Indicators of a quality assessment tool that will produce relevant and useable data; ways to use multiple tools and assessments that will provide a comprehensive picture of each student's creative potential and instructional needs.	Ask the right questions in order to design an assessment strategy that will provide the most complete picture possible of each student's present status in relation to creativity.
12	It is possible to identify students' creativity using different data sources and to help them appreciate their creative strengths and promote self-confidence and a commitment to learning.	Ways and tools to gather data from a variety of sources including parents, teachers, and peers, in order to identify each student's current level of performance (not yet evident, emerging, expressing, or excelling).	Design and use profiles that will provide data about each student's current level of creativity and update it on an ongoing basis and document each student's creative work using portfolios.
13	A strong foundation of skills and tools is necessary to build a solid structure for creative teaching and learning that includes differentiated instruction.	How to develop and use Creative Strengths Profiles to provide the information needed to differentiate instruction and when to serve as an instructor, coach or guide, or facilitator.	Have appropriate and varied lessons, activities, projects, and other opportunities on hand for students at all levels of creative development (not yet evident, emerging, expressing, or excelling).

Table 22, continued

	Educators Who Foster Creativity and Innovation		
Chapter	Believe That:	Know:	Do:
14	An effective foundation for productive thinking builds on deliberate guidelines for generating and focusing.	Four guidelines for generating and four for focusing and ways to help students learn and apply them.	Develop and use activities appropriate for students to gain understanding of the guidelines and their applications.
15	All students need to learn and use explicit generating and focusing tools.	The basic tools for generating and focusing and ways to use them in instruction.	Design and provide opportunities for students to learn and apply the tools.
16	Competent and confident problem solvers who are committed to effective thinking need to know and use an explicit process and tools.	CPS components and stages (or another explicit process model) and ways to help students learn the process; how to reinforce students' emerging skills through practice.	Design and provide well-structured opportunities and challenges that build competence in the use of an explicit problem-solving process.
17	Structured programs can provide realistic opportunities for students to apply their thinking and problem-solving skills.	How to include realistic activities through structured programs within the daily curriculum as opportunities to test students' skills as they work individually or collaboratively.	Choose one or more programs that lend themselves to the creative problem-solving process and the application of the problem-solving tools, engaging students in realistic problem-solving situations.
18	It is important for students to work on real challenges that go beyond the classroom and textbook in order to assume ownership of problems and challenges and to demonstrate expertise and imagination in dealing with a variety of complex tasks and opportunities.	Where and how to find real opportunities, how to help students find these opportunities, and how to help students identify whether they are more productive working alone or in groups.	Become a guide and facilitator as students work through challenges, providing them with time and materials, introducing new process tools when needed, facilitating follow through, and providing meaningful feedback where students share and celebrate their outcomes.
19	Many challenges facing education today are also creative opportunities that can lead to positive action for all students; these challenges include a growing need for mentoring, incorporating technology into instruction, supporting at-risk students, and addressing curriculum standards.	A variety of technology tools, mentoring principles and activities, ways to work with at-risk students, and ways to link creativity with curriculum or content standards.	Encourage mentoring for students for talent development; engage at-risk students and challenge them to discover their self-worth and creative potential; integrate content standards with creativity tools; use technology to enhance creative learning.
20	It is necessary and important to read, study, share, and discuss current research about creativity.	How to locate current research, how to read and understand published research; ways plan and carry out my own action research.	Read, share, discuss, and apply research and conduct action research in their own setting, individually and in collaboration with others.

References

Abra, J. (1997). *The motives for creative work*. Cresskill, NJ: Hampton Press.

Adams, K. (2005). *The sources of innovation and creativity*. Retrieved from http://www.skillscommission.org/pdf/commissioned_papers/Sources_of_Innovation_and_Creativity.pdf

Aleinikov, A., Kackmeister, S., & Koening, R. (2000). *Creating creativity: 101 definitions*. Midland, MI: Alden Dow Creativity Center.

Aljughaiman, A., & Mowrer-Reynolds, E. (2005). Teachers' conceptions of creativity and creative students. *Journal of Creative Behavior, 39,* 17–34.

Amabile, T. M. (1983). *The social psychology of creativity*. New York, NY: Springer-Verlag.

Amabile, T. M. (1989). *Growing up creative*. Buffalo, NY: Creative Education Foundation Press.

Anhorn, R. (2008). The profession that eats its young. *The Delta Kappa Gamma Bulletin, 74*(3), 15–26.

Associated Press. (2007, December 2). Trying to come up with ways to teach creativity. *Richmond Times Dispatch*. Retrieved from http://timesdispatch.com/ar/171656

Ausband, L. T., & Schultheis, K. (2010). Utilizing Web 2.0 to provide an international experience for pre-service elementary education teachers—the IPC project. *Computers in the Schools, 27,* 266–287.

Azzam, A. (2009). Why creativity now? A conversation with Sir Ken Robinson. *Educational Leadership, 67*(1), 22–26.

Baer, J. (1994a). Why you shouldn't trust creativity tests. *Educational Leadership, 51*(4), 80–83.

Baer, J. (1994b). Why you still shouldn't trust creativity tests. *Educational Leadership, 52*(2), 72–73.

Baer, J. (2011a). How divergent thinking tests mislead us: Are the Torrance Tests still relevant in the 21st century? The division 10 debate. *Psychology of Aesthetics, Creativity, and the Arts, 5,* 309–313.

Baer, J. (2011b). Four (more) arguments against the Torrance Tests. *Psychology of Aesthetics, Creativity, and the Arts, 5,* 316–317.

Baer, J. (2011c). Why teachers should assume creativity is very domain specific. *International Journal of Creativity and Problem Solving, 21,* 57–61.

Bailey, D. S. (2003). The "Sylvia Plath" effect. *Monitor on Psychology, 34*(10), 42–43.

Baker, P. A. (2008). An access enrichment model for an undergraduate teacher education program. *Gifted and Talented International, 23*(1), 17–22.

Baker, P. A., McCluskey, K. W., Bergsgaard, M., & Treffinger, D. J. (2005). Developing cross-cultural programs for at-risk students through creative problem solving. In E. Polyzoi, M. Bergsgaard, K. W. McCluskey, & O. A. Olifirovych (Eds.), *At-risk children and youth in Canada and Russia: A cross-cultural exchange for talent development* (pp. 167–185). Calgary, Alberta, Canada: University of Calgary-Gorbachev Foundation.

Balchin, T. (2009). Recognising and fostering creative production. In T. Balchin, B. Hymer, & D. Mathews (Eds.), *The Routledge international companion to gifted education* (pp. 203–209). New York, NY: Routledge.

Basadur, M. (1994). *Simplex®: A flight to creativity.* Buffalo, NY: Creative Education Foundation.

Batey, M., & Furnham, A. (2006). Creativity, intelligence, and personality: A critical review of the scattered literature. *Genetic, Social, and General Psychology Monographs, 132,* 355–429.

Beghetto, R. A. (2008). Prospective teachers' beliefs about imaginative thinking in K–12 schooling. *Thinking Skills and Creativity, 3,* 134–142.

Beghetto, R. A. (2010). Creativity in the classroom. In J. C. Kaufman & R. J. Sternberg (Eds.), *The Cambridge handbook of creativity* (pp. 447–463). New York, NY: Cambridge University Press.

Beghetto, R. A., & Kaufman, J. C. (2007). Toward a broader conception of creativity: A case for "mini-c" creativity. *Psychology of Aesthetics, Creativity, and the Arts, 1*, 73–79.

Beghetto, R. A., & Kaufman, J. C. (2009). Intellectual estuaries: Connecting learning and creativity in programs of advanced academics. *Journal of Advanced Academics, 20*, 296–324.

Bekhtereva, N. P., Danko, S. G., Starchenko, M. G., Pakhomov, S. V., & Medvedev, S. V. (2001). Study of the brain organization of creativity: III: Brain activation assessed by the local cerebral blood flow and EEG. *Human Physiology, 27*, 390–397.

Belanoff, P., & Dickson, M. (Eds.). (1991). *Portfolios: Process and product.* Portsmouth, NH: Heinemann.

Bender, W., & Shores, C. (2007). *Response to Intervention: A practical guide for every teacher.* Arlington, VA: Council for Exceptional Children.

Bennetts, C. (2004). The flight of the phoenix: Using hermeneutics to interpret the role of the mentor in the creative cycle. *International Journal of Lifelong Education, 23*(4), 367–383.

Besemer, S. (2006). *Creating products in the age of design: How to improve your new product ideas.* Stillwater, OK: New Forums Press.

Besemer, S., & O'Quin, K. (1986). Analyzing creative products: Refinement and test of a judging instrument. *Journal of Creative Behavior, 20*, 115–126.

Besemer, S., & Treffinger, D. (1981). Analysis of creative products: Review and synthesis. *Journal of Creative Behavior, 15*, 158–178.

Besemer, S. P., & O'Quin, K. (1987). Creative product analysis: Testing a model by developing a judging instrument. In S. G. Isaksen (Ed.), *Frontiers of creativity research: Beyond the basics* (pp. 341–357). Buffalo, NY: Bearly Limited.

Besemer, S. P., & O'Quin, K. (1993). Assessing creative products: Progress and potentials. In S. G. Isaksen, M. C. Murdock, R. L. Firestien, & D. J. Treffinger (Eds.), *Nurturing and developing creativity: The emergence of a discipline* (pp. 331–349). Norwood, NJ: Ablex.

Beyer, B. K. (1985). Teaching critical thinking: A direct approach. *Social Education, 49*, 297–303.

Blackbourn, J. M., Hamby, D., Hanshaw, L., & Beck, M. J. (1997). The total quality curriculum: A model for continuous improvement. *Applied Educational Research, 10*(1), 24–30.

Boling, C. J., & Evans, W. H. (2008). Reading success in the secondary classroom. *Preventing School Failure, 52,* 59–66.

Boyerand, A., & Hamil, B. W. (2008). Problems facing American education. *Focus on Colleges, Universities, and Schools, 2,* 1–9. Retrieved from http://www.nationalforum.com/Electronic%20Journal%20Volumes/Boyer,%20Ashley%20Problems%20Facing%20American%20Education.pdf

Brue, G. (2002). *Six Sigma for managers.* New York, NY: McGraw-Hill.

Buck Institute. (2011). *What is PBL?* Retrieved from http://www.bie.org/about/what_is/pbl

Buckmaster, L. (1994). Effects of activities that promote cooperation among seventh graders in a Future Problem Solving classroom. *Elementary School Journal, 95,* 49–62.

Burns, D. (1990). *Pathways to investigative skills.* Mansfield Center, CT: Creative Learning Press.

Callahan, C. M., Hertberg-Davis, H., & Missett, T. C. (2011). *Destination ImagiNation program evaluation report.* Charlottesville: University of Virginia, Curry School of Education.

Callahan, C. M., Lundberg, A. C., & Hunsaker, S. L. (1993). The development of the Scale for the Evaluation of Gifted Identification Instruments (SEGII). *Gifted Child Quarterly, 37,* 133–137.

Camp Invention. (n.d.). *Camp Invention activity descriptions.* Retrieved from http://www.invent.org/camp/parentsactivities.aspx

Carnevale, A. P., Gainer, L. J., & Meltzer, A. S. (1990). *Workplace basics: Skills employers want.* San Francisco, CA: Jossey-Bass.

Cattell, R. B., Eber, H. W., & Tatsuoka, M. M. (1970). *The handbook for the Sixteen Personality Factor Questionnaire.* Champaign, IL: Institute for Personality and Ability Testing.

Coleman, M. R., & Hughes, C. E. (2009). Meeting the needs of gifted students within an RtI framework. *Gifted Child Today, 32*(3), 14–17.

Common Core State Standards Initiative. (2012a). *Frequently asked questions.* Retrieved from http://www.corestandards.org/frequently-asked-questions

Common Core State Standards Initiative. (2012b). *Mission statement.* Retrieved from http://www.corestandards.org

Connell, V. (1991, October). *Factors contributing to creativity.* Paper presented at the International Networking Colloquium on Creativity Research, Center for Studies in Creativity, Buffalo, NY

Costa, A. (1984). Mediating the metacognitive. *Educational Leadership, 15*(2), 57–62.

Costa, A. L. (Ed.). (1991). *Developing minds: A sourcebook for teaching thinking* (2nd ed.). Alexandria, VA: Association for Supervision and Curriculum Development.

Coy, P. (2000, August 28). The 21st Century Corporation: The Creative Economy. *Business Week Magazine,* 76–82.

Craft, A. (2008). Tensions in creativity and education. In A. Craft, H. Gardner, & G. Claxton (Eds.), *Creative wisdom and trusteeship: Exploring the role of education* (pp. 16–34). Thousand Oaks, CA: Corwin Press.

Cramond, B. (1994). We can trust creativity tests. *Educational Leadership, 52*(2), 70–71.

Cramond, B., Martin, C., & Shaw, E. (1990). Generalizability of creative problem solving procedures to real-life problems. *Journal for the Education of the Gifted, 13,* 141–155.

Crenwelge, M. A. (1992). The meaningful use of literacy created by problem solving classroom environments. *Dissertation Abstracts International, 52*(8), 2872.

Creswell, J. W. (2012). *Educational research: Planning, conducting, and evaluating quantitative and qualitative research* (4th ed.). Upper Saddle River, NJ: Pearson.

Csikszentmihalyi, M. (1997). *Creativity: Flow and the psychology of discovery and invention.* New York, NY: HarperCollins.

Dacey, J. S. (1989). *Fundamentals of creative thinking.* Lexington, MA: Lexington Books.

Davis, G. (1987). What to teach when you teach creativity. *Gifted Child Today, 10*(1), 7–10.

Davis, G. A. (2005). *Creativity is forever* (5th ed.). Dubuque, IA: Kendall Hunt.

de Bono, E. (1970). *Lateral thinking: A textbook of creativity.* New York, NY: Penguin.

de Bono, E. (1981). *CoRT thinking lessons.* Blacklick, OH: Science Research Associates.

de Bono, E. (1983). The direct teaching of thinking as a skill. *Phi Delta Kappan, 64,* 703–708.

de Bono, E. (1985). *Six thinking hats.* New York, NY: Little, Brown.

Delcourt, M. A. B. (1993). Creative productivity among secondary school students: Combining energy, interest, and imagination. *Gifted Child Quarterly, 37,* 23–31.

Destination Imagination. (2012a). *The challenge program.* Retrieved from http://www.destinationimagination.org/what-we-do/challenge-program

Destination Imagination. (2012b). *Vision, mission, and history.* Retrieved from http://www.destinationimagination.org/who-we-are/vision-mission-history

Dewey, J. (1933). *How we think.* New York, NY: D. C. Heath.

Dewey, J. (1938). *Experience and education.* New York, NY: MacMillan.

Draze, D. (2005a). *Pickles, problems, and dilemmas.* Waco, TX: Prufrock Press.

Draze, D. (2005b). *Primarily problem solving.* Waco, TX: Prufrock Press.

DuBois, D. L., Holloway, B. E., Valentine, J. C., & Cooper, H. (2002). Effectiveness of mentoring programs for youth: A meta-analytic review. *American Journal of Community Psychology, 30,* 157–197.

Dunn, R., & Dunn, K. (1978). *Teaching students through their individual learning styles: A practical approach.* Englewood Cliffs, NJ: Prentice-Hall.

Easum, W. M. (1995). *Sacred cows make gourmet burgers.* Nashville, TN: Abingdon Press.

Eberle, B. (1971). *Scamper.* Buffalo, NY: DOK.

Eberle, B., & Stanish, B. (1996). *CPS for kids.* Waco, TX: Prufrock Press.

Eckhoff, A., & Urbach, J. (2008). Understanding imaginative thinking during childhood: Sociocultural conceptions of creativity and imaginative thought. *Journal of Early Childhood Education, 36,* 179–185.

Eger, J. M. (2004). *The future of education and work in the creative age.* Paper prepared for The World Foundation for Smart Communities, San Diego State University, San Diego, CA

Ekvall, G. (1983). *Climate, structure, and innovativeness of organizations: A theoretical framework and an experiment.* Stockholm, Sweden: Swedish Council for Management and Organizational Behavior.

Ennis, R. H. (1987). A taxonomy of critical thinking dispositions and abilities. In J. B. Baron & R. J. Sternberg (Eds.), *Teaching thinking skills: Theory and practice* (pp. 9–26). New York, NY: W. H. Freeman.

eSchool News Staff. (2006, October 10). *Survey reveals the skills employers covet.* Retrieved from http://www.eschoolnews.com

Experiment-Resources.com. (2012). *Definition of research.* Retrieved from http://www.experiment-resources.com/definition-of-research.html

Ferguson, R. F., & Snipes, J. (1994). Outcomes of mentoring: Healthy identities for youth. *Reclaiming Children and Youth, 3*(2), 19–22.

Fish, T. (2009). *School 2.0: Finding relevance in an "always-on" world.* Retrieved from http://www.nais.org/publications/ismagazinearticle. cfm?Itemnumber=151420&sn.ItemNumber=145956

Flanagan, J. C. (1963). The definition and measurement of ingenuity. In C. Taylor & F. Barron (Eds.), *Scientific creativity: Its recognition and development* (pp. 89–98). New York, NY: Wiley.

Franklin, T., & van Harmelen, M. (2007). *Web 2.0 for content for learning and teaching in higher education.* Retrieved from http://ie-repository.jisc. ac.uk/148/1/web2-content-learning-and-teaching.pdf

Freud, S. (1959). Creative writers and daydreaming. In J. Strachey (Ed. and Trans.), *The standard edition of the complete psychological works of Sigmund Freud* (Vol. 9, pp. 141–153). London, England: Hogarth Press. (Original work published 1908)

Frey, B. R., & Noller, R. B. (1992). *Mentoring for creative productivity.* Buffalo, NY: Buffalo State College, International Creativity Network.

Fromm, E. (1959). The creative attitude. In H. H. Anderson (Ed.), *Creativity and its cultivation* (pp. 44–54). New York, NY: Harper & Row.

Gallagher, S. (2009). Problem-Based Learning. In J. S. Renzulli, E. J. Gubbins, K. S. McMillen, R. D. Eckert, & C. A. Little (Eds.), *Systems and models for developing programs for the gifted and talented* (2nd ed., pp. 193–210). Mansfield Center, CT: Creative Learning Press.

Gardner, H. (1993a). *Creating minds: An anatomy of creativity as seen through the lives of Freud, Einstein, Picasso, Stravinsky, Eliot, Graham, and Gandhi.* New York, NY: Basic Books.

Gardner, H. (1993b). Seven creators of the modern era. In J. Brockman (Ed.), *Creativity* (pp. 28–47). New York, NY: Simon & Schuster.

Geist, E., & Hohn, J. (2009). Encouraging creativity in the face of administrative convenience: How our schools discourage divergent thinking. *Education, 130,* 141–150.

Gilson, L. L., & Madjar, N. (2011). Radical and incremental creativity: Antecedents and processes. *Psychology of Aesthetics, Creativity, and the Arts, 5,* 21–28.

Giroux, H. (2010, March 4). *Winter in America: Democracy gone rogue.* Retrieved from http://archive.truthout.org/winter-america-democracy-gone-rogue57353

Gisi, L., & Forbes, R. (1982). *The information society: Are high school graduates ready?* Denver, CO: Education Commission of the States.

Goffnett, S. P. (2004). Understanding Six Sigma: Implications for industry and education. *Journal of Industrial Technology, 20*(4), 1–9.

Goleman, D., Kaufman, P., & Ray, M. (1992). *The creative spirit.* New York, NY: Penguin.

Gordon, W. J. J. (1961). *Synectics.* New York, NY: Harper & Row.

Gordon, W. J. J., & Poze, T. (1979). *The metaphorical way of learning and knowing* (Rev. ed.). Cambridge, MA: Porpoise Books.

Gordon, W. J. J., & Poze, T. (1980). SES Synectics and gifted education today. *Gifted Child Quarterly, 24,* 147–151.

Gowan, J. C., Khatena, J., & Torrance, E. P. (1981). *Creativity: Its educational implications* (2nd ed.). Dubuque, IA: Kendall Hunt.

Gregorc, A. F. (1985). Matching teaching and learning styles. *Theory Into Practice, 23,* 51–55.

Grossman, J. B., & Tierney, J. P. (1998). Does mentoring work? An impact study of the Big Brothers/Big Sisters program. *Education Review, 22,* 403–426.

Guilford, J. P. (1950). Creativity. *American Psychologist, 5,* 444–454.

Guilford, J. P. (1980). Cognitive styles: What are they? *Educational and Psychological Measurement, 40,* 715–735.

Guilford, J. P. (1986). *Creative talents: Their nature, uses and development.* Buffalo, NY: Bearly Limited.

Haeger, W. W., & Feldhusen, J. F. (1989). *Developing a mentor program.* East Aurora, NY: D.O.K.

Hart, D. (1994). *Authentic assessment: A handbook for educators.* Reading, MA: Addison Wesley/Innovative Learning.

Hausman, J. (1992). On the use of portfolios in evaluation. *Art Education, 45,* 4.

Haynes, N. M. (1998). Creating safe and caring school communities: Comer School Development Program schools. *Journal of Negro Education, 65,* 308–314.

Haynes, N. M., & Comer, J. P. (1993). The Yale School Development Program process, outcomes, and policy implications. *Urban Education, 28,* 166–199.

Hebert, E. A. (1992). Portfolios invite reflection—from students and staff. *Educational Leadership, 49*(8), 58–61.

Hennessey, B. (2010). The creativity-motivation connection. In J. C. Kaufman & R. J. Sternberg (Eds.), *The Cambridge handbook of creativity* (pp. 342–365). New York, NY: Cambridge University Press.

Hennessey, B. A., & Amabile, T. M. (1987). *Creativity and learning.* Washington, DC: National Education Association.

Herman, J. L., Aschbacher, P. R., & Winters, L. (1992). *A practical guide to authentic assessment.* Alexandria, VA: Association for Supervision and Curriculum Development.

Hersh, R. H. (2009). A well-rounded education for a flat world. *Educational Leadership, 61*(1), 51–53.

Hilgersom-Volk, K. (1987). Celebrating students' diversity through learning styles. *OSSC Bulletin, 30*(9).

Honawar, V. (2008, April 2). Working smarter by working together. *Education Week, 27,* 25–27.

Hulsheger, U., Anderson, N., & Salgado, J. (2009). Team-level predictors of innovation at work: A comprehensive meta-analysis spanning three decades of research. *Journal of Applied Psychology, 94,* 1128–1145.

Isaac, S., & Michael, W. B. (1997). *Handbook in research and evaluation.* San Diego, CA: Educational and Industrial Testing Service.

Isaksen, S. (Ed.). (1987a). *Frontiers of creativity research: Beyond the basics.* Buffalo, NY: Bearly Limited.

Isaksen, S. (1987b). Introduction: An orientation to the frontiers of creativity research. In S. Isaksen (Ed.), *Frontiers of creativity research: Beyond the basics* (pp. 1–26). Buffalo, NY: Bearly Limited.

Isaksen, S., & Treffinger, D. (1985). *Creative problem solving: The basic course.* Buffalo, NY: Bearly Limited.

Isaksen, S. G. (2007). The Situational Outlook Questionnaire: Assessing the context for change. *Psychological Reports, 100,* 455–466.

Isaksen, S. G., & Ekvall, G. (2007). *Assessing the context for change: A technical manual for the Situational Outlook Questionnaire®* (2nd ed.). Buffalo, NY: The Creative Problem Solving Group.

Isaksen, S. G., Dorval, K. B., & Treffinger, D. J. (2011). *Creative approaches to problem solving* (3rd ed.). Thousand Oaks, CA: SAGE.

Isaksen, S. G., Murdock, M. C., Firestien, R. L., & Treffinger, D. J. (Eds.). (1993a). *Nurturing and developing creativity: The emergence of a discipline.* Norwood, NJ: Ablex.

Isaksen, S. G., Murdock, M. C., Firestien, R. L., & Treffinger, D. J. (Eds.). (1993b). *Understanding and recognizing creativity: The emergence of a discipline.* Norwood, NJ: Ablex.

Isaksen, S. G., Stein, M. I., Hills, D. A., & Gryskiewicz, S. S. (1984). A proposed model for the formulation of creativity research. *Journal of Creative Behavior, 18,* 67–75.

Isaksen, S. G., Treffinger, D. J., & Dorval, K. B. (2000). *Climate for creativity and innovation: Educational implication.* Sarasota, FL: Center for Creative Learning.

Isop, L. (2011). *How do you hug a porcupine?* New York, NY: Simon & Schuster Books for Young Readers.

Jalongo, M. R., & Heider, K. (2006). Editorial: Teacher attrition: An issue of national concern. *Early Childhood Education Journal, 33,* 379–380.

Johnsen, S. K., & Goree, K. (2005). *Independent study for gifted learners.* Waco, TX: Prufrock Press.

Johnsen, S. K., & Johnson, K. L. (2007). *Independent study program: Complete kit* (2nd ed.). Waco, TX: Prufrock Press.

Jung, C. G. (1923). *Psychological types* (H. B. Baynes, Trans.). New York, NY: Harcourt, Brace.

Jung, C. G. (1971). *The portable Jung* (R. F. C. Hull, Trans.). New York, NY: Viking.

Kaufman, A., Kornilov, S., Bristol, A., Tan, M., & Grigorenko, E. (2010). The neurobiological foundations of creative cognition. In J. C. Kaufman & R. J. Sternberg (Eds.), *The Cambridge handbook of creativity* (pp. 216–232). New York, NY: Cambridge University Press.

Kaufman, J., & Beghetto, R. (2009). Beyond big and little: The four c model of creativity. *A Review of General Psychology, 13,* 1–12.

Keller-Mathers, S., & Murdock, M. (1999). Research support for a conceptual organization of creativity. In A. S. Fishkin, B. Cramond, & P. Olszewski-Kubilius (Eds.), *Investigating creativity in youth: Research and methods* (pp. 49–71). Cresskill, NJ: Hampton Press.

Keller-Mathers, S., & Murdock, M. (2002). Teaching the content of creativity using the Torrance Incubation Model: Eyes wide open to the possibilities of learning. *Celebrate Creativity (NAGC Creativity Division Newsletter), 13*(2), 7–9.

Khatena, J., & Torrance, E. P. (1973). *Thinking creatively with sounds and words: Technical manual* (Research Ed.). Lexington, MA: Personnel Press.

Khatena, J., & Torrance, E. P. (2006). *Khatena-Torrance Creative Perception Inventory.* Bensenville, IL: Scholastic Testing Service.

Kim, K. (2006). Can we trust creativity tests? A review of the Torrance Tests of Creative Thinking (TTCT). *Creativity Research Journal, 18,* 3–14.

Kim, K. H. (2011a). The Division 10 debate—Are the Torrance Tests still relevant in the 21st century? Torrance Tests are still relevant in the 21st century. *Psychology of Aesthetics, Creativity, and the Arts, 5,* 302–308.

Kim, K. H. (2011b). Proven reliability and validity of the Torrance Tests of Creative Thinking. *Psychology of Aesthetics, Creativity, and the Arts, 5,* 314–315.

Kirschenbaum, R., & Armstrong, D. (1999). Diagnostic assessment of creativity in students. In A. S. Fishkin, B. Cramond, & P. Olszewski-Kubilius (Eds.), *Investigating creativity in youth: Research and methods* (pp. 329–348). Cresskill, NJ: Hampton Press.

Kirton, M. J. (1961). *Management initiative.* London, England: Action Society Trust.

Kirton, M. J. (1976). Adaptors and innovators: A description and measure. *Journal of Applied Psychology, 61,* 622–629.

Kirton, M. J. (1987). Cognitive styles and creativity. In S. G. Isaksen (Ed.), *Frontiers in creativity research: Beyond the basics* (pp. 282–304). Buffalo, NY: Bearly Limited.

Klijn, M., & Tomic, W. (2010). A review of creativity within organizations from a psychological perspective. *Journal of Management Development, 29,* 322–343.

Klimoviene, G., Urboniene, J., & Barzdziukiene, R. (2010). Creative classroom climate assessment for the advancement of foreign language acquisition. *Kalbu Studies: Studies About Languages, 16,* 114–121.

Kohn, A. (2010, January 14). Debunking the case for national standards: One-size-fits-all mandates and their dangers. *Education Week.* Retrieved from http://www.alfiekohn.org/teaching/edweek/national.htm

Kolb, D. (1981). Disciplinary inquiry norms and student learning styles: Diverse pathways for growth. In A. Chickering (Ed.), *The modern American college* (pp. 57–76). San Francisco, CA: Jossey-Bass.

Kopkowski, C. (2008). Why they leave. *NEA Today, 26*(7), 21–25.

Kowaltowski, D., Bianchi, G., & de Paiva, V. (2010). Methods that may stimulate creativity and their use in architectural design education. *International Journal of Technology & Design Education, 20,* 453–476.

Kuperminc, G. P., Leadbeater, B. J., Emmons, C., & Blatt, S. J. (1997). Perceived school climate and difficulties in the social adjustment of middle school students. *Applied Developmental Science, 1,* 76–88.

Lauer, K. J. (1994). *The assessment of creative climate: An investigation of Ekvall's Creative Climate Questionnaire* (Unpublished master's thesis). State University College, Buffalo, NY.

Law, E. L.-C. (2007). Technology-enhanced creativity. In A. Tan (Ed.), *Creativity: A handbook for teachers* (pp. 363–383). Hackensack, NJ: World Scientific.

Lawrence, G. (1997). *Looking at type and learning styles.* Gainesville, FL: Center for Applications of Psychological Type.

Lawrence, G. (2009). *People types and tiger stripes* (4th ed.). Gainesville, FL: Center for Applications of Psychological Type.

Lee, S., Luppino, J., & Plionis, E. (1990). Keeping youth in school: A follow-up report. *Children Today, 19,* 4–7.

Leung, A. K., & Chiu, C. (2008). Interactive effects of multicultural experiences and openness to experience on creative potential. *Creativity Research Journal, 20,* 376–382.

Leung, A. K., Maddux, W. W., Galinsky, A. D., & Chiu, C. (2008). Multicultural experience enhances creativity: The when and how. *American Psychologist, 63,* 169–181.

Lieberman, A., & Miller, L. (2011). Learning communities. *Journal of Staff Development, 32*(4), 16–20.

Linn, R. L., & Gronlund, N. E. (1995). *Measurement and assessment in teaching* (7th ed.). Columbus, OH: Charles E. Merrill.

Litterst, J. K., & Eyo, B. A. (1993). Developing classroom imagination: Shaping and energizing a suitable climate for growth, discovery, and vision. *Journal of Creative Behavior, 27,* 270–282.

LoSciuto, L., Rajala, A. K., Townsend, T. N., & Taylor, A. S. (1996). An outcome evaluation of Across Ages: An intergenerational mentoring approach to drug prevention. *Journal of Adolescent Research, 11,* 116–129.

MacKinnon, D. (1987). Some critical issues for future research in creativity. In S. Isaksen (Ed.), *Frontiers of creativity research: Beyond the basics* (pp. 120–130). Buffalo, NY: Bearly Limited.

Maddux, W. M., Leung, A. K., Chiu, C., & Galinsky, A. D. (2009). Toward a more complete understanding of the link between multicultural experience and creativity. *American Psychologist, 64,* 156–158.

Marshall, M. L. (2004). *Examining school climate: defining factors and educational influences* [White paper]. Retrieved from http://education.gsu. edu/schoolsafety

Martin, C. R. (1997). *Looking at type: The fundamentals.* Gainesville, FL: Center for Applications of Psychological Type.

Martinsen, O., & Kaufmann, G. (1999). Cognitive style and creativity. In M. A. Runco & S. R. Pritzker (Eds.), *Encyclopedia of creativity* (Vol. I, pp. 273–282). New York, NY: Academic Press.

Marx, G. (2001). Educating children for tomorrow's world. *The Futurist, 35*(2), 43–48.

Maslow, A. H. (1958). Emotional blocks to creativity. *Journal of Individual Psychology, 14,* 51–56.

Maslow, A. H. (1976). Creativity in self-actualizing people. In A. Rothenberg & C. Hausman (Eds.), *The creativity question* (pp. 86–92). Durham, NC: Duke University Press.

McCluskey, K. W. (2000). Setting the stage for productive problem solving. In S. G. Isaksen (Ed.), *Facilitative leadership: Making a difference with creative problem solving* (pp. 77–101). Dubuque, IA: Kendall Hunt.

McCluskey, K. W. (2008). *Thoughts about tone, educational leadership, and building creative climates in our schools.* Ulm, Germany: ICIE.

McCluskey, K. W., Baker, P. A., Bergsgaard, M., & McCluskey, A. (2001). *Creative problem solving in the trenches: Interventions with at-risk populations*

(Monograph #308). Williamsville, NY: Creative Problem Solving Group.

McCluskey, K. W., Baker, P. A., & McCluskey, A. (2005). Creative problem solving with marginalized populations: Reclaiming lost prizes through in-the-trenches interventions. *Gifted Child Quarterly, 49,* 330–341.

McCluskey, K. W., Baker, P. A., O'Hagan, S. C., & Treffinger, D. J. (Eds.). (1995). *Lost prizes: Talent development and problem solving with at-risk students.* Sarasota, FL: Center for Creative Learning.

McCluskey, K. W., Baker, P. A., O'Hagan, S. C., & Treffinger, D. J. (1998). Recapturing at-risk, talented high-school dropouts: A summary of the three-year Lost Prizes project. *Gifted and Talented International, 13*(2), 73–78.

McCluskey, K. W., & Mays, A. M. (Eds.). (2003). *Mentoring for talent development.* Sioux Falls, SD: Augustana College, Reclaiming Youth International.

McCluskey, K. W., & Treffinger, D. J. (1998). Nurturing talented but troubled children and youth. *Reclaiming Children and Youth, 6,* 215–219, 226.

McGilchrist, I. (2010, January 2). The battle of the brain. *The Wall Street Journal,* p. 9W.

McLellan, R., & Nicholl, B. (2008, September). *Creativity in crisis in D&T: Are classroom climates conducive for creativity in English secondary schools?* Paper presented at the British Educational Research Association Annual Conference, Heriot-Watt University, Edinburgh

Meador, K. S., Fishkin, A. S., & Hoover, M. (1999). Research-based strategies and programs to facilitate creativity. In A. S. Fishkin, B. Cramond, & P. Olszewski-Kubilius (Eds.), *Investigating creativity in youth* (pp. 389–415). Cresskill, NJ: Hampton Press.

Mednick, S. A. (1962). The associative basis of the creative process. *Psychological Review, 69,* 220–232.

Metzl, S., & Morrell, M. (2008). The role of creativity in models of resilience: Theoretical exploration and practical applications. *Journal of Creativity in Mental Health, 3,* 303–318.

Millar, G. W. (1995). *E. Paul Torrance: "The creativity man."* Norwood, NJ: Ablex.

Mölle, M., Marshall, L., Lutzenberger, W., Pietrowsky, R., Fehm, H. L., & Born, J. (1996). Enhanced dynamic complexity in the human EEG during creative thinking. *Neuroscience Letters, 208*(1), 61–64.

Mueller, J. (2011). *Authentic assessment toolbox.* Naperville, IL: North Central College. Retrieved from http://jfmueller.faculty.noctrl.edu/toolbox/portfolios.htm

Murdock, M., & Keller-Mathers, S. (2002a). Teaching for creativity: Where there's a will, there's a way. *Celebrate Creativity (NAGC Creativity Division Newsletter), 13*(2), 3–4, 10–12.

Murdock, M., & Keller-Mathers, S. (2002b). The foundation of the Torrance Incubation Model: Identifying and using a creativity skill set. *Celebrate Creativity (NAGC Creativity Division Newsletter), 13*(2), 5–6, 13.

Nash, D. (2001, December). Enter the mentor. *Parenting for High Potential,* 18–21.

Nash, D., & Treffinger, D. J. (1993). *The mentor kit: A step-by-step guide to creating an effective mentor program in your school.* Waco, TX: Prufrock Press.

National Science Board Commission on Precollege Education in Mathematics, Science, and Technology. (1983). *Educating Americans for the 21st Century: A plan of action for improving mathematics, science and technology education for all American elementary and secondary students so that their achievement is the best in the world by 1995.* Washington, DC: Author.

Nickerson, R., Perkins, D., & Smith, E. (1985). *The teaching of thinking.* Hillsdale, NJ: Lawrence Erlbaum.

Noller, R. B. (1997). *Mentoring: A voiced scarf* (2nd ed.). Mt. Holly, NJ: Snedley Group.

Noller, R. B., & Frey, B. R. (1983). *Mentoring: An annotated bibliography.* Buffalo, NY: Bearly Limited.

Noller, R. B., & Frey, B. R. (1994). *Mentoring: An annotated bibliography (1982–1992).* Sarasota, FL: Center for Creative Learning.

Noller, R. B., & Frey, B. R. (1995). Mentoring for the continued development of lost prizes. In K. W. McCluskey, P. A. Baker, S. C. O'Hagan, & D. J. Treffinger (Eds.), *Lost Prizes: Talent development and problem solving with at-risk students* (pp. 203–212). Sarasota, FL: Center for Creative Learning.

Norris, S. P., & Ennis, R. H. (1989). *Evaluating critical thinking.* Pacific Palisades, CA: Critical Thinking Press and Software.

O'Quin, K., & Besemer, S. (1989). The development, reliability, and validity of the Revised Creative Product Semantic Scale. *Creative Research Journal, 2,* 267–278.

Olenchak, F. R. (1994). Future Problem Solving: A sample of effects on students. *Research Briefs, 9,* 61–66.

Osborn, A. F. (1953). *Applied imagination: Principles and procedures for creative thinking.* New York, NY: Charles Scribner's Sons.

Osborn, A. F. (1963). *Applied imagination: The principles and procedures of creative problem-solving* (3rd ed.). New York, NY: Charles Scribner's Sons.

Ozturk, M., & Debelak, C. (2008). Academic competitions as tools for differentiation in middle school. *Gifted Child Today, 31*(3), 47–53.

Parnes, S. J. (1967). *Creative behavior guidebook.* New York, NY: Charles Scribner's Sons.

Parnes, S. J., Noller, R. B., & Biondi, A. M. (1977). *Guide to creative action.* New York, NY: Charles Scribner's Sons.

Partnership for 21st Century Skills. (2007). *Beyond the three Rs: Voter attitudes toward 21st century skills.* Retrieved from http://www.p21.org/storage/documents/P21_pollreport_singlepg.pdf

Partnership for 21st Century Skills. (2009). *P21 framework definitions.* Retrieved from http://www.p21.org/storage/documents/P21_Framework_Definitions.pdf

Place, D., McCluskey, K. W., McCluskey, A., & Treffinger, D. J. (2000). The second chance project: Creative approaches to developing the talents of at-risk native inmates. *Journal of Creative Behavior, 34,* 165–174.

Plucker, J. A., Beghetto, R. A., & Dow, G. T. (2004). Why isn't creativity more important to educational psychologists? Potentials, pitfalls, and future directions in creativity research. *Educational Psychologist, 39,* 83–96.

Polya, G. (1957). *How to solve it* (2nd ed.). Princeton, NJ: Princeton University Press.

Prentky, R. A. (1980). *Creativity and psychopathology: A neurocognitive perspective.* New York, NY: Praeger.

Prince, G. M. (1970). *The practice of creativity.* New York, NY: Harper & Row.

Purcell, J. H., Renzulli, J. S., McCoach, D. B., & Spottiswoode, H. (2001, December). The magic of mentorships. *Parenting for High Potential,* 22–26.

Rank, J., Pace, V., & Frese, M. (2004). Three avenues for future research on creativity, innovation, and initiative. *Applied Psychology: An International Review, 53*, 518–528.

Renzulli, J. S. (1977a). *The Enrichment Triad Model.* Mansfield Center, CT: Creative Learning Press.

Renzulli, J. S. (1977b). What makes giftedness? Reexamining a definition. *Phi Delta Kappan, 59*, 180–184.

Renzulli, J. S. (1982). What makes a problem real: Stalking the illusive meaning of qualitative differences in gifted education. *Gifted Child Quarterly, 26*(4), 137–156.

Renzulli, J. S., Smith, L. H., White, A. J., Callahan, C. M., Hartman, R. K., Westberg, K. L., . . . Sytsma, R. E. (2004). *Scales for Rating the Behavioral Characteristics of Superior Students: Technical and administration manual* (Rev. ed.). Mansfield Center, CT: Creative Learning Press.

Reuter, M., Panksepp, J., Schnabel, N., Kellerhoff, N., Kempel, P., & Hennig, J. (2005). Personality and biological markers of creativity. *European Journal of Personality, 19*, 83–95.

Reynolds, A. (2009). Why every student needs critical friends. *Educational Leadership, 67*(3), 54–57.

Rhodes, M. (1961). An analysis of creativity. *Phi Delta Kappan, 42*, 305–310.

Rich, G. J. (2009). Big C, little c, Big M, little m. *American Psychologist, 64*, 155–156.

Richards, R. (2007). *Everyday creativity.* Washington, DC: American Psychological Association.

Richards, R. (2010). Everyday creativity: Process and way of life—Four key issues. In J. C. Kaufman & R. J. Sternberg (Eds.), *Cambridge handbook of creativity* (pp. 189–215). New York, NY: Cambridge University Press.

Ripple, R. E. (1989). Ordinary creativity. *Contemporary Educational Psychology, 14*, 189–202.

Roberts, J., & Inman, T. (2001, December). Mentoring and your child: Developing a successful relationship. *Parenting for High Potential*, 8–10.

Rogers, C. (1954). Toward a theory of creativity. *ETC: A Review of General Semantics, 11*, 250–258.

Rogers, C. (1959). Toward a theory of creativity. In H. H. Anderson (Ed.), *Creativity and its cultivation* (pp. 69–82). New York, NY: Harper & Row.

Royce, D. (1998). Mentoring high-risk minority youth: Evaluation of the Brothers Project. *Adolescence, 33,* 145–158.

Ruff, M. (n.d.). *Using Six Sigma to solve issues in a public school system.* Retrieved from http://www.isixsigma.com/index.php?option=com_ k2&view=item&id=167:using-six-sigma-to-solve-issues-in-public-school-system&Itemid=184

Runco, M. (2003a). Creativity, cognition, and their educational implications. In J. Houtz (Ed.), *The educational psychology of creativity* (pp. 25–56). Cresskill, NJ: Hampton Press.

Runco, M. (2003b). Education for creative potential. *Scandinavian Journal of Education Research, 47,* 317–324.

Runco, M., & Acar, S. (2010). Do tests of divergent thinking have an experiential bias? *Psychology of Aesthetics, Creativity, and the Arts, 4,* 144–148.

Russ, S. W., & Fiorelli, J. A. (2010). Developmental approaches to creativity. In J. C. Kaufman & R. J. Sternberg (Eds.), *The Cambridge handbook of creativity* (pp. 233–249). New York, NY: Cambridge University Press.

Ryser, G. R. (2007). *Profile of Creative Abilities.* Austin, TX: PRO-ED.

Sapp, D. D. (1997). Problem parameters and problem finding in art education. *Journal of Creative Behavior, 31,* 282–298.

Saxon, J. A., Treffinger, D. J., Young, G. C., & Wittig, C. V. (2003). Camp Invention®: A creative, inquiry-based summer enrichment program for elementary students. *Journal of Creative Behavior, 37,* 64–74.

Schoonover, P. (1996). The preference for and use of Creative Problem Solving tools among adaptors and innovators. *Creative Learning Today: Center for Creative Learning Newsletter, 6*(3), 10–11.

Schoonover, P. F., & Treffinger, D. J. (2003). Implications of style differences for explorers and developers in use of CPS tools. *Creative Learning Today, 12*(3), 2–3.

Schoonover, P., Treffinger, D., & Selby, E. (2012). *Linking technology and creative learning.* Sarasota, FL: Center for Creative Learning.

Selby, E. (1997). Lucy and Michael: Case studies of creative styles in teenagers. *Creative Learning Today: Center for Creative Learning Newsletter, 7*(2), 4–6.

Selby, E., Shaw, E., & Houtz, J. (2005). The creative personality. *Gifted Child Quarterly, 49,* 300–314.

Selby, E., Treffinger, D., & Isaksen, S. (2007a). *Facilitator guide—VIEW: An assessment of problem solving style* (2nd ed.) Sarasota, FL: Center for Creative Learning.

Selby, E., Treffinger, D., & Isaksen, S. (2007b). *Technical manual—VIEW: An assessment of problem solving style* (2nd ed.). Sarasota, FL: Center for Creative Learning.Silvia, P. J., & Kaufman, J. C. (2010). Creativity and mental illness. In J. C. Kaufman & R. J. Sternberg (Eds.), *The Cambridge handbook of creativity* (pp. 381–394). New York, NY: Cambridge University Press.

Simon, H., & Newell, A. (1970). Human problem solving: The state of the theory in 1970. *American Psychologist, 26,* 145–159.

Simonton, D. K. (2010). Creativity in highly eminent individuals. In J. C. Kaufman & R. J. Sternberg (Eds.), *The Cambridge handbook of creativity* (pp. 174–188). New York, NY: Cambridge University Press.

Simpson, R. (1922). Creative imagination. *American Journal of Psychology, 33,* 234–243.

Sitler, H. C. (2007). The lived experience of new teachers, or why should I stay in this profession? *Phi Kappa Phi Forum, 87*(4), 22.

Smith, J. K., & Smith, L. F. (2010). Educational creativity. In J. C. Kaufman & R. J. Sternberg (Eds.), *The Cambridge handbook of creativity* (pp. 250–264). New York, NY: Cambridge University Press.

Stanish, B., & Eberle, B. (1997). *Be a problem solver.* Waco, TX: Prufrock Press.

Sternberg, R. J. (2006). Creating a vision of creativity: The first 25 years. *Psychology of Aesthetics, Creativity, and the Arts, S*(1), 2–12.

Sternberg, R. J., & Lubart, T. I. (1995). *Defying the crowd: Cultivating creativity.* New York, NY: Free Press.

Sternberg, R. J., Jarvin, L., & Grigorenko, E. L. (2009). *Teaching for wisdom, intelligence, creativity and success.* Thousand Oaks, CA: Corwin Press.

Swartz, R., & Parks, S. (1994). *Infusing the teaching of critical and creative thinking into content areas.* Pacific Grove, CA: Critical Thinking Press and Software.

Tallent-Runnels, M. K. (1993). The Future Problem Solving Program: An investigation of effects on problem solving ability. *Contemporary Educational Psychology, 18,* 382–388.

Tauber, R. (1991). Praise "strikes" out as a classroom management tool. *Contemporary Education, 62,* 194–198.

Thomas, C., Blackbourn, J., Papason, B., Britt, P., Blackbourn, R., Tyler, J. L., & Williams, F. (2004–2005). Portfolio assessment: A guide for teachers and administrators. *National Forum of Educational Administration and Supervision Journal, 23*(4E). Retrieved from http://www.nationalforum.com/Electronic%20Journal%20Volumes/Thomas,%20Conn-Portfolio%20As

Torrance, E. P. (1974). *Torrance Tests of Creative Thinking: Norms and technical manual.* Bensenville, IL: Scholastic Testing Service.

Torrance, E. P. (1979). An instructional model for enhancing incubation. *Journal of Creative Behavior, 13*, 23–35.

Torrance, E. P. (1984). *Mentor relationships: How they aid creative achievement, endure, change, and die.* Buffalo, NY: Bearly Limited.

Torrance, E. P. (1987). Teaching for creativity. In S. G. Isaksen (Ed.), *Frontiers of creativity research: Beyond the basics* (pp. 189–215). Buffalo, NY: Bearly Limited.

Torrance, E. P. (1995). *Why fly? A philosophy of creativity.* Norwood, NJ: Ablex.

Torrance, E. P. (2006). *Torrance Tests of Creative Thinking.* Bensenville, IL: Scholastic Testing Service.

Torrance, E. P., & Safter, H. T. (1990). *Incubation model of teaching: Getting beyond the aha.* Buffalo, NY: Bearly Limited.

Treffinger, D. J. (1986). Research on creativity. *Gifted Child Quarterly, 30*, 15–19.

Treffinger, D. J. (1988). Components of creativity: Another look. *Creative Learning Today, 2*(5), 1–4.

Treffinger, D. J. (1991). Creative productivity: Understanding its source and nature. *Illinois Council for the Gifted Journal, 10*, 6–8.

Treffinger, D. J. (1994). Productive thinking: Toward authentic instruction and assessment. *Journal of Secondary Gifted Education, 6*(1), 30–37.

Treffinger, D. J. (1996). *Dimensions of creativity.* Sarasota, FL: Center for Creative Learning.

Treffinger, D. J. (1997). Editorial: Toward a more precise, concise, and consistent language for productive thinking instruction. *Creative Learning Today, 7*(1), 1, 8–9.

Treffinger, D. J. (2000). *Practice problems for creative problem solving.* Waco, TX: Prufrock Press.

Treffinger, D. J. (2003a). Assessment and measurement in creativity study. In J. Houtz (Ed.), *The educational psychology of creativity* (pp. 59–93). Cresskill, NJ: Hampton Press.

Treffinger, D. J. (2003b). The role of mentoring in talent development. In K. W. McCluskey & A. M. Mays (Eds.), *Mentoring for talent development* (pp. 1–11). Sioux Falls, SD: Reclaiming Youth International.

Treffinger, D. J. (2004). Introduction to creativity and giftedness: Three decades of inquiry and development. In D. J. Treffinger (Ed.), *Creativity and giftedness* (pp. xxiii–xxx). Thousand Oaks, CA: Corwin Press.

Treffinger, D. J. (2008). Preparing creative and critical thinkers. *Educational Leadership, 65*(9). Retrieved from http://www.ascd.org/publications/educational_leadership/summer08/vol65/num09/Preparing_Creative_and_Critical_Thinkers.aspx

Treffinger, D. J. (2009). Myth: Creativity is too difficult to measure. *Gifted Child Quarterly, 53,* 245–247.

Treffinger, D. J. (2011). *Creativity, creative thinking, and critical thinking: In search of definitions* (Rev. ed.). Sarasota, FL: Center for Creative Learning.

Treffinger, D. J., & Feldhusen, J. F. (1998). *Planning for productive thinking and learning.* Waco, TX: Prufrock Press.

Treffinger, D. J., Isaksen, S. G., & Dorval, K. B. (2006). *Creative problem solving: An introduction* (4th ed.). Waco, TX: Prufrock Press.

Treffinger, D. J., Isaksen, S. G., & Dorval, K. B. (2011). *Climate for creativity and innovation: Educational implications* (3rd ed.). Sarasota, FL: Center for Creative Learning.

Treffinger, D. J., & Nassab, C. A. (2011a). *Facilitator's guide: Focusing tools.* Sarasota, FL: Center for Creative Learning.

Treffinger, D. J., & Nassab, C. A. (2011b). *Facilitator's guide: Generating tools.* Sarasota, FL: Center for Creative Learning.

Treffinger, D. J., Nassab, C. A., Schoonover, P. F., Selby, E. C., Shepardson, C. A., Wittig, C. V., & Young, G. C. (2006). *The creative problem solving kit.* Waco, TX: Prufrock Press.

Treffinger, D. J., Nassab, C. A., & Selby, E. C. (2009). Programming for talent development: Expanding horizons for gifted education. In T. Balchin, B. Hymer, & D. Matthews (Eds.), *The Routledge international companion to gifted education* (pp. 210–217). London, England: Routledge.

Treffinger, D. J., & Selby, E. C. (1993). Giftedness, creativity, and learning style: Exploring the connections. In R. Milgram, R. Dunn, & G.

Price (Eds.), *Teaching and counseling gifted adolescents through their learning styles: An international perspective* (pp. 87–102). New York, NY: Praeger.

Treffinger, D. J., Selby, E. C., & Crumel, J. H. (in press). Evaluation of the Future Problem Solving Program International (FPSPI). *International Journal of Creativity and Problem Solving.*

Treffinger, D. J., Selby, E. C., & Isaksen, S. G. (2008). Understanding individual problem-solving style: A key to learning and applying creative problem solving. *Learning and Individual Differences, 18,* 390–401.

Treffinger, D. J., Selby, E. C., Isaksen, S. G., & Crumel, J. H. (2007). *An introduction to problem solving-style.* Sarasota, FL: Center for Creative Learning.

Treffinger, D. J., Selby, E. C., & Schoonover, P. F. (2004). *Evaluation report, Phase I: The Destination ImagiNation® program.* Sarasota, FL: Center for Creative Learning.

Treffinger, D. J., & Shepardson, C. A. (2012). *The real problem solving handbook* (2nd ed.). Manuscript in preparation.

Treffinger, D. J., Young, G. C., Nassab, C. A., Selby, E. C., & Wittig, C. V. (2008). *Talent development planning handbook.* Thousand Oaks, CA: Corwin Press.

Treffinger, D. J., Young, G. C., Nassab, C. A., & Wittig C. V. (2004). *Enhancing and expanding gifted programs: The levels of service approach.* Waco, TX: Prufrock Press.

Treffinger, D. J., Young, G. C., Selby, E. C., & Shepardson, C. A. (2002). *Assessing creativity: A guide for educators.* Storrs: University of Connecticut, The National Research Center on the Gifted and Talented.

Treffinger, D., Nassab, C., Schoonover, P., Selby, E., Shepardson, C., Wittig, C., & Young, G. (2003). *Thinking with standards: Preparing for tomorrow (Elementary level).* Waco, TX: Prufrock Press.

United States Department of Labor. (1991). *What work requires of schools: A SCANS report for America 2000.* Washington, DC: Author.

Vernon, P. E. (1989). Giftedness and construction of a creative life. In J. A. Glover, R. R. Ronning, & C. R. Reynolds (Eds.), *Handbook of creativity* (pp. 93–110). New York, NY: Plenum Press.

Vygotsky, L. S. (1978). *Mind and society: The development of higher psychological processes.* Cambridge, MA: Harvard University Press.

Wagner, T. (2007). Five "habits of mind" that count. *Education Week, 26*(45), 29–30.

Wallace, D. R., & Gruber, H. E. (1989). *Creative people at work.* New York, NY: Oxford University Press.

Wallas, G. (1926). *The art of thought.* New York, NY: Franklin Watts.

Weisberg, R. W. (1986). *Creativity: Genius and other myths.* New York, NY: W. H. Freeman.

Weisberg, R. W. (1994). Genius and madness? A quasi-experimental test of the hypothesis that manic-depression increases creativity. *American Psychological Society, 5,* 361–367.

Wiggins, G. P. (1989). A true test: Toward more authentic and equitable assessment. *Phi Delta Kappan, 70,* 703–713.

Wiggins, G. P. (1993). *Assessing student performance.* San Francisco, CA: Jossey-Bass.

Williams, F. E. (1968, February). *Helping the child develop his creative potential.* Paper presented at Wilder Child Guidance Clinic Symposium, St. Paul, MN

Witkin, H. A., & Goodenough, D. R. (1981). *Cognitive styles: Essence and origins.* Madison, WI: International University Press.

Woolfolk, A. (2010). *Educational psychology* (11th ed.). Upper Saddle River, NJ: Merrill.

Young, G. (1995). Becoming a talent spotter. *Creative Learning Today, 5*(1), 4–5.

Zeng, L., Proctor, R., & Salvendy, G. (2011). Can traditional divergent thinking tests be trusted in measuring and predicting real-world creativity? *Creativity Research Journal, 23,* 24–37.

About the Authors

Donald J. Treffinger, Ph.D., LL.D., is president of the Center for Creative Learning, Inc., in Sarasota, FL. He has authored or coauthored more than 400 books, monographs, and articles. He served as a faculty member at Purdue University, The University of Kansas, and Buffalo State College. Dr. Treffinger received the National Association for Gifted Children's Distinguished Service Award, the E. Paul Torrance Creativity Award, and in 2011, the Ann F. Isaacs Founder's Award and the Educator of Distinction (Legacy Series) Award. He also received the Risorgimento Award from Destination ImagiNation, Inc. and the International Creativity Award from the World Council for Gifted and Talented Children. Dr. Treffinger also served as editor of *Gifted Child Quarterly* and *Parenting for High Potential*.

Patricia F. Schoonover, Ph.D., is an associate of the Center for Creative Learning who works with schools and other organizations. Dr. Schoonover also teaches undergraduate and graduate courses in creativity and creative problem solving at the University of Wisconsin-Stevens Point, where she was the director for Wisconsin Creative Problem Solving Programs. Dr. Schoonover worked for many years in the area of gifted education and talent development, was an elementary gifted education teacher and director of gifted programming, and was a lecturer at the University of Wisconsin-Green Bay. She is the author of several books and articles on creativity and CPS in education.

Edwin C. Selby, Ph.D., is an associate with the Center for Creative Learning and an adjunct professor at Fordham University's Graduate School of Education. He is the principal author of *VIEW: An Assessment of Problem Solving Style*. He offers seminars and workshops to help individuals and groups to become more effective problem solvers. Dr. Selby is also the author of several articles on creativity and individual style. He has been a public school music and drama teacher, founded and directed the Sussex Student Theater, served as president of the Sussex County Teen Arts Festival, and was a member of the Sussex County Technical School Board of Education. He currently serves as president of the Board of Trustees for the Sussex County Charter School for Technology. Dr. Selby's professional interests include learning styles, talent development, and developing creativity and problem solving among students and staff.